Praise for *New York and Slavery*

"An inspired high school teacher … unearths the long-buried history of slavery, complicity, and resistance in New York state, from the Wall Street slave market to the fiery rhetoric of Frederick Douglass. Singer provides useful strategies to help teachers navigate racially charged curriculum and discussions, making this an invaluable resource."

—*Chronogram*

"*New York and Slavery* resists the all-consuming drive to make scoring well on standardized tests the goal of education, emphasizing rather the importance of focusing on the realities of history and helping young people become savvy critical thinkers … An absolute 'must-read' supplementary resource for junior high, high school, and even college American History educators."

—*Wisconsin Bookwatch*

"Singer sheds light on slavery by providing an insightful historical examination."

—*CHOICE*

"*New York and Slavery* is a singular gift to New York teachers and children, and a milestone in the battle for historical truth. How else, Singer's book seems to ask, are we ever going to solve our racial nightmare, educate our children for a multicultural world, and provide future citizens with the knowledge they need?"

—*In Motion Magazine*

New York and Slavery

New York and Slavery

Time to Teach the Truth

Alan J. Singer

excelsior editions

State University of New York Press
Albany, New York

Cover engraving courtesy of I. N. Phelps Stokes Collection, Miriam and Ira D. Wallach Division of Art, Prints and Photographs, The New York Public Library, Astor, Lenox and Tilden Foundations. (colorized)

Published by State University of New York Press, Albany

For information, contact State University of New York Press,
www.sunypress.edu

Production by Kelli LeRoux
Marketing by Fran Keneston

Library of Congress Cataloguing-in-Publication Data

Singer, Alan J.
    New York and Slavery : time to teach the truth / Alan J. Singer.
        p. cm.
    ISBN 978-0-7914-7509-6 (hardcover : alk. paper) — ISBN 978-0-7914-7510-2 (pbk. : alk. paper) 1. Slavery—New York (State)—New York—History—Study and teaching. 2. Slave trade—New York (State)—New York—History—Study and teaching. 3. New York (N.Y.)—History—Colonial period, ca. 1600–1775—Study and teaching. 4. New York (N.Y.)—History—1775–1865—Study and teaching. 5. Slavery—New York (State)—New York—History. 6. Slave trade—New York (State)—New York—History. 7. New York (N.Y.)—History—colonial period, ca. 1600–1775. 8. New York (N.Y.)—History—1775–1865. I. Title.

F128.4.S58 2008
306.3'620899607307471—dc22

                                                                            2007035783

10 9 8 7 6 5 4 3 2 1

This book is dedicated to the accused 1741 "conspirators" and Colonel Tye, Henry Highland Garnet, and the thousands of other freedom fighters, both Black and White, whose names have been virtually erased from history. May the truth about their struggle to end slavery in New York, the North, and the nation finally be taught in our schools.

Contents

Preface   ix

Acknowledgments   xi

Chapter 1   Erased from History   1

Chapter 2   Teaching About Slavery   13

Chapter 3   Complicity and Resistance   27

Chapter 4   Settlement   37

Chapter 5   Control   49

Chapter 6   Making Choices in a New Nation   65

Chapter 7   Debate   75

Chapter 8   Profiting for Human Misery   89

Chapter 9   Resistance!   99

Chapter 10   What Students Understand About Slavery   111

Chapter 11   Time to Teach the Truth   117

Chapter 12   Books, Movies, and Web sites   121

Chapter 13   Classroom Ideas for Teaching About Slavery   127

References   143

Biographical Note   155

Index   157

Preface

This book was inspired and supported by a number of people, some of whom are not even aware of my work. The most important contributors were the thousands of secondary school students and their teachers who corrected me when I was off base and made sure my ideas made sense to them.

Milton Borome, who taught "Negro History" at the City College of New York in the 1960s, showed me that American history was much more complex with many more major participants than I had dreamed. William L. Katz, an independent historian who is also a close friend, has always shared materials and ideas.

The New York State Council for the Social Studies and the New Jersey Council for the Social Studies and their local subsidiaries provided venues for presenting and writing about slavery in the United States, particularly New York's relationship with the slave system. A "Teaching American History" grant that brought the New York City Department of Education, Hofstra University, and the Brooklyn Historical Society together as collaborators introduced me to teachers interested in this project who were willing to develop and use a curriculum guide (http://www.nyscss.org) on slavery and New York in their classrooms.

A number of social studies teachers affiliated with the Hofstra University New Teachers Network helped research and design lessons discussed in this book and included in the *New York and Slavery: Complicity and Resistance* curriculum guide. Special contributions to the project were made by Mary Carter, a retired social studies teacher and Hofstra University student teaching field supervisor; Kerri Creegan, a high school teacher in the Massapequa, New York school district; Douglas Cioffi, a middle school teacher in the Long Island, New York Roman Catholic diocese school system; April Francis, a middle school teacher in the Uniondale, New York school district; Stephanie Sienkiewicz, a middle school in McLean, Virginia; and Michael Pezone, a high school teacher in Queens, New York.

Students from Law, Government, and Community Service Magnet High School in Queens, New York deserve special recognition for organizing the New York and Slavery Walking Tour in lower Manhattan.

William Katz, Michael Pezone, Mary Carter, and two middle school teachers, Adeola Tella (Uniondale, New York) and Rachel Thompson (Queens, New York), read and commented on drafts of this book.

Two colleagues provided ongoing intellectual and emotional support on this project and deserve special recognition. Maureen Murphy, Professor of Secondary Education and the director of the English Education program in the Hofstra University School of Education and Allied Human Services, and Judith Y. Singer, Associate Professor of Early Childhood and Elementary Education at the Long Island University–Brooklyn Campus, listened, questioned, critiqued, and cajoled far beyond normal human endurance. Without them as professional partners, my work would never have reached this point.

Errors of fact and interpretation, of course, are my own.

Acknowledgments

An earlier version of chapter 2 was originally published as Singer, A. (2001, Summer–Fall), "Teaching About Slavery in the Americas," *Social Science Docket, 1* (2).

An earlier version of chapter 8 was originally published as Singer, A. (January–April, 2003), "19th Century New York City's Complicity with Slavery: The Case for Reparations," *The Negro Educational Review, 54* (1/2).

An earlier version of chapter 11 was originally published as Singer, A. (2005, September/October), "Strange Bedfellows: The Contradictory Goals of the Coalition Making War on Social Studies," *The Social Studies, 96* (5).

Chapter 1

Erased from History

If there is no struggle, there is no progress.

—Frederick Douglass (1857)

In May 2006, students in Michael Pezone's twelfth-grade United States Government and Politics class were discussing the conflict over slavery in the early years of the Republic, the history of enslavement in New York City, and the involvement of local merchants in the trans-Atlantic slave trade. They were an especially knowledgeable group of young people, as many had participated in field-testing lessons from the award-winning *New York and Slavery: Complicity and Resistance* curriculum guide (Nanji, 2005; Evans, 2005).

The students decided they wanted to take a walking tour of the sites they learned about in Lower Manhattan. The difficulty was that other than the colonial-era African American Burial Ground, which was uncovered during excavations for a federal office building in 1991, these sites, and slavery in New York in general, have been erased from historical memory. There is not even a historical marker at the South Street Seaport in the financial district of Manhattan where enslaved Africans were traded in the seventeenth and eighteenth centuries and where illegal slaving expeditions were planned and financed up until the time of the American Civil War.

New York City has eighty-five museums listed on a popular Web site for tourists (http://www.ny.com). They celebrate art, science, culture, and history, including the histories of numerous ethnic groups. But other than a recently completed exhibit and monument at the burial ground site, there are no museums or permanent exhibits on slavery in New York City or the city's role in the trans-Atlantic slave trade.

The more I began to dig into the past as I edited the *New York Slavery: Complicity and Resistance* curriculum and prepared this book, the more I realized the extent to which historical knowledge about New York's involvement with

1

slavery and the trans-Atlantic slave trade has been erased from our memory. In January 1895, an article by Thomas A. Janvier appeared in *Harper's New Monthly Magazine* (pp. 293–305) describing "New York Slave Traders" during the colonial era. What is most striking about the article is its tone. It is a matter-of-fact, almost cavalier, account of the history of slavery in the city. While it can provide teachers, students, and historians with some useful information, and it is the source of a much replicated drawing of the Wall Street slave market, its greatest value is as an indicator of White insensitivity towards racial issues at the end of the nineteenth century.

According to Janvier, and remember, this article was written for an educated, but general readership, "[f]rom the very foundation of the New Netherland colony slavery was part and parcel of its economic organization" because "[a] colonial establishment of that period, to be well equipped, required slaves in just the same way that it required horses and cows" (293). It is as if greater awareness about the problems of race in the United States, and the need to be politically sensitive to the demands of a large and increasingly activist minority group, has led to the suppression of the true history of the city, state, and nation.

In June 2007, the Democratic Party dominated New York State Assembly finally approved a symbolic resolution (A00273B) "acknowledging that the institution of slavery was an appalling tragedy," apologizing for the state's role, and establishing a "commemorative day in tribute to persons enslaved in New York." However, Republicans blocked the legislation in the State Senate, concerned that it might be used to support a campaign for reparations (Associated Press, 2007).

Michael and I met with the students and as a group we decided that the problem of this missing history was largely political rather than historical or educational. An op-ed piece by *New York Times* columnist David Brooks had just declared "The Death of Multiculturalism" (Brooks, 2006, p. A27), partly, he claimed, because "civil rights groups" had "become stale and uninteresting."

As a response to the article and the absence of historical markers, we suggested a bit of guerrilla theater that would combine the study of history with political action. With our help, the students mapped out the walking tour and designed poster-size placards including information about the "Slave Market" on Wall Street, the bank that financed the slave trade, the meeting house where "blackbirders" (slave traders) planned their voyages, and sites of Black insurrections in 1712 and 1741. The students wrote a press release, invited local politicians to join them, and then visited the sites and posted their own historical markers. At each site they passed out literature explaining to office workers and tourists why they were there (Pezone and Singer, 2006, pp. 32–35).

Black History Is American History

In 1903, W. E. B. DuBois began *The Souls of Black Folk* (1961) with "The Forethought," a letter to his audience in which he explained the issues he hoped to clarify. He asked each "Gentle Reader" to "receive my little book in all charity, studying my words with me, forgiving mistake and foible for the sake of the faith and passion that is in me, and seeking the grain of truth hidden there." Unlike Dr. DuBois, I am a White man and not "bone of the bone and flesh of the flesh" of those subject to the harshness of American slavery and racism. I will need the forbearance of both "gentle" and not-so-gentle readers as I present an approach to teaching American history centered on the institution of slavery and racism and the roles they played in shaping the country and world we live in today.

In the spring of 2006 I was teaching demonstration lessons in a Brownsville, Brooklyn middle school as part of a federal Teaching American History grant. Every student in the school was African American, Caribbean American, or Hispanic, as were most of the teachers and administrators. After one lesson, a twelve-year-old Black girl in a seventh-grade class came up and thanked me for "teaching us about our history." She also asked me why as a White person I had decided to focus on Black history. It was a good question that merited a thoughtful answer. I explained that my field of study was the history of the United States rather than Black history, but that I did not believe you could understand this country in the past or present without focusing on the African American experience. Black history is American history.

Readers have a right to ask why a book on the subject of teaching about slavery in the United States focuses on Northern complicity with slavery in the United States, particularly New York's relationship with slavery and participation in the trans-Atlantic slave trade over one-hundred and fifty years ago. Part of the answer lies in the subtitle of this book, *Time to Teach the Truth*.

In *The Discovery of India*, Jawaharal Nehru (1946), a future Prime Minister of India, wrote, "History is almost always written by the victors and conquerors and gives their viewpoint." Similar quotes have been attributed to Napoleon, Joseph Stalin, and Winston Churchill. The victor's history is a distorted history. It is time to teach the truth about slavery and the settlement of what would become New York and the United States so we can finally understand what happened in the past and the way these events reverberated through time and shape the present.

Discovering the "truth" about the past can be exceedingly difficult. The issue is not just whether the information historians report is correct, but whether the assembled narrative, the historical story, accurately portrays and explains events.

Too often the public or "official" version of history follows one of three fundamentally unreliable and predictable models. There is the uncritical patriotism presented at national monuments such as the Alamo or Mount Vernon, which has been documented by James Loewen in his book *Lies Across America: What Our Historic Sites Get Wrong* (Touchstone, 2000). The "truth" is that at the Alamo, slaveholders from the American South fought for the right to own other human beings in violation of Mexican law. At Mount Vernon, the work of the plantation, and the profit that made it possible for George Washington to evade the British army for five years, were provided by enslaved Africans. At the end of the war, Washington had the nerve to petition the British to return the human "property" that had escaped to freedom. Later, as President of the United States and a resident of Philadelphia, he circumvented a Pennsylvania gradual abolition act by rotating enslaved Africans back to his plantation in Virginia every six months (Koppel, 2007: p. A10).

The "Disney" version of history roughly draws on the past as a starting point to present entertaining and marketable stories that tells little about actual events or people. One of its most egregious "historical" movies is *Songs of the South* (1946), an early blending of live action and animation where enslaved Black people express happiness with their condition by periodically breaking out into joyous songs. The "truth" is that music played a major role in African American work, religion, and community, but it never celebrated racism and slavery.

Meanwhile, for the so-called History Channel, history is most often reduced to blood and gore, a whirlwind of war, natural disasters, and other kinds of mayhem. In this version, which markets the past, the American Civil War is about weapons and battlefields, not union, nation building, the triumph of Northern capital, or the end of human enslavement.

Because of such sanitized, biased, or commercialized versions of "history," many secondary school students I work with, especially students from inner-city African American, Caribbean, and Hispanic communities, are deeply skeptical about what they learn in school. They generally want to believe what they read or hear about the past or current events, but it just doesn't seem "true" to them. They react against what James Loewen (1995) describes in the title to another one of his books as *Lies My Teacher Told Me*.

Another problem that teachers face when teaching about a topic such as slavery is that the word "history" has multiple meanings. What the general public commonly refers to as history are events from the past. But history also means the process of gathering and organizing information, explanations about the relationships between events, and broader explanations or "theories" about how and why change takes place. History is the past, the study of the past, and explanations about the past. To be historically literate, to be practicing historians rather than consumers of prepackaged propaganda, teachers and students must commit themselves to constantly formulate and reformulate their own explanations as they learn more and more about events. Knowing the "truth" about slavery means figuring out why things happened and considering the impact of these events on the future.

Of course there are other problems with history as well. Sometimes not enough information is available to effectively tell the story. On other occasions, either consciously or unconsciously, important information is ignored because it does not fit the theses, or explanations, about the past that the narrators and their stories are trying to present. And far too often, in classrooms and works of history, the essential kernel of meaning is buried in an avalanche of data, quotes, and footnotes intended for specialists. When this happens—and unfortunately it happened more and more as the Bush administration pushed for increased content testing for students and teachers—history becomes inaccessible to public viewing.

Yet despite all of these drawbacks, the study of history is a powerful force for human understanding and social change. Franz Fanon, who wrote about the Algerian War for Independence, described "the plunge into the chasm of the past" as both the "condition and source of freedom" (Williams & Harris, 1970, p. 266).

Slavery was a national system, and conflict over its abolition eventually led to disunion and Civil War. However, to both sharpen our focus and correct misconceptions about the history of slavery in the United States and the Northern states, most of the examples cited in this book are from the history of New York State. New England abandoned slavery and the slave trade earlier than in New York; the slave system was never as developed in Pennsylvania; New Jersey was much smaller; and slavery was banned by the Ordinance of 1787 in the Northern states that entered the Union as European American settlement spread westward. The focus of this book is on people and events in the City of New York and the surrounding downstate region during the period leading up to the end of slavery in New York State in 1827. However, with the movement of people west along the Erie Canal from the 1820s onward, resistance to slavery increasingly became a statewide phenomenon. Kerri Creegan, one of the high school teachers who assisted in the development of the *New York and Slavery: Complicity and Resistance* curriculum guide, concluded, "New York was really a microcosm of the debate engulfing the nation and leading to civil war" (Creegan, 2007, p. 62). Most historical research involves relatively narrow case studies that provide insight into broader historical forces. By looking at the microcosm, it is easier to see and understand what took place in the past.

This book and the curriculum guide it draws from are rich in historical detail because without supporting evidence, we are stuck with mere opinion. At the same time, without historical opinions we have information without explanation. Historians, teachers, and students have an obligation, to themselves and to each other, to both test their theories and to make them explicit so that others can examine them. This intellectual obligation is most directly discussed in chapter 8, "Profiting from Human Misery," which explores how merchants and bankers and their political allies profited from human misery. In the nineteenth century, New York City merchants and bankers financed the illegal trans-Atlantic slave trade and trafficked in goods produced by human beings living and working under dire circumstances in the South and the Caribbean. They were not innocents tricked into complicity with an evil force. They knew exactly what they were doing. Chapter 8 presses teachers, students, and general readers to think about slavery and racism as global systems shaping the world and creating the powerful institutions that govern today. It challenges them to consider their own underlying explanations or theories of history. Was slavery a tragic mistake or an underlying pillar of capitalist industrial development?

Historical Explanation

My approach to history came be placed within a tradition that is identified with Karl Marx, a nineteenth-century philosopher, economist, historian, and radical political commentator. Historical explanation, from this perspective, must focus on the ways that societies are organized to produce and distribute goods and services, including the food, clothing, and shelter that people need to survive. This does not mean that every cultural practice or institution in a society is determined solely by economic concerns, or that individual decisions are always motivated by money or greed. It does mean that social systems that are unable to satisfy the basic needs of their populations, adjust to changing technologies and environmental conditions, or fall behind the productive capacities of their neighbors or competitors face serious crises.

In addition, the ways societies are organized to produce and distribute goods and services generate conflict between competing social, political, and economic groups. These conflicts are the dynamic force propelling social change. They are both constructive and destructive. They build powerful supporting institutions and promote massive resistance. In the Hindu religion, this unity of creation and destruction are identified with the goddess Shiva.

Few realize that Karl Marx was a European correspondent for the *New York Tribune* and wrote regularly about the American Civil War for the *Tribune* and the Austrian newspaper *Die Presse*. From the start of the war, Marx argued that it was fundamentally about slavery, not union.

Marx first commented on the economic role of slavery in the American and world economies in the 1840s. In *The Poverty of Philosophy* (1847), he argued, "slavery is just as much the pivot of bourgeois industry as machinery, credits, etc. Without slavery you have not cotton; without cotton you have no modern industry. It is slavery . . . and it is world trade that is the pre-condition of large-scale industry . . . Wipe slavery off the map of the world, and you will have . . . the complete decay of modern civilization and commerce" (Easton & Guddat, 1967, p. 482).

As an historian working within a Marxian tradition, I focus on slavery as an economic system that generated enormous wealth at the expense of people denied basic human rights. Wealth was created by the forced labor of enslaved people who built the physical infrastructure of colonial America and produced agricultural products on its plantations. In this slave-based economic system, shippers, boatbuilders, bankers, and insurance houses made huge profits from the trade in human beings and by the resale of slave-produced commodities as raw materials and finished goods.

The impact of slavery, however, was actually much greater. The enslavement of Africans provided work for White textile workers, barrel-makers, and sailors, and opened markets for a wide assortment of products produced by free labor. Profits generated by the slave system supplied money or capital for clearing marshland in Holland, building canals in England, creating global trade networks and empires, financing the Industrial Revolution, and for the development of New York City as an international financial center. Social and political institutions and cultural practices developed in order to maintain this slave system. These included oppressive laws and racist practices, as well as an ideology that justified dehumanization and death and the transformation of people into commodities in the name of profit.

This book includes tales of heroic resistance, because the same society that prospered from human misery also generated opposition to it. Black resistance to oppression played a fundamental role in contributing to abolition in New York and the Northern states, and to the movement to abolish slavery in the country as a whole. Within White society, political and religious turmoil in a revolutionary era lent support to the struggle against slavery, as did the rapid growth in free White immigrant labor in the North, the emergence of more democratic political institutions, and conflicts between different sectors of the nation's economic elite.

The trans-Atlantic slave trade transformed human beings into commodities to be bought and sold for profit. Even after it was declared illegal, and involvement in the trade was made a crime punishable by death, business interests continued to participate. They shifted the trans-Atlantic slave trade's center of operation from Bristol and Liverpool in the United Kingdom to New York City, where they employed euphemism, legal loopholes, and financial manipulation to avoid prosecution.

Essential Questions

As a social studies teacher, I use a methodology in my classroom designed to engage students as historians and help them explore events from the past in an effort to answer essential questions about humanity and history. It is an approach directly concerned with ideas and issues being discussed today. For example, among the essential questions that need to be considered by citizens, as well as historians, are: What was the nature of capitalist economic development in the nineteenth century, and how does this system operate today? and Was slavery peripheral to American economic, social, and political development, or was it central?

A study of New York City's involvement in the trans-Atlantic slave trade forces us to consider other questions as well: Can unfettered capitalist production for profit be trusted to protect human rights and meet human needs (or are we doomed to a continuing series of environmental and social disasters like the hurricane relief fiasco in New Orleans in September, 2005, and mega-electrical power failures such as plagued California in the last decade)? And, if it was profitable, as I argue, why did New York's complicity with slavery ultimately end?

Human beings who embraced values very similar to our own also justified the bartering of other human beings and condemned them and their descendants to perpetual exploitation. The social impact and profits from this illicit trade contributed to the inequalities and injustices in this country and the world today, inequalities and injustices that many in our society, including some of our highest-ranking public officials, prefer to overlook. An examination of New York City's role in the trans-Atlantic slave trade and society's unwillingness to acknowledge it raises the questions: What is our fundamental nature as human beings? and Are humans condemned to live in a world rife with racism and exploitation?

In *The Souls of Black Folk*, W. E. B. DuBois wrote: "the problem of the Twentieth Century is the problem of the color line." The general silence on the impact of slavery on the United States and the world, the difficulty in developing and disseminating curricula on slavery and the trans-Atlantic slave trade, and continuing social and economic inequality in this country and the world, demonstrate that the gap described by Dr. DuBois is still with us as we proceed into the twenty-first century. This introduces the essential question, Can the United States ever become a more just society and finally bridge its racial divide?

A major debate that continually reemerges in discussion of the teaching of social studies and history is whether teachers should be permitted to express their own views in class. While I try to hold myself to the standard for research and analysis expected of an historian, I have a point of view. I am not neutral. As they analyze the past, I want students in my classes and readers of this book to challenge me and to challenge people with authority in our society. An examination of essential questions such as the ones posed in this chapter is crucial for protecting and promoting democracy. The ultimate test of whether this book contributes to telling the "truth" about history will be the extent to which it stimulates broad public debate involving people who are often shut out of the discussion.

I often speak with students, teachers, and community groups who are interested in the history of New York's complicity with slavery. Sometimes I am the only White person in the room. I usually begin by saying, "Just in case you haven't noticed, I know that I am White." In the United States today, many White people argue that they are color blind and claim that they do not see race. Very few, if any, Black people believe them. I do not believe them either. No one raised and educated in the United States in the second half of the twentieth century and the beginning of the twenty-first century can honestly assert that race is not a factor in the way they see the world and other people. I acknowledge being White, not because the audience does not recognize it, but so that they understand that I realize the historical baggage I bring to the topic of slavery, to raise the issue that race does not determine political perspective, and because I value their views on the material I will present.

The narrative thread that runs through this book is the story of New York's complicity with slavery and the struggle to overturn the slave system as told from my perspective. It is not the only perspective, but I am convinced that it is a useful one.

This book opens and closes with discussions concerning teaching about slavery, and, by extension, about race in American society. In the racially and ethnically charged atmosphere of contemporary America, currently in the midst of a national debate over the status of undocumented immigrants, many White teachers, especially if they work in schools with predominately African American student populations, are hesitant to enter into conversations about slavery, oppression, and racism in the classroom. They are uncertain about their own biases and worry about potential student reactions. These concerns are legitimate and actually helpful to a teacher. Once you see a problem, you can begin to address it. The worst teachers are those who refuse to recognize the reality of race and its continuing impact on themselves and others.

An examination of secondary school student attitudes toward what they have learned about slavery in chapter 10 is based on interviews with hundreds of students from diverse racial and ethnic backgrounds. While Black and White students who attended racially segregated schools had similar levels of content knowledge about slavery and racism, they had very different attitudes toward them. Their divergent responses raise serious questions about the future of the United States as a nation.

Local elites, from the time of the Dutch settlement in 1624 up until New York State Emancipation Day in 1827, supported a labor system that exploited an enslaved Black population. While the overall Black population of New York and the Northern states was small, they made up as much as 30 percent of the population in some counties near New York City. This story is presented in four chapters that describe the settlement of Dutch New Netherland (chapter 4), the systemization of enslavement in the British colony of New York (chapter 5), and attitudes toward slavery and African Americans in New York and the new nation (chapters 6 and 7).

A second concern is how New York merchants, bankers, and their political allies profited from human misery (chapters 7 and 8). In the nineteenth century, New York City merchants and bankers financed the illegal trans-Atlantic slave trade and trafficked in goods produced by human beings living and working under dire circumstances in the South and the Caribbean. During this period New York City became a dominant force in world commerce and the mores of modern American capitalism were established.

There was heroic resistance to slavery by both Black and White New Yorkers (chapters 7 and 9). Theirs is the third story told in this book. Some of the names, such as John Brown and Frederick Douglass, are well known from standard historical sources. Others, including William Wells Brown, Henry Highland Garnet, Harriet Jacobs, Jermain Loguen, Gerrit Smith, and Lewis Tappan, have largely been forgotten outside the circle of professional historians. Many of these people left behind powerful memoirs that detail life under slavery and the struggle for freedom. Solomon Northup of Saratoga Springs and Frederick

Douglass of Rochester tell the most useful stories. Northup was a free Black New Yorker kidnapped and sold into slavery in 1841. His autobiography, written after his escape twelve years later, explains conditions faced by free Blacks in the North and details life and work on plantations in the Deep South. It is a unique historical document.

Frederick Douglass is best known for his escape from slavery in Maryland, but what I find most interesting in his memoirs are his reflections on his life as a free man of color and on political struggle. Douglass was involved with John Brown in planning a slave insurrection in the American South, but withdrew his support when Brown decided to target the federal arsenal at Harpers Ferry. Despite this, Douglass was indicted for treason in the state of Virginia and was forced to flee the country. Douglass's involvement in the planning stages of the Harpers Ferry assault, and his material support for Brown, compel readers to consider other essential questions confronting us in the modern world, such as: What does it mean to be patriotic? and Who is a terrorist?

Powerful Voices

This book resurrects these people and their struggles from the wastebasket of the past in order to show how human efficacy can reshape historical possibility (Thompson, 1963). As Frederick Douglass powerfully noted in an 1857 speech commemorating West Indian emancipation, "If there is no struggle, there is no progress. Those who profess to favor freedom and yet deprecate agitation are people who want crops without plowing up the ground. They want rain without thunder and lightning. . . . That struggle might be a moral one, it might be a physical one; it might be both moral and physical, but it must be a struggle" (Foner, 1950, p. 437).

The words of these freedom fighters continue to resonate today. Reverend Henry Highland Garnet, who was born enslaved, escaped to the North and freedom at age eleven. He later graduated from Oneida Institute in Utica, New York and became a minister in the city of Troy. In 1843, he issued a call for a slave rebellion in a speech at a National Negro Convention in Buffalo, New York. Garnet beseeched his enslaved brethren to "Awake, awake; millions of voices are calling you! Your dead fathers speak to you from their graves. Heaven, as with a voice of thunder, calls on you to arise from the dust. Let your motto be resistance! resistance! resistance! No oppressed people have ever secured their liberty without resistance. Trust in the living God. Labor for the peace of the human race, and remember that you are four millions" (Aptheker, 1951/1973, pp. 232–233). In the spirit of Reverend Garnet, I humbly ask readers of this book to share his motto and join the resistance against injustice.

In the first issue of *The Liberator*, published in Boston, Massachusetts, on January 1, 1831, William Lloyd Garrison (Seldes, 1960, p. 270) declared that on the issue of human enslavement: "I *will* be as harsh as truth, and as uncompromising as justice . . . I will not equivocate—I will not excuse—I will not retreat a single inch—AND I WILL BE HEARD. The apathy of the people is enough to make every statue leap from its pedestal, and to hasten the resurrection of the dead." In the spirit of William Lloyd Garrison, activists need to cease equivocation and to struggle, as did the abolitionists, until our voices are heard.

Frederick Douglass was born in Maryland, the son of a White man and an enslaved African woman. As a young man he escaped to the North where he became a prominent abolitionist and champion of full citizenship rights for African Americans. In 1852, Douglass was invited to give a Fourth of July speech in Rochester, New York. His audience was probably surprised when he charged them with mocking him and declared, "This Fourth of July is *yours*, not *mine*. You may rejoice, *I* must mourn" (Aptheker, 1951/1973, pp. 330–334).

"What to the American slave is your Fourth of July?" Douglass asked the crowd. "I answer, a day that reveals to him more than all other days of the year, the gross injustice and cruelty to which he is the constant victim. To him your celebration is a sham; your boasted liberty an unholy license; your national greatness, swelling vanity; your sounds of rejoicing are empty and heartless; your denunciation of tyrants, brass-fronted impudence; your shouts of liberty and equality . . . There is not a nation of the earth guilty of practices more shocking and bloody than are the people of these United States at this very hour."

While the "hour" of slavery was "back in the day," we must, as citizens and as activists, ask ourselves and our nation if the "gross injustice" and "brass-fronted impudence" that Douglass decried are things best relegated to the past or if they are problems that still must be confronted.

Chapter 2

Teaching About Slavery

If the law is of such a nature that it requires you to be an agent of injustice to another, then, I say, break the law.

—Henry David Thoreau

"Mock" Slave Auction

In October 1994, in an effort to fulfill its responsibilities as a major public historical resource and provide a more accurate portrait of the American past, Colonial Williamsburg conducted a "mock" slave auction. It was intended "to educate visitors about a brutal yet important part of black American history" (Janofsky, 1994, p. 7; *New York Times*, 1994, p. A16).

According to spokesperson Christy Coleman, who directed the project and participated in the reenactment as a pregnant slave sold to pay her "master's" debts, "this is a very, very sensitive and emotional issue. But it is also very real history." Ms. Coleman felt that "only by open display and discussion could people understand the degradation and humiliation that blacks felt as chattel" (Janofsky, 1994, p. 7).

Critics, mobilized by the Virginia chapters of the National Association for the Advancement of Colored People and the Southern Christian Leadership Conference, protested that the auction trivialized slavery by depicting scenes "too painful to revive in any form" (Janofsky, 1994, p. 7). A small group of demonstrators stood witness at the reenactment. Later, one of the demonstrators, who initially charged Colonial Williamsburg with turning Black history into a "sideshow," changed his mind. As a result of witnessing the "mock" auction, he now felt that "(p)ain had a face. Indignity had a body. Suffering had tears" (*New York Times*, 1994, p. A16).

The controversy following the "mock" auction at Colonial Williamsburg is a reflection of larger debates about slavery and racism taking place in classrooms across the United States. These involve both historical issues and pedagogical questions. Our society continues to argue over the nature of chattel slavery itself, the treatment of enslaved people, and the long-term impact of slavery on American society (Foner, 1991/1997). There are disputes over the reliability of sources such as the autobiographical narratives of enslaved Africans that may have been ghostwritten and usually were published by abolitionist organizations.

Curriculum and Pedagogy

Teachers grapple with ways to help students understand the impact of slavery and the slave trade on American society and on the human beings who were its victims. They must decide whether to assign fictional works such as Harriet Beecher Stowe's *Uncle Tom's Cabin* or show Hollywood-produced movies like *Amistad*. There are also disagreements about the accuracy, sensitivity, and efficacy of teaching approaches such as role-playing and historical reenactments, especially given continuing racial segregation and ethnic tension in classrooms, schools, and communities.

A flair for the dramatic is often necessary to capture and hold the attention of students. In the fall of 2005 and spring of 2006, the New York Historical Society widely advertised an exhibit on slavery in New York City. The advertisements focused on the idea that *"it happened here,"* and that enslaved Africans had constructed many of the city's earliest landmarks. The exhibit drew record crowds.

Over the years, I have presented workshops about slavery on Long Island and New York to audiences of overwhelmingly White, suburban, high school students (*New York Times,* January 1, 2006, section 14, p. 1). At one school, I started by displaying primary source documents from the history of their town. In his last will and testament, dated April 26, 1720, Richard Smith, a founder of Smithtown, New York, wrote "I give unto my son Richard my young Negro boy called Stephen," and "I give unto my son Nathaniel my Negro boy called John." Another document was a 1773 inventory from the farm of Mary Platt Treadwell, on whose land one of the town's high schools was later built. It listed twenty-six enslaved Africans and their value in English pounds. Later in the lesson, I delivered a summary of the presentation in the form of a "rap" song that included references to local communities. One line was repeated again and again. "Time to learn the truth / Our local his-tor-y / Lon' islan was land of sla-ver-y. Time to learn the truth / Our local his-tor-y / Lon' islan was land of sla-ver-y."

My singing is "bad"—bad in the traditional sense—and certainly the subject was serious, but students responded with heightened interest and a meaningful examination of a series of documents about New York's involvement in slavery and the trans-Atlantic slave trade. After the program, one student told a local newspaper reporter, "I always thought it was just the South. It feels like everything you have been taught has been wrong and you have to change it now" (Associated Press, 2006).

I also performed the "rap" song for students at a largely minority high school in Freeport, New York. Months later, I was approached by an African American teenager who said, "You're the guy who does the slavery rap." He thanked me for visiting his class.

My own experience as a secondary school teacher illustrates some of the difficulties teaching about topics like slavery (Singer, 2001, pp. 2–4). I am a White male and an ethnic Jew. For most of my career, I taught in schools where the majority or plurality of students was African American. Usually the remaining students were either of Caribbean ancestry or Latino/a. I often found slavery was one of the most difficult topics to address because students and I were all uncomfortable. Over the years, a number of African American students raised the point that they resent continually learning about slavery and how their people were oppressed. These challenges forced me to reconsider how I felt as a teenager learning about the history of my own people, especially the devastation that I felt because Eastern European Jews, including my relatives, had died in the gas chambers of Nazi Germany. Knowledge of oppression did not satisfy me then. I felt humiliated and I wanted to scream out, "Why didn't we fight back?"

What finally helped me come to terms with the Holocaust was reading about Jewish resistance in *Mila 18,* Leon Uris's (1961) book about the Warsaw Ghetto, and the creation and defense of the State of Israel. I realize that the key for my coming to terms with the twentieth-century history of Jews was recognition of human resistance.

In response to my students and the lessons they helped teach me about my own life, I shifted the focus on Black history in my classroom from the burdens of oppression to an exploration of the history of people's struggles for justice. Among other things, this meant that study about the horror of slavery and the slave trade was always combined with examination of the way people fought to establish their humanity.

Stacey Cotten, an African American woman who is a high school social studies teacher and a former student of mine, has a similar understanding of what it means to constantly learn about the past in this way. Stacey remembers that as a middle school and high school student she always felt uncomfortable when the subject of slavery was introduced. According to Stacey, "It generally was the first time, and often the only time, my classmates and I would learn about the history of Black people. Teachers never handled the topic or our feelings with sensitivity. They made it seem, at least to us, that slavery was proof that Black people were inferior and our inferiority was the reason for our continuing subordinate position in society. It also sounded like we would have remained as slaves forever if not for sympathetic Whites who secured our freedom for us. As a social studies teacher, one of my primary goals is to put an end to these humiliating myths that degrade Black students and mislead White ones" (Cotten, 2001, p. 12).

One way to address my own experience with the importance of human resistance to oppression, and Stacey's feeling that instruction about slavery has been used to diminish people of African ancestry, is to make social struggle and efforts to achieve freedom and human dignity major themes in all areas of historical study. It was not until I began research for the New York and Slavery curriculum that I learned how the original Black population of New Amsterdam had negotiated with the Dutch West India Company to obtain land and freedom (chapter 4); about consistent small acts of resistance that contributed to panic among the White population in British colonial New York (chapter 5); about Colonel Tye and his antislavery, pro-British raiders during the American Revolution (chapter 5); or about William W. Brown, Jermain Loguen, and the informal African American militia that would suddenly mobilize and physically obstruct "slave catchers" along the Erie Canal underground railroad route to Canada (chapter 9). Africans in New York and the Americas had always resisted the bonds of servitude—but their stories were not told.

Which Version of the Story

Part of the problem is that the standard historical narrative in American history is distorted to give the impression that the United States was always destined to triumph as a land of the free. Slavery, at worst, was a tragic mistake. In *The American Reader* (1990a, p. 3), Diane Ravitch wrote that the "settling of America began with an idea. The idea was that the citizens of a society could join freely and agree to govern themselves by making laws for the common good." She argued that this idea was embedded in the Mayflower Compact and came to the New World on November 11, 1620.

But the history of America did not start on November 11, 1620 (even excluding native people and Spanish colonial settlements), and it did not start with only one idea. Jamestown, Virginia was established in 1607, and in 1619, the year before the Pilgrims landed in New England, captured Africans were sold as slaves in that colony. Using Ravitch's logic, American history began there with the idea of social and racial inequality.

Another problem is that the social studies curriculum is compartmentalized by geographical regions. For Africans in the Americas, however, who were treated as commodities to be bought and sold, it made little difference whether a slave ship deposited them in Santo Domingue (Haiti), Brazil, Jamaica, or the mainland British colonies that would become the United States.

If we look at the Americas as a whole, we see active, armed resistance to enslavement in era after era. In 1630, over ten thousand Africans rebelled against European control and slavery and established the independent African Republic of Palmares in Brazil. Between 1734 and 1739, Jamaican Maroons living in the interior of the island battled British forces until they were declared legally free forever. Under the leadership of Toussaint L'Ouverture, the African population of Santo Domingue rose in rebellion, abolished slavery, defeated British and Spanish invading armies and blocked Napoleon's effort to reestablish French control (Bell, 2007). In the United States, between 1810–1860, as many as 100,000 enslaved Africans escaped North to freedom on the Underground Railroad. Other escaped Africans joined the Seminole nation and helped resist efforts to force Native Americans to move from the east coast to Oklahoma. Two hundred thousand men and women of African ancestry served in the Union army and navy during the Civil War and nearly 40,000 died in the battle to preserve the union and end slavery.

Nichole Williams, an African American woman, a former social studies teacher, and currently a high school assistant principal, shares this commitment to focusing on "complicity and resistance" when teaching about slavery. Nichole finds that "students are usually more comfortable talking about how people have struggled against oppression than how they were oppressed, while most teachers prefer discussing the economic impact of slavery instead of exploring the reality of slave life and struggles in America. To my knowledge, teachers rarely introduce discussions of the justification for slavery or the impact of slavery on the North. My students are usually under the mistaken impression that all northerners were abolitionists" (Williams, 2001, p. 11).

Nichole believes that "an examination of slavery in the United States should include discussion of Africa and Eurocentric influences on the writing of history." She constantly had to struggle with other members of her department to justify including West African culture and Native Americans at the beginning of the United States History course. Because of the focus on preparing students for standardized assessments, "Teachers are encouraged to start with the colonists' struggle against the English. I always respond that the history of the United States has three roots, not just one."

For Nichole, symbols of oppression and struggle are more powerful than words alone. She took a high school social studies class to the Schomburg Library in New York City to witness a special exhibit on slavery and the slave trade. It included artifacts from slavery like chains, branding irons, and whips. Her students, who were primarily African American, Caribbean, and Latino, were overwhelmed by what they saw at the exhibit and had extended conversations about what they witnessed.

While Nichole Williams is an African American woman who was teaching in a minority school district, she also taught in a school where a plurality of the students were European American. In her advice to teachers, she emphasizes that "no matter how uncomfortable the situation can become, students must be allowed to talk with each other and discuss their feelings, otherwise we risk losing their trust and interest."

Many school districts are pushing for expanded document-based instruction in history and social studies. One problem for teachers involves deciding which documents and which points about history to present to students Such decisions depend on the teacher's own understanding of slavery and of history.

William Katz (1995, pp. 133–134), in *Eyewitness: A Living Documentary of the African American Contribution to American History,* presents excerpts from an article by Dr. Samuel Cartwright, a highly respected Southern authority on medical issues that was published in *De Bow's Review* in September 1851. Without an historical context provided by the teacher, these quotes support racism. With explanation, they show how a commitment to human enslavement distorted science and blinded Americans to the impact of the slave system.

Cartwright identified two "psychological diseases" that he claimed to observe among enslaved Africans in the United States South. The first mental disorder, which he called "Drapetomia," was a tendency to runaway. The second was called "Dysaethesia Aethiopica" or "Rascality," and was marked by a careless indifference to their owners' property. Cartwright classified the enslaved Africans' resistance to enslavement and desire for freedom as "mental alienation" or diseases curable by "whipping the devil out of them."

Cartwright wanted to provide insight into the operation of the mind of the enslaved, and these excerpts do, although not in the way that Cartwright intended. They are based on the assumption that slavery is a justifiable, if not benevolent, institution. Of course if slavery violates human nature, and if Africans are understood as fully human, then their resistance to bondage would be expected. The diseased minds in this case, if they exist at all, belong to members of a racist "master class."

The denial of the humanity of enslaved Africans was pervasive and embedded in the science of the time. One of nineteenth-century New York City's most noted physicians, Dr. James Marion Sims, performed experimental gynecological operations on countless enslaved African women in the American south, including over thirty-four experimental operations on a single woman without the benefit of anesthesia or any type of antiseptic. Many of the women he experimented on lost their lives to infection (Lerner, 2003, p. F7).

Teaching Ideas

Some of my most successful lessons as a teacher have dealt with slavery, but also one of my greatest disasters. At the start of my teaching career, while working with African American middle-school–age students in a summer program, I presented material on the Southern biblical defense of slavery. The youngsters believed these were my ideas and they were furious with me; it took weeks to reestablish a relationship of trust with them. Today I know effective, well-intentioned teachers who reenact the middle passage and slave auctions in their social studies classes. One African American woman continually reorganizes the classroom, pushing students and their desks into smaller and smaller spaces, as they read Olaudah Equiano's account of the "Middle Passage." She does not stop pushing until they start to complain of the overcrowded conditions and make a connection to what they are reading.

However, based on my experience as a teacher, I think this type of activity is a mistake. While students may tolerate these reenactments and participate in them, it is not clear whether they can be done with either sufficient sensitivity or authenticity. White students end up thinking they have experienced and learned more about slavery than they have any right to believe, while Black students are left embarrassed or alienated by the attempted reenactments (Singer, 2001, 3).

While I reject role-playing and reenactments about an issue as controversial and painful as slavery, I have participated in very effective dramatic presentations with students on different academic levels. I prefer dramas because a prepared script provides structure to the activity and content on the history of slavery. One summer, I worked with teens who performed scenes from Martin B. Duberman's documentary play about the Black struggle for freedom and civil rights, *In White America* (1964). Based on this experience, I had my high school social studies students edit and present to other classes' excerpts from the speeches and writings of African American and White abolitionists.

In an after-school program where I assisted, a multiracial group of fifth graders performed a version of Virginia Hamilton's story about slavery and the undying desire for freedom, "The People Could Fly" (Hamilton, 1985). In this story, an elderly African remembers magic words that allow enslaved people to soar off into the sky and return to Africa. A scene upset the children where a White overseer and a Black driver whip a young mother while she is holding her infant because she will not work harder. After discussing the meaning of the story and the fact that they "don't treat people that way," the children decided to perform it. However, they also decided not to cast the parts according to the race of the characters or of the actors. Later, I worked with a middle school class that performed the same play. The students were African American, Caribbean, and Latino/a. Following a similar discussion, the students decided that none of them would play the oppressors. Instead, they built giant puppets to represent the overseer and driver.

Another group of middle school students took primary source material from the New York and Slavery curriculum guide about a 1741 slave conspiracy trial and translated the transcript of the case into a "hip-hop rap opera." In the introduction to their performance, a seventh grader declared:

Slavery in New York was crazy,
For people of African ancestry,
Life was different from the South,
Let me communicate to you by mouth.
In the year 1741,
Blacks thought about freedom,
Whites in the city were afraid
A slave revolt would be made.
Rumors went on throughout the night,

They tried and killed Blacks and Whites,
Torture, exile, burn, or hang,
Hundreds punished by this gang.
Looking back many doubt
What these accusations were about,
The real target was not the Whites,
But African American human rights.

What each of these productions had in common was not the production itself, but student discussion of the meaning of the dramatization, how they wanted to cast it, what they believed about race and ethnicity in the United States, and what they had learned about slavery. In each case, the play served as the vehicle for promoting the discussion.

A simple symbol can be much more powerful than a reenactment. One of the most successful depictions of a human catastrophe similar to slavery in the Americas is the United States Holocaust Memorial in Washington, DC. One of the most powerful exhibits in the memorial is the pile of thousands of shoes standing in stark reminder of what happened to their owners. Another is the gradual narrowing and darkening of the corridor as museum visitors prepare to enter a model of a cattle car that transported European Jews to death camps. Significantly, the memorial is able to evoke what happened during the Holocaust without reenacting what happened in a gas chamber, displaying a pile of human bodies, or having actors dressed in prison garb digging their own graves. Similarly, at the Schomburg Center for Research in Black Culture in New York City, one of the best exhibits on slavery in the Americas was simply a display of chains, metals collars, wooden yokes, metal rods, and other instruments for branding and imprisoning enslaved Africans.

No activity or exhibit by itself substitutes for the context created by a teacher and the relationship that exists in the classroom among students and between students and their teacher. "The New York City Slave Conspiracy Trial (1741) Hip-Hop Rap Opera" worked because the teacher, April Francis, invested time and energy studying about slavery and translating her own discoveries into lessons. She also successfully built a classroom community where students were not afraid to take intellectual and emotional risks as they rewrote the trial text and performed their interpretations in front of her, guests, and each other.

Despite the outstanding qualities of the Holocaust Memorial, there were problems with it as an educational tool. Even as I was moved by what I saw and felt, it was disconcerting to watch a group of high school students running through the exhibits without reflection or even "seeing" the displays, as they raced to the next historical site on their itinerary. The exhibit itself was insufficient to capture the imaginations of students who were disengaged from the material. A lesson, a museum visit, or a classroom activity may seem like a good idea in the abstract, but this does not mean it will achieve its intended goals with a particular group of students. For a lesson to be meaningful it has to take into account who the students are, what they already know, and how they will react.

Some of the most effective tools available for exploring the meaning of slavery, the longing for freedom, and resistance to oppression, are traditional African American folk songs. Among these songs are "All the Pretty Little Horses," "Go Down Moses," and "Follow the Drinking Gourd." "All the Pretty Little Horses," as sung by Odetta, is a haunting lullaby. The key to understanding it is to recognize that she is singing about two babies.

> Hush-a-bye, don't you cry, go to sleep my little baby,
> When you wake, you shall have, all the pretty little horses,
> Blacks and bays, dapples and grays, all the pretty little horses.
> Way down yonder, in the meadow, lies my poor little lambie,
> With bees and butterflies peckin' out its eyes,
> The poor little things crying Mammy. (Singer, 2003a, p. 167)

A useful teaching technique is to have students listen to the entire song and then read this stanza aloud repeatedly for effect. On a number of occasions, when students realized that the woman was a "wet-nurse" breast-feeding the White child while her own child was neglected, they responded in outrage that she was being treated like a cow, not like a human being.

A powerful depiction of enslavement is presented in Solomon Northup's autobiographical narrative, *Twelve Years a Slave* (Eakin & Logsdon, 1967; Eakin, 1990). Northup was a free Black man and a citizen of New York State who lived in Saratoga Springs with his wife and three children. Northup, a skilled carpenter and violinist, was kidnapped by slave traders while on a trip to Washington, DC. He was transported to Louisiana were he worked on cotton plantations until he was able to smuggle a letter to his wife and friends in New York. Using a New York State law designed to protect free Black citizens from being sold into slavery, they secured his freedom through the courts. When he returned to New York, abolitionists helped him publish his memoirs as part of their campaign to abolish slavery. Solomon Northup's account is especially important as a historical document because he is able to describe slavery on plantations in the "deep" South from the point of view of a free man and a skilled worker. Students can read excerpts and watch segments from the PBS version of his life, *Solomon Northup's Odyssey*.

In recent years, I have even revived my lesson on the Biblical defense of slavery, although I am very careful to introduce the lesson with a White abolitionist's attack on slavery and a challenge to students that they respond to the quotations based on their own religious and moral beliefs. Henry David Thoreau, a Northern abolitionist, declared, "I cannot for an instant accept a political organization that is the slave's government also. If [the law] is of such a nature that it requires you to be an agent of injustice to another, then,

I say, break the law" (Thoreau, 1849). After we discuss this quotation and the question of when it is legitimate to break the law, and I establish my agreement with Thoreau, we turn to the Southern apologists for slavery.

During the lesson, students, many of whom are religious Christians, are challenged to construct responses to Representative Charles Pinckney of South Carolina and Thomas Dew, a member of the Virginia state legislature, who argued that both the Old and New Testaments endorsed slavery (Bailey & Kennedy, 1984, pp. 203–205; Feder, 1967, p. 123).

Michael Pezone, a White man who turned to teaching as a second career in his mid-thirties, works in an inner-city high school where the student population is overwhelmingly Black, an ethnic mixture of African American and Caribbean American youth. It was his class that organized the lower Manhattan walking tour discussed in the opening to chapter 1. Michael is an especially thoughtful teacher with a deep understanding of both history and ways to reach young people. He cautions social studies teachers to avoid the danger of "antiquarianism." He argues that we must "guard against the tendency to limit the realities of slavery to the past, and to deny the fact that slavery still conditions our lives in the present-day United States." Michael believes the Civil War abolished slavery as a legal institution, "but not the systematic dehumanization of African-Americans (and others) that was the necessary condition of slavery" (Pezone, 2001, p. 12).

Michael supplements documents that present the history of slavery with material that addresses the oppressive reality of modern day America in all its forms, functions, and effects. In his classes, a unit on slavery will also include reading selections from authors such as W. E. B. DuBois, Manning Marable, Mumia Abdul-Jamal, Howard Zinn, Michael Parenti, and Angela Davis. He recommends a particularly powerful essay by James Baldwin, written in 1963, that was directed to teachers. In the essay, Baldwin says that if he were a teacher working with minority youth, "I would try to teach them—I would try to make them know—that those streets, those houses, those dangers, those agonies, by which they are surrounded, are criminal. I would try to make each child know that these things are the results of a criminal conspiracy to destroy him. I would teach him that if he intends to get to be a man, he must at once decide that he is stronger than this conspiracy and that he must never make his peace with it" (Baldwin, 1998, p. 685).

Ten Main Ideas About Slavery in the Americas

I share Michael Pezone's concern with the continuing impact of slavery and racism on American society and urge teachers to start planning units for their classes by asking themselves what is important to know and why. It will be helpful to consider these ten main ideas about slavery in the Americas (Singer, 2001, p. 5):

1. West Africans were experienced agricultural workers whose labor was used to exploit the resources of the American continents. Profits generated by the trans-Atlantic slave trade and trade in

slave-produced commodities financed the commercial and industrial revolutions in Europe and the United States. Global inequality today is a direct result of this history.

2. European societies and their American colonies accepted hierarchy, injustice, and exploitation as a normal condition of human life. Color and religious differences made it easier to enslave Africans. Europeans justified this slavery by denying the humanity of the African. These attitudes were reinforced by nineteenth-century Social Darwinism and are the root of contemporary racist ideas.

3. Africans had slaves and participated in the slave trade. But although slavery existed in many times and cultures throughout human history, slavery in the Americas, including the United States, was a fundamentally different institution. There was no reciprocal obligation by the elite to the enslaved. Enslavement, with denial of humanity, was a permanent hereditary status; there was an impassable racial barrier.

4. Democracy and community among White, male, Christian property holders in the early American republic rested on the exploitation of other groups, especially the enslavement of the African. The founders of the United States were aware of the hypocrisy of owning slaves. Slavery was intentionally not addressed in the Declaration of Independence and the U.S. Constitution.

5. Africans in the Americas resisted slavery in many different ways. They built families, communities, and religious institutions that asserted their humanity. In the United States, enslaved Africans developed an emancipatory Christianity based on the story of Exodus and laced it with African symbols. In Haiti and Brazil, there were successful slave rebellions. Historians W. E. B. DuBois and C. L. R. James believe the rebellion in Haiti was the impetus for the final decisions by Great Britain and the United States to support the suppression of the trans-Atlantic slave trade (DuBois, 1896, pp. 70–93; Williams & Harris, 1970, pp. 124–125).

6. White and African-American abolitionists struggled for decades against slavery. Most White abolitionists based their beliefs on their Protestant religion. *Uncle Tom's Cabin* was the "Common Sense" of the antislavery crusade because it presented the humanity of the enslaved African. The story of the complicity of some New Yorkers with slavery and resistance of others to oppression is not the story of White villainy. Many White New Yorkers took strong political stands against what they perceived of as a fundamental moral evil.

7. While Christian religious beliefs were used to challenge slavery, they were also used to justify it. Defenders of slavery, particularly in the South, used biblical citations to defend the "peculiar institution."

8. Slavery was a national, rather than a southern, institution. There was limited slavery in the North until 1840 and prosperity in the North rested on the slave trade and the processing of slave-produced raw materials.
9. The Civil War was not fought by the north to free Africans; it was fought to save the Union. It ended legal bondage, but not the racist ideas that supported the system.
10. With over 200,000 African Americans in the Union army and navy, the American Civil War should be seen as part of an African-American liberation struggle.

Ten Main Ideas About Slavery and the North

These ten main ideas are based on the history of slavery in New York and the North:

1. Slavery, until its abolition in New York State in the beginning of the nineteenth century, the trans-Atlantic slave trade, even after it was declared illegal in 1808, the financing of slave plantations in the South and the Caribbean, the shipping of slave-produced products, and the manufacture of goods using the commodities of slavery, were all integral to the prosperity of New Netherland, the British colony of New York, and New York State.
2. Many New Yorkers implicated in the slave system were politically influential and economically powerful. They shaped the policies of the state and nation. A number of prominent individuals and the founders of the state and national governments were participants in and profited from the slave system.
3. In order to preserve the Union and protect their own profits from products produced by enslaved workers, many New York and national leaders who opposed the expansion of slavery into the West were willing to compromise with Southern slave owners and to support the slave system in the South even after the outbreak of the Civil War.
4. Despite the Declaration of Independence's promise of human equality, there were ideological inconsistencies in the early nation. Many leading New Yorkers, including some White opponents of slavery, believed in the racial inferiority of African Americans, opposed full political rights for African Americans, and endorsed their recolonization in Africa. Some of the most radical abolitionists in New York who accepted Black equality were unwilling to support equal rights for women. Significantly, Frederick Douglass and Susan B. Anthony were major allies in the struggles for rights for both African Americans and women.

5. The slave system and racism contributed to an endemic fear of uprisings by New York's African population during the colonial era. Rumors of potential rebellion led to "witch hunts." Africans who fought for their freedom in the colonial era were summarily tried, tortured, and executed. Suspects were tortured until they confessed to "crimes" and implicated others. Minor infractions of the slave code were severely punished. On a number of occasions violent mobs attacked African Americans and White abolitionists.

6. At the same time, New York State offered a safe haven to many Africans who escaped from slavery and a place where free African Americans could organize politically with White allies to end the slave system and achieve full citizenship. New Yorkers, both Black and White, were active participants and national leaders in political campaigns to end slavery and to resist the oppression of Black people.

7. African Americans in New York resisted slavery through active and passive means. They resisted slavery by running away to freedom, organizing their own cultural and religious institutions, building families and communities, openly or surreptitiously disobeying slaveowners, and through open revolt.

8. Resistance to slavery was often violent. Enslaved Africans in New York openly rebelled against slavery during the colonial era. Many supported the British against forces fighting for American independence in an effort to achieve their own emancipation. Leading New York abolitionists, both Black and White, violated the law and physically prevented the recapture of runaway slaves. Some New York abolitionists were supporters of John Brown's military campaigns against the slave system and were implicated in his armed assault on a federal weapon's arsenal in 1859.

9. The histories of many parts of New York were influenced by slavery, the slave trade, and the struggles to end them. Because of the pattern of settlement in the seventeenth and eighteenth centuries, slavery in New York State was concentrated on Long Island, in New York City and its surroundings, and in the Hudson River Valley up through Albany. In the nineteenth century, the port of New York functioned as a major international center for financing the slave trade and the trade in goods produced by slave labor.

10. New York was a major center for abolitionist and anti-abolitionist movements and publications. Due to their proximity to Canada, to work opportunities, and to religious and other social movements, regions of New York State and cities located along the route of the Erie Canal played major roles on the underground railroad and in antislavery agitation during the nineteenth

century. Toward the middle of the nineteenth century, the availability of land in the North Country made it a safe haven for free Blacks and for escaped slaves who sought a place where they could build families and communities.

Any educator who wants to effectively teach about a subject as sensitive and controversial as the history of slavery in the North has to see her- or himself as a political activist willing to fight to ensure that these main ideas are included in the curriculum. Teachers often express reluctance to deviate from topics that traditionally have been found on standardized tests. They are afraid supervisors will target them if their students score below expectations. However, experienced teachers know that students who are engaged by what they are learning will have greater conceptual understanding, more content knowledge, and higher academic skills than students who learn by rote and fail to see the relevance of what is being presented to them. If we allow the tests (and the test-makers) to determine what we teach, we undermine ourselves and our ability, and the ability of our students, to become thinkers, teachers, learners, historians, and effective citizens. It is a heavy price to pay for acquiescence to ignorance, inaccuracy, and injustice. To paraphrase and slightly modify the quote from Henry David Thoreau that opens this chapter, if the *curriculum* is of such a nature that it requires you to be an agent of injustice to another, then, I say, change the *curriculum*.

Chapter 3

Complicity and Resistance

My paramount object in this struggle is to save the Union, and is not either to save or destroy slavery.

—Abraham Lincoln

In her book *Uncle Tom's Cabin,* Harriet Beecher Stowe (1852/1981) attacked the institution of slavery, rather than Southerners. Her primary goal was to humanize enslaved Africans forced to endure physical, psychological, and sexual abuse from plantation owners and slave traders. Stowe was an activist as well as an author, and she wanted to promote the abolitionist cause and rally support against the Fugitive Slave Act of 1850. In one of the more powerful scenes in the book, the enslaved Tom, an honest man and devout Christian, is ordered beaten by a sadistic master, Simon Legree, when Tom refused Legree's order to whip a fellow slave (Stowe, 1852/1981, pp. 506–509).

After initial serialization in an abolitionist newspaper in Washington DC, *Uncle Tom's Cabin* was published as a novel in 1852. Within five years, over half a million copies were sold, an incredible number for that time. According to legend, on meeting Harriet Beecher Stowe in 1862, Abraham Lincoln described her as "the little woman who wrote the book that started this great war!" (Stowe, C., 1911, p. 203).

While most of *Uncle Tom's Cabin* described conditions in the South and the brutality of slavery, Harriet Beecher Stowe shifted focus in her "Concluding Remarks" (chapter XLV, p. 624). In a political statement aimed at readers who were overwhelmingly from the North and Europe, she charged that the people of the northern states had "defended, encouraged, and participated" in the enslavement of Africans and were therefore "more guilty for it, before God, than the South. . . ."

Stowe believed that if only "the mothers of the free states" had opposed slavery, their sons "would not have connived at the extension of slavery, in our national body; the sons of the free states would not, as they do, trade the souls and bodies of men as an equivalent to money, in their mercantile dealings."

In a tone more reminiscent of abolitionists such as William Lloyd Garrison than of her own narrative, Harriet Beecher Stowe declared, "Northern men, northern mothers, northern Christians, have something more to do than denounce their brethren at the South; they have to look to the evil among themselves."

In these statements, Stowe addressed a number of the essential questions, about humanity and history, and themes about slavery that should be discussed in social studies classrooms. While she is especially concerned about the nature of evil and the essence of humanity, she also writes about slavery as a national system and about the possibility of resistance.

National System

In 2000, two opinion essays in the *New York Times* challenged historians and teachers to rethink the way we teach about slavery in the United States, especially slavery and the Northern states. According to Eric Foner (2000, p. A29), a prominent historian, "(o)n the eve of the Civil War, the economic value of slaves in the United States was $3 billion in 1860 currency, more than the combined value of all the factories, railroads, and banks in the country. Much of the North's economic prosperity derived from what Abraham Lincoln, in his second inaugural address, called 'the bondman's two hundred and fifty years of unrequited toil.'"

In "History Lessons From the Slaves of New York," Brent Staples (2000, section IV, p. 18), a member of the *New York Times* Editorial Board, described how New York City's ties with slavery go back deep into its colonial past. The Dutch, who built New Amsterdam, "recruited settlers with an advertisement that promised to provide them with slaves who 'would accomplish more work for their masters, at less expense than [white] farm servants, who must be bribed to go thither by a great deal of money and promises.'" Enslaved Africans helped build Trinity Church, the streets of the early city, and a wooden fortification located where Wall Street is today.

Staples's essay reported the findings of biological anthropologists from Howard University who studied "the skeletal remains of more than four hundred African slaves whose graves were accidentally uncovered during the construction of a federal office tower in lower Manhattan nine years ago." When it was closed in 1794, the African Burial Ground, which was outside that era's city limits, probably contained between 10,000 and 20,000 bodies. Staples believed the research team's work showed that "colonial New York was just as dependent on slavery as many Southern cities, and in some cases even more so."

In addition, "the brutality etched on these skeletons easily matches the worst of what we know of slavery in the South. . . . Of the 400 skeletons taken to Howard, about 40 percent are of children under the age of 15, and the most common cause of death was malnutrition. . . . The adult skeletons show that many of these people died of unrelenting hard labor. Strain on the muscles and ligaments was so extreme that muscle attachments were commonly ripped away from the skeleton—taking chunks of bone with them—leaving the body in perpetual pain."

In "Slavery's Fellow Travelers," Eric Foner reminded readers "of the usually glossed-over participation of the North in America's slave system. . . , even after Northern states no longer allowed slaveholding within their own borders." According to Foner, "Nowhere did the connection go deeper than in New York City," where, as the nation approached Civil War, "Mayor Fernando Wood proposed that New York declare itself a free city, so as to be able to continue to profit from slavery."

Foner argued:

"Accounts of the city's rise to commercial prominence in the 19th century rightly point to the Erie Canal's role in opening access to produce from the West, but they don't talk about the equal importance to the city's prosperity of its control over the South's cotton trade. Because of this connection, New York merchants and bankers were consistently pro-slavery, pressing during the 1840's and 1850's for one concession to the South after another in order to maintain their lucrative access to cotton."

In response to this forgotten history, Foner proposed that "when New York's history is taught in public schools, the city's intimate link with slavery should receive full attention." In addition, "(t)he city should have a permanent exhibition —perhaps even an independent museum—depicting the history of slavery and New York's connection with it."

As of this writing, Foner's challenge at best has been addressed only partially. The reasons, of course, are largely political.

Curriculum Wars

Since the late 1980s, when New York State Education officials convened a committee to develop a "Curriculum of Inclusion," there have been sharp and at times nasty debates over how to address ethnic diversity among the state's students and over whose history would be included in the social studies curriculum. New York's troubling relationship with slavery has been one of the more sticky subjects to resolve (Cornbeth and Waugh, 1995).

In 1996, the state legislature decided to shift the focus of the social studies curriculum away from diversity and inclusion and substituted a requirement that the state Board of Regents have public schools devote attention to human rights issues. The New York State Human Rights curriculum is supposed to include guidelines and material for teaching about the European Holocaust, the Great Irish Famine, and Slavery and the trans-Atlantic slave trade. An award winning 1,000-page interdisciplinary fourth- through twelfth-grade curriculum on the Great Irish Famine was completed and distributed by the state in 2001. A number of Holocaust curricula developed by museums, local school districts, and nonprofit agencies were already in use. However, an official—or even an officially recommended—curriculum for teaching about Slavery and the trans-Atlantic slave trade was entrapped in a web of racial politics.

Part of the problem was that the State Department of Education envisioned the slavery and the trans-Atlantic slave trade curriculum as a celebration of "New York's Freedom Trail," its role on the underground railway, and as a base of operations for abolitionists. Many historians, however, especially those from the African American community, wanted students to take a much more critical look at the state's role in promoting and profiting from human bondage. Finally, in September 2005, the New York State Legislature acted again and established an Amistad Commission to examine whether the "physical and psychological terrorism" against Africans in the slave trade was being adequately taught in the state's schools. But the battle over what gets taught is certainly not over. A year after the law was approved, only two people had been appointed to the commission.

Important steps have been taken by the New York Historical Society toward the possible creation of a museum on New York's participation in the slave system, but so far its widely reviewed and visited exhibits on "Slavery in New York" are only temporary. The first exhibit focused on the colonial era up until New York's emancipation day in 1827. It included hundreds of artifacts, documents, paintings, and maps. The second exhibit, "Commerce and Conscience," extended the chronicle on slavery into the era after the Civil War (Collins, 2005, p. E1).

A logical place for a permanent museum would be at New York City's South Street Seaport restoration site. At the seaport, enslaved Africans were unloaded from cargo vessels and sold or rented out at the Wall Street slave market. It is also the site of the building that housed the restaurant, Sweet's, where in the first half of the nineteenth-century slavers, who were known as "blackbirders," met to discuss smuggling the illegal cargo they called "black ivory." Nearby is 55 South Street (now part of the 111 Wall Street complex), the office of Moses Taylor, the nineteenth-century banker who helped finance the illegal trade. Currently, none of these sites is marked.

Lower Manhattan
"Slavery in New York" Walking Tour

1. Distributed by African American History and United States government students from Law, Government and Community Service Magnet High School, Cambria Heights, Queens.
2. Based on the *New York and Slavery: Complicity and Resistance* curriculum guide (http://www.nyscss.org).

   Other than at the colonial era African American Burial Ground, which was uncovered during excavations for a federal office building in 1991, these sites, and slavery in New York in general, have been erased from historical memory. There is not even a historical marker at the South Street Seaport in the financial district of Manhattan where enslaved Africans were traded in the seventeenth century and where illegal slaving expeditions were planned and financed up until the time of the American Civil War.

New York and Slavery
African American Heritage Trail Markers

1. Wall Street Slave Market (Wall and Water Streets). A market for the sale and hire of enslaved Africans and Indians was established here at the Meal (Grain) Market in 1711 by the New York Common Council.
2. Amistad Defense Committee (122 Pearl Street near Hanover Street). Offices of silk merchants Lewis and Arthur Tappan, abolitionists who organized the defense committee to free enslaved Africans on the Amistad. The Tappans were among the founders of the American Anti-Slavery Society in December 1833. In 1834, it was attacked by a pro-slavery mob.
3. Financier of the Slave Trade (55 South Street). Moses Taylor was a sugar merchant and banker with offices at 55 South Street. Taylor became a member of the board of the City Bank in 1837, and served as its president from 1855 until his death in 1882. Taylor's personal resources and role as business agent for the leading exporter of Cuban sugar to the United States was invaluable to the growth of the institution now known as Citibank.
4. Slave Traders' Meeting Place (Fulton and South Streets). The men who smuggled enslaved Africans referred to themselves as "blackbirders" and to their illegal human cargo as "black ivory." Their favorite New York City meeting place was Sweet's Restaurant at the corner of Fulton and South streets.

(*continued*)

5. Abolitionist Meeting House (118 Williams Street between Fulton and John). Site of a boarding house operated by Asenath Hatch Nicholson, an ardent abolitionist. Starting in 1835, abolitionists met here to plan campaigns to end slavery.

6. African Free School (William and Beekman Streets). The first African Free School was established at 245 Williams Street in 1787 by the New York Manumission Society. Forty boys and girls were taught in a single room. It was destroyed in 1814 and replaced by a new building on William Street near Duane Street.

7. 1712 Slave Rebellion (Maiden Lane near Broadway). In 1712, a group of over twenty enslaved Africans set fire to a building on Maiden Lane in Manhattan and ambushed Whites who tried to put out the blaze. Eight White men were killed in this abortive rebellion. In response, thirteen Black men were hanged, one was starved to death, four were burned alive at the stake, and another broken on the wheel.

8. Hughson's Tavern (Liberty and Trinity streets). The location of the tavern where enslaved Africans, free Blacks, and White supporters are supposed to have plotted the 1741 Slave Conspiracy. White New Yorkers, afraid of another slave revolt, responded to rumors and unexplained fires with the arrest of 146 enslaved Africans, the execution of thirty-five Blacks and four Whites, and the transport to other colonies of seventy enslaved people. Historians continue to doubt whether a slave conspiracy ever existed.

9. New York City Hall. William Havemeyer, elected mayor of New York City in 1845, 1848 and 1872, launched his political career with wealth from the family's sugar refining business. The sugar was produced in the South and in Cuba by enslaved African labor. Fernando Wood, as Mayor of New York City in 1861, called on the city to secede from the Union along with the South. As a congressman, he opposed the Thirteenth Amendment to the United States Constitution.

10. African Burial Ground. The African Burial Ground is an approximately five-acre cemetery that was used between the late 1600s and 1796 and originally contained between ten thousand and twenty thousand burials. Despite the harsh treatment that these African people in colonial America received, the 427 bodies recovered from the site were buried with great care and love. They were wrapped in linen shrouds and methodically positioned in well-built cedar or pine coffins that sometimes contained beads or other treasured objects.

(continued)

11. 1741 Execution of Enslaved Africans (Foley Square). The site where enslaved Africans, free Blacks, and White supporters accused of plotting the 1741 Slave Conspiracy were executed. White New Yorkers, afraid of another slave revolt, responded to rumors and unexplained fires with the arrest of 146 enslaved Africans, the execution of thirty-five Blacks and four Whites, and the transport to other colonies of seventy enslaved people. Historians continue to doubt whether a slave conspiracy ever existed.

Other Important Manhattan Sites

- David Ruggles's Home (36 Lispendard Street, one block south of Canal Street at the corner of Church Street). In 1838, Ruggles harbored a fugitive slave here named Frederick Washington Bailey who later became known as Frederick Douglass.
- Land of the Blacks (Washington Square Park). In 1644, eleven enslaved African men petitioned the local government and obtained their freedom in exchange for the promise to pay an annual tax in produce. They each received the title to land on the outskirts of the colony where they would be a buffer against attack from native forces. Black farmers soon owned a two-mile long strip of land from what is now Canal Street to Thirty-fourth Street in Manhattan. This is the site of the farm of Anthony Portugies.
- Seneca Village (Central Park). Seneca Village was Manhattan's first prominent community of African American property owners. From 1825 to 1857, it was located between Eighty-second and Eighty-ninth streets at Seventh and Eighth Avenues in what is now a section of Central Park (Pezone and Singer, 2006, pp. 32–35).

Faculty, students, and alumni from the Hofstra University School of Education and Allied Human Services were part of the team that wrote the New York State Great Irish Famine curriculum. Starting in 2001, members of this team used resources provided by a federal Department of Education Teaching American History Grant to develop a curriculum guide for the teaching of slavery with a focus on New York State. With added support from the New York and New Jersey Councils for the Social Studies, it published 268- and 84-page versions of "New York and Slavery: Complicity and Resistance" and posted the entire guide on the Internet at http://www.nyscss.org and http://people.hofstra.edu/faculty/alan_j_singer/. The curriculum guide received a National Council for the Social Studies Program of Excellence Award in 2005 and, as a result of renewed political pressure generated by the Amistad legislation, the State Education Department put a link to the guide on its Web site.

The accounts of slavery in New York and the North presented by Staples and Foner powerfully echo the famous front-page editorial by William Lloyd Garrison in the introductory issue of *The Liberator* (Seldes, 1960, p. 270) where he argued "that a greater revolution in public sentiment was to be effected in the free states . . . than at the south." He also related that in the North, he "found contempt more bitter, opposition more active, detraction more relentless, prejudice more stubborn, and apathy more frozen, than among slave owners themselves."

In response to this reception, Garrison "determined, at every hazard, to lift up the standard of emancipation in the eyes of the nation, within sight of Bunker Hill and in the birth place of liberty." He warned readers that he would not be silenced "till every chain be broken, and every bondman set free" and declared, "Let southern oppressors tremble—let their secret abettors tremble—let their northern apologists tremble—let all the enemies of the persecuted blacks tremble."

In Brooklyn, New York, Reverend Henry Ward Beecher of Plymouth Church espoused similar sentiments. In a sermon delivered in January, 1861, in the midst of the nation's secession crisis, Beecher declared that "(w)e who dwell in the North are not without responsibility for this sin. . . . When our Constitution was adopted; . . . All the institutions were prepared for liberty, and all the public men were on the side of liberty." However, because of the "delinquency of the North," the nation's commitment to liberty was "sacrificed." He calls the North's failure to preserve liberty "an astounding sin! It is an unparalleled guilt!" (Jensen, 2000, p. B11).

Drawing Connections

The antebellum North's "secret abettors" and "apologists" for slavery are under attack on a number of other fronts at the start of the twenty-first century. Deadria Farmer-Paellmann, a lawyer who grew up in Brooklyn, New York, has uncovered documentary evidence that prominent corporations still in operation profited from the nineteenth-century slave trade (Finn, 2000, B2; Farmer-Paellmann, 2006). According to Farmer-Paellmann, Providence Bank of Rhode Island, a predecessor of the modern FleetBoston Financial Corporation, was one of the most serious offenders. One of its founders borrowed money from the bank to finance business operations that included slaving expeditions. He was eventually prosecuted in federal court for participating in the international slave trade after it became illegal under United States laws.

A team of reporters from the *Hartford Courant* in Connecticut has documented that state's complicity with slavery, as a supplier of food to Southern and Caribbean plantations and as a purchaser of slave-produced cotton for use in its mills. Because of these efforts, two Connecticut companies have publicly apologized for supporting the slave system. The Aetna Insurance Company of Hartford insured slave owners against the loss of their human property. The horrors of slavery emerge in a rider to insurance policies that declares the company did not have "to pay the premium for slaves who were lynched, worked to death or who committed suicide." The *Hartford Courant,* founded in 1764 and the oldest continuously published newspaper in the United States, disclosed that it had published advertisements for the sale of slaves in the eighteenth and nineteenth centuries (Zielbauer, 2000; Farrow, Lang, & Frank, 2005).

Churches have also started to acknowledge the role of their parishioners in promoting African slavery. In Rhode Island, the United Church of Christ publicly repented for the participation of Northerners, particularly Bristol and Newport, RI merchants, who profited from the slave system (Niebuhr, 1999, p. A14). While this denomination was historically tied to antislavery abolitionists, one of the church's buildings was named after a family involved in the slave trade.

On a political level, Representative John Conyers Jr., Democrat of Michigan, has spearheaded a decade-long campaign to recognize broader national participation in slavery and slavery's long-term impact on American society (Cardwell, 2000, B7). Conyers has repeatedly introduced a bill in Congress to establish a commission to study reparations for slavery. While the bill has never emerged from committee, the issue has garnered support from intellectuals like Randall Robinson, the president of TransAfrica, a lobbying group, and the author of *The Debt: What America Owes to Blacks* (2001), and Harvard University professors Charles T. Ogletree and Henry Louis Gates.

In New York City, City Council member Charles Barron has pushed for hearings on the "'Queen Mother Moore' Reparations Resolution for Descendants of Enslaved Africans." It would mandate annual New York City "Reparations Awareness Day" and a "Declaration of Slavery and the Trans-Atlantic Slave Trade as Crimes Against Humanity." He has also questioned whether streets, parks, and public buildings should continue to be named after slaveholders and participants in the trans-Atlantic slave trade (Rivera, 2007, B3).

Henry Louis Gates, Jr. (2001, Section 4, p. 15) has proposed that since "many Western nations reaped large and lasting benefits from African slavery, while African nations did not," the industrialized West bears a collective responsibility for the condition of Africa today. He calls for massive investment to stop the spread of AIDS in Africa and to economically develop the continent. There should be similar investment in rebuilding American cities and for the development of the Caribbean islands, home to millions of displaced Africans. While this may seem radical to some, the idea of rebuilding American cities echoes the Great Society program proposed by President Lyndon Johnson in a speech at the University of Michigan in 1964. President Johnson declared, "We have the opportunity to move not only toward the rich society and the powerful society, but upward to the Great Society. The Great Society rests on abundance and liberty for all. It demands an end to poverty and racial injustice, to which we are totally committed in our time." He warned his audience that, "Our society will never be great until our cities are great" (Johnson, 1964).

Whatever your position on reparations, an issue that certainly opens a whole new realm of debate, New York, the North, and the nation certainly need to confront the actual history of slavery in this country.

A reevaluation of the history of slavery will challenge some of our country's most sacred myths. Remember that Abraham Lincoln wrote, "If there be those who would not save the Union unless they could at the same time destroy slavery, I do not agree with them. My paramount object in this struggle is to save the Union, and is not either to save or destroy slavery. If I could save the Union without freeing any slave, I would do it; and if I could save it by freeing all the slaves, I would do it; and if I could do it by freeing some and leaving others alone, I would also do that" (Stern, 1940, pp. 718–719).

Chapter 4

Settlement

And for the advancement of the cultivation of the land there, it would not be unwise to allow, at the request of the patroons, colonists and other farmers, the introduction, from Brazil there, of as many negroes as they would be disposed to pay for at a fair price; which negroes would accomplish more work for their masters, and at a less expense, than farm servants, who must be bribed to go thither by a great deal of money and promises.

—Report of the Board of Accounts on New Netherland (1644)

My wife Judi and I visited the Dutch city of Amsterdam during the summer of 2002. Amsterdam is a beautiful city in which to walk, and it is especially hospitable to bicyclists. Guidebooks praise its cafés, canals, churches, and small museums. Its older sections, Amsterdam Centrum, were built in the seventeenth century when the city was the center of a global trading network and the Netherlands was Europe's leading economic power. The cobblestoned streets and canals are lined with thousands of narrow three-story buildings topped by fanciful gables. According to legend, the narrowness of the buildings was to avoid property taxes determined by square footage, and the design of the gables was a way to distinguish the buildings from each other before the advent of a system of street addresses. The lack of interior space meant that anything but the most crowded stairwell was considered wasteful. Each building came equipped with an external beam and pulley projecting from an upper story, which was used to hoist furniture and goods into the house. A late-sixteenth-century population explosion, fueled by refugees from religious wars waged across Europe, left the city extremely crowded.

The overcrowding was exacerbated because much of the Netherlands, including Amsterdam, is below sea level and was initially unsuitable for habitation and agriculture. Because of this, many of the early houses and public buildings had to be constructed on stilts. In 1613, local governors and merchants launched a canal and dike building project that within a hundred years virtually tripled the usable land area inside the city limits. Today, Amsterdam has over 100 kilometers of interlocking canals (a little less than seventy miles) that lead into the Amstel River to the east and the old harbor and the inland sea in the north. The seven main canals form concentric rings around the old city and are spanned by over 1,200 bridges.

It is neither an accident nor a quaint historical anecdote that the first European settlers on Manhattan Island were the Dutch. In 1728, Daniel Defoe, author of *Robinson Crusoe* and an investor in the trans-Atlantic slave trade, described the Dutch as "the Carryers of the World, the middle Persons in Trade, the Factors and Brokers of Europe" (DeFoe, 1728, p. 192). The story of New York's complicity with slavery and the pivotal role of slavery in the development of modern capitalist economies begin with the canals, dikes, and ponders (reclaimed land) of Amsterdam and The Netherlands (Postma, 1990, p. 9).

In 1579, the Union of Utrecht established the United Provinces (later known as the Dutch Republic and the Netherlands). It was a time of immense economic expansion, new global interaction, enormous local turmoil, and unbridled potential for exploitation and profit. Spain and Portugal, with the approval of the Roman Catholic Church, were carving up a vastly larger world and the Dutch, as well as the British and French, wanted a share.

For a new and small country with a limited population and scarce military power, the key to success in the race for the world's resources was control over trade. Building on their experience as financiers and middlemen in the exchange of goods between the Baltic region and the Mediterranean Sea, Dutch merchants and bankers entered the East Asian, African, and American trade. In 1585, 65 pecent of Amsterdam's richest businessmen were overseas merchants. By 1631, the figure was over 80 percent (Israel, 1995, p. 347).

The organization of the Dutch East India Company (known as the VOC) in 1602 and the Dutch West India Company (WIC) in 1621 led to Dutch dominance over the trade of New World silver and gold—looted by the Spanish from Native American empires—for East Asian spices. To facilitate trade around the southern coast of Africa, the VOC constructed a series of fortified trading posts on the west or Gold Coast of Africa. By 1634, these trading posts had propelled Dutch merchants into involvement in, and eventual dominance over, the trans-Atlantic slave trade. Temporary Dutch control over Brazil in the middle of the seventeenth century coupled with the labor of enslaved Africans gave Dutch merchants and bankers control over the early New World sugar trade. Later, Dutch merchants secured a monopoly over the Spanish colonial slave trade (known as the *asiento*).

By the end of the seventeenth century, the Portuguese, Dutch, English, French, and Danish were all involved in the trans-Atlantic slave trade. While the Netherlands had a relatively small population, approximately 1.5 million people, its merchant fleet, based on the round-sided *vlieboot* or *fluyt* (which allowed for greater storage space and a smaller crew) was probably equal in size to the fleets of the rest of Europe put together. A major portion of its cargo included 1.6 million Africans transported across the Atlantic Ocean between 1601 and 1700. This "cargo" contributed to what historians have described as a "Golden Age" for the Dutch (Braudel, 1979, p. 190; Postma, 1990, pp. 7–33; Blackburn, 1997, pp. 326–327).

Profits from the spice trade with Asia, the trans-Atlantic slave trade, and New World sugar production financed the growth of Dutch industry, including fine ceramics, papermaking, and tobacco products. They paid for the development of the Amsterdam canal system and supported the urbanization of the Netherlands. Between 1570 and 1647, the population of Amsterdam grew from 30,000 to 140,000, an increase of almost five times in less than eighty years. Other Dutch towns experienced similar dynamic growth. Dutch dominance over trade in this era provided the capital for physically building a nation. Windmills, one of the bigger tourist attractions today, were built to drain and reclaim marginal land, transforming it into productive farmland (Israel, 1995, pp. 313–335; Postma, 1990, pp. 7–33).

Dutch merchants may have been involved in the slave trade with Spanish colonies as early as 1528, but the first successful Dutch slaving expedition on the coast of Africa was probably not until 1606, when over four hundred enslaved Africans were transported to Trinidad in the Caribbean. With the conquest of Portugal's Brazilian colony and its renaming as New Holland in 1630, Dutch merchants entered the slave trade on a regular basis. Curaçao in the Caribbean, with its natural harbor, was established as a Dutch trading station in the trans-Atlantic slave trade. The peak years for Dutch involvement in the trans-Atlantic slave trade were 1670–1674, when Dutch vessels transported an average of 4,940 captives per year across the Atlantic. The region around Amsterdam, which included Amsterdam, Haarlem, Leiden, and Gouda, was the home port for approximately one-third of the slave trade vessels and accounted for the transport of nearly 50,000 Africans (Braudel, 1979, pp. 12–14; Israel, 1995, pp. 313–335; Postma, 1990, pp. 7–8).

Selecting a Starting Point

Where an historian or teacher begins the story of the trans-Atlantic slave trade and slavery in the territory that became the United States is of fundamental importance. It defines the rest of the story, and it determines how you will present what you teach. As students at Law, Government, and

Community Service Magnet High School learned during their campaign to have historical markers about New York's involvement with slavery posted in lower Manhattan, many historical and educational decisions are made based on political considerations.

During the antebellum era, Southern apologists for slavery repeatedly cited its roots in the ancient Greco-Roman world and pointed to references in the Old and New Testaments in order to justify the "peculiar institution." Eugene Genovese and Elizabeth Fox-Genovese (2005) dedicate a chapter in *The Mind of the Master Class* to the scriptural justification of slavery (pp. 473-504). Thomas Jefferson, in his *Notes on the State of Virginia* (1785), argued the legitimacy of slavery based on the fact that the status of Roman slaves had not prevented them from making intellectual contributions in the arts and sciences. At the United States Constitutional Convention, Charles Pinckney of South Carolina declared, "If slavery be wrong, it is justified by the example of all the world, including the case of Greece and Rome" (Koch, 1966, p. 505). Later, during congressional debate over the Missouri Compromise, Pinckney challenged opponents of slavery to cite "a single line in the Old or New Testament either censuring or forbidding it" (Annals of Congress, 1820).

Prominent historians have looked deeply into the European past to explain the origins of the slave system. Pulitzer Prize–winning historian David Brion Davis (2006) offers an extensive discussion of slavery in the ancient world and argues that attitudes and institutions from Roman times shaped the legal foundation of modern slavery. Winthrop Jordan (1968) focuses more on the European cultural conception of "blackness" and "otherness" and argues for an inherent racism that preceded and determined African enslavement.

On the other hand, Eric Williams (1944/1994) in *Capitalism & Slavery* argues that the enslavement of the African was directly related to the development of capitalism in the post-Columbian era. According to Williams, slavery was primarily a solution to the "Caribbean labor problem." Without a slave labor force "the great development of the Caribbean sugar plantation . . . would have been impossible" (29).

Robin Blackburn (1997) in *The Making of New World Slavery* also examines slavery in the ancient world. He concludes that, while New World slave systems drew on "traditional ingredients," they were "radically new in character compared with prior forms of slavery" (3). Its scale, destructiveness, "businesslike methods," and "thoroughly commercial character differentiated it from earlier practices" (10). According to Blackburn, the traditional European slave system atrophied with the collapse of the Roman Empire (83). New World slavery was a modern enterprise recognizable for its market entrepreneurs and captains of industry. Roman slaves were sold because they were captured, usually in war. Enslaved Africans in the trans-Atlantic slave trade were captured with the express purpose of being sold to feed the New World labor market. Blackburn argues that post-Columbian slavery was part of an emerging capitalist economic system within an increasingly European-dominated world.

Another argument made by apologists of slavery, in some ways even more insidious than the biblical and classical justification is to blame Africans for the trans-Atlantic slave trade. Although there was slavery in Africa prior to the arrival of Europeans, traditional African slavery did not strip people of their humanity and turn them into commodities to be shipped halfway around the world. Once the trans-Atlantic slave trade had been established, Africans did capture and sell other Africans into slavery, but they did not capture and sell their "own," members of their own tribe or nation. Explaining slavery by blaming Africans is as absurd as justifying the murder of Europeans because White people killed other White people during World War I and II.

Students should know that there are different explanations of the origins of New World slavery, but at the same time, teachers have an obligation to examine the issues, read extensively, and take a stand on historical interpretation. I think the evidence strongly supports the connection between slavery in the post-Columbian world and capitalism, although some important historians disagree. In any event, it is unacceptable for teachers to justify the enslavement of Africans by citing African involvement in the slave trade and slavery.

Main Ideas and Essential Questions

The history of slavery in the Dutch New Netherland colony illustrates a series of issues in the study of history that need to be integrated into our understanding of the world as well as into the social studies curriculum. The first issue concerns the importance of overcoming regional compartmentalization when presenting an historical narrative. This is a significant problem in the study of history, where areas of expertise tend to be narrowly defined. Few historians, let alone high school teachers and students, draw a clear connection between the development of the Netherlands, the settlement of the Dutch North American colonies, and the trans-Atlantic slave trade.

Following the Colombian encounter at the end of the fifteenth and beginning of the sixteenth centuries, the histories of different parts of the globe were increasingly interwoven. In the seventeenth century, the New Netherland colony developed as part of an emerging global economic system that tied together Europe, Africa, Asia, South America, the Caribbean, and North America and promoted trade in enslaved human beings. Until they were displaced by the English, Dutch merchants were among the principal players in this system. Traditional instruction in history, with its focus on single regions and narrow time frames, fails to make necessary connections.

The second issue involves the problem of reading the present into the past as if historical developments were predetermined. Today, New York City is one of the world's major cultural and economic centers and its metropolitan area is home to nearly twenty million people. However, prior to the first quarter of the nineteenth century, New York City, and the European colonies on the North America mainland in general, were not that important on the world stage. In 1667, the Dutch were willing to trade their territorial claims to New Amsterdam for Surinam in South America. The British later granted their North American colonies independence rather than risk losing more highly valued colonies in the Caribbean such as Jamaica and Barbados to the Spanish or French. While the enslavement of Africans was central to the history of the Dutch New Netherland colony and later to the British colony of New York, the settlement itself was never more than an outpost on the periphery of an increasingly European-dominated world.

The third issue is related to what I call the "Fallacy of Athena." According to Greek legend, the Goddess of Wisdom emerged fully formed from the head of Zeus. But history does not work that way. In the Dutch New Netherland colony there is a gradual definition of the status of Africans out of uncertain legal beginnings, a codification that is not completed until after the British seizure of power. At least at the start of European settlement in North America, people with African ancestry could be (though they usually were not) accepted as free and contributing members of the community (Horton & Horton, 2005, pp. 28–30; Moore, 2005, pp. 38–48).

The fourth issue has to do with the lingering effect of cultural institutions and beliefs. Once slavery became associated with race and took on a permanent dimension, it became increasingly difficult for Africans in America to secure any rights or to challenge White domination.

A Brief History of Dutch New Amsterdam

As part of this post-Columbian global economic expansion, the Dutch, who were much better at establishing trading posts than permanent settlements, founded the colony of New Netherland along a river valley in North America. Its main trading post, New Amsterdam, was built on an island in a protected harbor where the river flowed into the Atlantic Ocean.

The first documented European visitor to what would become New York harbor was probably Giovanni da Verrazano. An Italian navigator, he arrived in 1524 while exploring the North American coast for France (Ellis, 1966, p. 11). The bridge that vessels pass under today as they enter the harbor bears his name and honors his voyage. It is one of the longest and most elegant suspension bridges in the world. Once a year in the spring it is briefly closed to vehicular traffic and bicyclists can peddle across and savor its panoramic views.

The next European explorer who is believed to have arrived in New York harbor was not even European. In 1525, Estéban Gómez, who was of at least partial African ancestry, arrived in the service of Portugal. He was one of many people of African and mixed African and European backgrounds involved in the Atlantic naval trade during the sixteenth and seventeenth century, a period before the final institutionalization of race-based chattel slavery (Moore, 2005, p. 33).

The first two European-sponsored voyages to the New York area left nothing behind and, as a result, are of limited historical importance. It was more than eighty years later that the arrival of an English ship's captain, sailing for the Dutch in search of a northwest water route from Europe to Asia, led to permanent European settlement in the region.

In 1609, African seamen might have been among the sailors who helped Henry Hudson navigate the *Half Moon*, a sixty-three-foot-long *galliot* (flat-bottomed boat), into New York's bay (Ellis, 1966, p. 15). The historical record does not identify who these men were. However, we do know that Africans often served on these voyages. Matthieu da Costa, a free Black man who translated for French traders in Canada, was later hired by the Dutch and may have visited the New York area with one of the early expeditions (Moore, 2005, p. 33; Katz, 1997, p. 1).

The first Dutch agent of African ancestry who can be documented in the New York region was Jan Rodriguez. In either 1612 or 1613, a Dutch ship's captain named Thijs Mossel built a temporary wooden trading post on Manhattan Island. When Mossel returned to the Netherlands, Rodriguez remained behind to trade with local natives as the region's first merchant and nonnative resident (Katz, 1997, p. 2; Moore, 2005, p. 34).

The permanent European settlement on the site of what would become New York City began in 1625 when the Dutch West India Company (WIC) established the village of New Amsterdam on Manhattan Island. The colony was set up by WIC as a business whose main goal was to profit from selling beaver furs and other American goods in Europe. From the start, the Dutch settlement suffered from a labor shortage. The solution, to merchants who were already engaged in the trans-Atlantic slave trade, was to employ enslaved Africans to clear land, plant and harvest crops, and to build houses, roads, bridges, and fortifications (Burrows & Wallace, 1999, p. 21).

In 1626, a WIC ship brought eleven enslaved male Africans to the colony. Based on some of their names—Paul d'Angola, Simon Congo, Anthony Portuguese, and John Francisco—they were probably Africans from the southwest coast of Africa who were captured or purchased from the Portuguese. Two years later, three enslaved Angolan women arrived. At the time, New Amsterdam was a small village with about thirty wooden houses and fewer than two hundred people (Katz, 1997, p. 2).

In 1629, in order to attract European settlers to the New Netherland colony, WIC promised them that they would be able to purchase African slaves. The company later promised that each "patroon" would be allotted twelve Black men and women and allowed its North American colonists to sell food to Dutch-controlled Brazil in exchange for enslaved Africans. In July, 1646, instructions from the Dutch West India Company office in Amsterdam to the Director General and Council in New Netherlands recognized that "the promotion of agriculture" required "the conveyance thither of as many Negroes as they [patroons, colonists, and other farmers] are willing to purchase at a fair price." In 1648, WIC suggested that under certain restrictions the colony might even be able to trade for slaves directly with Angola (Donnan, 1932/1969, p. 411).

Teaching About Slavery in Dutch New Amsterdam

The importance of African slavery in the plans for developing the Dutch colony is clearly presented in a 1643 woodcut labeled with the banner "Nieu Amsterdam." This image lends itself to an introductory lesson on the economic importance of slavery in the northern colonies that I have taught to middle school students. They work in teams of three or four and make three lists: What do you see? What do you learn? What questions do you have?

In the foreground are two Dutch farmers, probably a married couple. They are standing on an elevated ridge in what is possibly Brooklyn Heights. The man, who is on the right, is plainly dressed in breeches, a coat, a cape, and a broad-brimmed hat. His right arm points toward his wife and his left hand holds what looks to be tobacco leaves. The woman's clothing is a little more stylized than her husband's, tucked in at the waist and billowing at the shoulders and feet. She holds a box of farm produce. In the distance are sailing ships and a wooden settlement (possibly representing the southern tip of Manhattan Island).

What students immediately focus on are four Africans in the background just behind and below the Dutch woman. Two of them, men, appear to be talking together. The other two, a man and a woman, are carrying large bundles on their heads as they do the work of the settlement (Hodges, 1999, p. 11). In 1644, Willem Kieft, the Dutch Governor, commented that "Negroes would accomplish more work for their masters and at less expense, than [Dutch] farm servants, who must be bribed to go thither by a great deal of money and promises" (Hodges, 1999, p. 25; O'Callaghan, 1856, v. I, pp. 123, 154, 162).

Every teacher on any level from junior high school through college knows that human sexuality is the one subject of constant interest to students, regardless of the specific topic being examined. Students always wonder how people did "*it*" in the past (to which I always answer—"Pretty much the same way we do '*it*' now"). For this reason alone, an examination of sexual relationships is a useful window into the culture and values of a community.

The issue of sex between Blacks and Whites came up early in the short history of the Dutch colony and again in eighteenth-century British New York. In 1638, Governor Kieft ordered European settlers not to have "Adulterous intercourse with Heathens [and] Blacks." But from the start, interracial sexual relationships were impossible to avoid. At least one of the early settlers, Anthony Jansen van Vaes, was a free Black of mixed African and European ancestry who was married to a Dutch woman. At one point, WIC banned the couple from Manhattan Island and they lived on Long Island near the area now known as Coney Island. Jan de Fries, whose father was a Dutch ship's captain and mother an African woman, was another settler of mixed race. He was a member of the Dutch Reformed Church and he and his wife, a Dutch woman originally from the Fort Orange settlement on the Hudson River about 150 miles north of New Amsterdam, had four children (Hodges, 1999, pp. 10–12).

Documentary Evidence

The documentary record for the Dutch colony of New Amsterdam is at best sketchy. Peter Stuyvesant served as Director-General of New Netherland from 1647 to 1664, and was the largest private owner of enslaved Africans; he claimed ownership of forty men and women. WIC remained the largest slave-holder in New Amsterdam as long as the company and the Dutch controlled the colony.

Under Stuyvesant's direction, a number of enslaved Africans became skilled caulkers, blacksmiths, bricklayers, and masons. In some cases, they were granted "half-freedom," which meant they were still obligated to provide WIC with labor when needed and that their children were not born free. Stuyvesant even offered the colony's Black population the right to serve in the militia, although it is uncertain whether anyone joined.

Stuyvesant, however, was in no way committed to freedom or equality. In 1660, after a shipment of enslaved Africans landed in New Amsterdam, Stuyvesant supervised what was probably the colony's first public auction of human beings (Burrows & Wallace, 1999, p. 55; Katz, 1997, p. 12).

The legendary, irascible, and combative Stuyvesant, who has many New York sites named after him, including one of the country's leading public high schools, has been described in many other places. Edward Ellis (1966) dedicated a chapter to him, "Peter Stuyvesant Takes Command," in his accessible one-volume *The Epic of New York City, A Narrative History* (pp. 41–70). What is of interest here is the correspondence between Stuyvesant and WIC directors in New Amsterdam that sheds light on conflicting ideas for the development of slavery in the colony. The letters from WIC keep promising shipments of enslaved Africans to address New Amsterdam's chronic labor shortage. The letters from Stuyvesant read like a series of complaints. While he is cautious—after all these are his employers—Stuyvesant blames WIC directors for failing to seriously invest in the colony.

In 1657, WIC directors wrote to Stuyvesant, "We would have liked to send you now two masons and as many ship carpenters," but, "[t]o engage such people is expensive for the Company and therefore trades as carpenting, bricklaying, blacksmithing and others ought to be taught to the negroes, as it was formerly done in Brazil and now is in Guinea and other Colonies of the Company: this race has sufficient fitness for it and it would be very advantageous" (O'Callaghan, 1856, v. III, p. 387). A letter sent in 1660 advised Stuyvesant that enslaved Africans sent from Curaçao on the Eyckenboon must be "sold at public auction" and "used for the cultivation of the soil," so that "the country and in consequence also the Company may . . . reap the imagined and hoped for fruits" (O'Callaghan, 1856, v. III, p. 480).

In a 1659 letter, Stuyvesant wrote company directors in Amsterdam that "Negroes purchased at Curaçao . . . cannot be sold here again at that price, either in Beaver or Tobacco, so that all the expenses and risk of going and returning are entirely lost" (Donnan, 1932/1969, p. 420). In 1660, he complained that in the latest shipment of enslaved Africans "one of the five died on the passage hither; some were sick or have become so after arriving" (Donnan, 1932/1969, pp. 420–421). In 1664, an apparently exasperated Stuyvesant wrote, "The negroes and negresses have all arrived safely and in health, but were, on an average, quite old, and as the skipper alleges, rejected by the Spaniards. . . . They would have brought more, had they not been so old. Five of the negro women, who were, in our opinion, unsalable, have been kept back and remain unsold" (Donnan, 1932/1969, p. 429).

An Ambiguous Legal Status

Part of the problem faced by WIC in establishing a slave society in New Amsterdam was the ambiguous legal status of Africans in the Dutch colony. In 1634, five Africans petitioned directors in the Netherlands, unsuccessfully, for unpaid wages. Some Africans converted to Dutch Calvinism. They married in the Dutch Reformed Church and had their children baptized. In 1638, Dutch colonists petitioned for a "school master to teach and train the youth of both Dutch and Blacks in the knowledge of Jesus Christ." The first officially sanctioned church wedding between Africans in New Amsterdam was between Anthony van Angola and Lucie d'Angola in 1641. In 1644, the Dutch Reformed Church in Holland ordered the colony to provide for the "instruction of Negroes in the Christian religion" (Katz, 1997, p. 4).

Unlike the legal systems in other slave colonies, Dutch laws did not mandate racial discrimination in New Amsterdam. Africans in the Dutch New Netherland colony could meet in groups, walk around town without passes, and own property. People of African ancestry could appeal to the Dutch courts for redress of grievances and even testify against Whites. According to an English ship's captain who visited the Dutch colony, Africans in New Amsterdam were "free and familiar." They could be seen "sauntering about among the whites at meal time" and "freely joining occasionally in conversation, as if they were one and all of the same household" (Katz, 1997, p. 10).

A murder case in January 1641 illustrates the peculiar relationship between colonial officials and enslaved Africans whose work was vital to the prosperity and survival of the Dutch New Netherland colony. When an enslaved African was found dead, nine of his compatriots were suspected of participating in the murder. Officials threatened the suspects with torture and they all confessed. In what can only be described as justice mitigated by economic necessity, the colonial council ordered the nine men to draw lots to see who would be executed. Manuel de Gerritt, also known as the "Giant," was the man condemned to hang. However, when the rope snapped under his weight, Governor Kieft pardoned him and the others (Katz, 1997, p. 5).

On February 25, 1644, in the midst of a war between colonists and a local Algonquian tribe, eleven enslaved Africans, including some of the 1641 murder suspects, petitioned Dutch officials for their freedom and secured the first group manumission in colonial North America. Each freedman was given farmland on the border of the community where they would grow food for the colony and serve as a buffer between Dutch settlers and the Algonquians. The "Land of the Blacks," as it was known, covered the area that stretches from Greenwich Village north to Herald Square in midtown Manhattan today. Manuel de Gerritt's land grant included part of what is now Washington Square Park. Simon Congo's farm incorporated what is now Union Square. In exchange for their freedom and land, each family agreed to pay taxes to WIC in corn, wheat, and hogs every year (Katz, 1997, pp. 7–8).

International events often determined what happened in the seventeenth-century Dutch New Netherland colony. When Portugal, with the support of England, drove the Dutch out of Brazil, WIC hoped to shift its slave-trading operation to New Amsterdam. Beginning in 1655, colonial authorities increased restrictions on the rights and privileges of African residents of the colony. WIC also began to encourage the sale of the enslaved Africans to individual Dutch colonists. In 1655 and 1659, Dutch vessels brought hundreds of African women, children, and men to Manhattan, some of whom were re-shipped to other European colonies (Burrows & Wallace, 1999, pp. 48–49; Katz, 1997, pp. 13–14; Donnan, 1932/1969, p. 415).

WIC plans for the expansion of New Netherland and New Amsterdam as part of a New World empire based on slavery and the slave trade were never successfully implemented. Between 1654 and 1674, England and the Netherlands fought a series of naval wars over economic supremacy in the Atlantic trade. During the Anglo-Dutch wars, jurisdiction over New York shifted from the Dutch to England in 1664, back to the Dutch in 1673, and back to the English in 1674. In one of the worst trades in world history, the Dutch accepted English rule in New York in exchange for Dutch sovereignty over Surinam, a potential source of sugar on the Atlantic coast in the northern region of South America. This provision of the Treaty of Breda (1667) was reconfirmed in the 1674 Treaty of Westminster that ended the Anglo-Dutch wars.

In 1664, about eight thousand Whites and seven hundred Africans (about 8% of the population) lived in New Amsterdam. Again, while the enslavement of these Africans was central to the history of the colony of New Netherland and later to the British colony of New York, the settlement itself was never more than an outpost on the periphery of the European world (Katz, 1997, p. 15).

Chapter 5

Control

That liberty is a great thing, we may know from our own feelings, and we may likewise judge from the conduct of the white people in the late war. How much money has been spent, and how many lives have been lost to defend their liberty. I must say that I hoped that God would open their eyes, when they were so much engaged for liberty, to think of the state of the poor blacks, and to pity us.

—Jupiter Hammon (1786)

Who is the freedom fighter and who is the terrorist? Who is the patriot and who is the traitor? Who is the hero and who is the villain?

As Martin Luther King Jr. reminded Americans in his speech during the 1963 March on Washington, although the *Declaration of Independence* declared all men equal and promised protection for inalienable rights, equality and equal rights had still not been achieved. While King called for nonviolent civil disobedience against oppression, others, including John Brown and Malcolm X, promoted struggle by any means necessary. The debate over the legitimacy of armed resistance to injustice and enslavement has been an ongoing one since the colonial era.

On November 22, 1775, a New Jersey Quaker named John Corlis posted a runaway slave advertisement in a Philadelphia newspaper. He was searching for "Titus," an enslaved African "about 22 years of age, not very black, near 6 feet high." Corliss offered a three-pound reward to "Whoever takes up said Negroe, and secures him in any gaol, or brings him to me" (Hodges,1999, p. 185). Titus escaped to the British lines where he took up arms in the struggle for freedom—his freedom and the freedom of other enslaved Africans. Between 1776 and 1783, the years covering the Revolutionary War, more than two hundred and fifty runaway slave advertisements, offering rewards for the return of over three hundred formerly enslaved Africans from New York and New Jersey, appeared in local newspapers (Hodges & Brown, 1994). Many of these runaways served in the British Ethiopian Regiment, the Black Pioneers, or in less formal guerrilla units. Others worked in British-occupied New York City.

Despite Jupiter Hammon's prayer, many of the nation's founders did not "open their eyes" or reconsider their views on Africans and slavery. In his memoir, Boston King, an escaped African who fought for the British in order to protect his freedom, wrote that at the end of the American Revolution the restoration of peace "issued universal joy among all parties, except us, who had escaped from slavery, and taken refuge in the English army" (King, 1798, p. 157). Rumors circulated in New York, where most of the Black troops were stationed, "that all the slaves . . . were to be delivered up to their masters, altho' some of them had been three or four years among the English." Many were filled with "inexpressible anguish and terror, especially when we saw our old masters coming from Virginia, North-Carolina, and other parts, and seizing upon their slaves in the streets of New-York, or even dragging them out of their beds" (157).

Their fears were not unwarranted. George Washington and Thomas Jefferson, as well as all four of the New Yorkers who signed the *Declaration of Independence,* owned enslaved Africans. Washington, in correspondence with the British commander of New York City, General Guy Carleton, and in a meeting held at Orange Town, New York, objected to the British plan to allow escaped Africans to leave the city and resettle in Canada. He claimed this was a violation of the peace treaty provision requiring the return of all confiscated property. Carleton refused to surrender any of the refugees and about four thousand people who had escaped to the British lines were able to remain free. Among the formerly enslaved Africans who left New York with the British were Harry and Deborah Squash. The manifest for the British ships headed for Canada, which is known as the "Book of Negroes," described Mrs. Squash, as "20, stout wench, thick lips, pock marked. Formerly slave to General Washington, came away about 4 years ago" (Hodges, 1999, pp. 155–158; Burrows & Wallace, 1999, pp. 259–261).

During the eighteenth century, New York moved from being a British colony to becoming part of an independent nation allegedly committed to ideas expressed in the *Declaration of Independence* that "all men are created equal" and that they are "endowed by their creator with certain inalienable rights." Yet even after independence from Great Britain was achieved, the enslavement of people of African ancestry continued in New York and other parts of the North. The contradiction between the promise of America—freedom—and the reality of American life—enslavement—is at the heart of this chapter. As students read historical documents and secondary sources they should constantly consider the "revolutionary" idea that enslaved Africans were human beings, just like them, with the same emotions, concerns for their loved ones, and hopes for the future.

Important Issues

As a British colony, and later as the first capital of the newly independent nation, eighteenth-century New York was torn by contradictions. The demands of British colonists for the rights of Englishmen and later for independence were based on the enslavement of others. In some ways the situation was best summarized by a Virginian, Patrick Henry, who is remembered for his 1775 "Give me liberty or give me death" speech calling for open rebellion against the mother country. In 1773, Henry described slavery as a "lamentable Evil." However, it was an evil with which he and other White colonists were prepared to live. He wrote to a friend, "Would any one believe that I am Master of Slaves of my own purchase! I am drawn along by ye [*sic*]. general inconvenience of living without them, I will not, I cannot justify it" (Meade, 1957, pp. 299–300).

Contemporary New York City is littered with statues and monuments commemorating people who owned slaves or were complicit with the slave trade. Schools are named after them. There is a larger-than-life statute of George Washington on Wall Street at the site where he was inaugurated as president. New York City's flagship high school is named after Peter Stuyvesant. Under the circumstances, students and teachers should feel compelled to question who should legitimately be considered a hero during this time period.

The history of New York during the colonial era calls into question our society's fundamental notion of rule by law. As the slave system stabilized and the rules of slavery were codified, law was used to suppress human freedom. For Black New Yorkers, the legal and judicial systems were tools of oppression, not institutions for achieving justice. Fear of Black sexuality and the African's desire for freedom became weapons to justify enslavement, enrage mobs, and mete out harsh punishment.

Another issue that should be raised concerns sacred beliefs about the origins of a free press. Newspapers that challenged the corruption of British officials financed their operations by printing advertisements for the return of escaped slaves.

An important theme during the eighteenth century is increasing resistance to bondage by enslaved Africans in the New York colony. Sometimes in the open, sometimes beneath the surface, sometimes individually, and sometimes collectively, Africans in New York challenged bondage. Jupiter Hammon, the first black poet published in the United States, is one of the most interesting figures in the history of colonial New York and the early years after independence. His poetry reflected his deep religious beliefs and what appears to be acceptance of his enslavement. This may well explain why the Whites in control of the society were willing to publish his work.

The details of Jupiter Hammon's life are not well established, but he was probably born in 1711, died in 1806, and was "owned" by the Lloyd family of Lloyd's Neck. In 1684, a Boston merchant named James Lloyd purchased a peninsula on the north shore of Long Island, and a royal land grant later made his property the "Lordship and Manor of Queen's Village." His son Henry Lloyd inherited the land and constructed the first manor house. Upon Henry Lloyd's death in 1763, his four sons, Henry, John, Joseph, and James, inherited the estate and its human chattel. "Ownership" of Jupiter Hammon appears to have passed to Henry (Brown, 1997, p. A15).

In 1786, just after the Revolutionary War, Hammon wrote, "An Address to the Negroes in the State of New York" (Katz, 1997, p. 29; Hammon, 1787, p. 13). In it he spoke out against rebellion and for honesty, faithfulness, and obedience toward "masters." It is a document that on the surface appears to show Hammon's acquiescence to his fate. However, it can also be read on another level. Hammon argued "That liberty is a great thing, we may know from our own feelings, and we may likewise judge from the conduct of the White people in the late war. How much money has been spent, and how many lives have been lost to defend their liberty. I must say that I hoped that God would open their eyes, when they were so much engaged for liberty, to think of the state of the poor blacks, and to pity us." While it is not a call for rebellion, it is also not a simple acceptance of injustice and enslavement.

As we look at the history of slavery in the British colony of New York, and during the early years of American independence, we find that many things are not exactly as they first appear. The codification of slave laws during this period is certainly a sign of increasing repression, but it also suggests growing resistance to oppression. Every new law and every advertisement that called for the return of a runaway slave, was a signal that African people, sometimes with support from Whites, were fighting back against human bondage.

In teaching about slavery in the British colony and during the early years of American independence, I emphasize themes that are important for understanding not only the history of slavery, but also history in general. The first, as noted above, is that oppression and resistance go hand in hand; they are two sides of the same coin. Increasingly restrictive laws generally mark increasingly intense resistance to illegitimate authority. We can see this in the way White America responded to British policies that led up to the American Revolution, and we can see it in the way Black America responded to enslavement in colonial New York. Because so much of the history of oppression and resistance is told through the history of laws, the judicial process exposes much of the tension that might otherwise have gone undocumented.

A continuing theme is New York's place in a broader global slave-system after Great Britain replaced the Dutch as the colonial power in the region and as the dominant slave-trading nation. Although local merchants played a more active role in the slave trade than in the Dutch era, New York remained on the world's economic margins during this period.

The eighteenth century is often identified with the European intellectual Enlightenment. American Revolutionary War era thinkers like Thomas Paine, Thomas Jefferson, James Madison, Alexander Hamilton, and John Jay and the supporters of documents such as *the Declaration of Independence* and the *Constitution* are usually placed within this tradition. Madison, Hamilton, and Jay are included because of their authorship of the *Federalist Papers* during debate over ratification of the federal Constitution in New York State. Another theme in this chapter is the inconsistency of the nation's founders as they debated the meaning of the American Revolution.

Defining Slavery

In August 1664, four British ships carrying approximately 2,000 soldiers arrived in New Netherland and demanded that Peter Stuyvesant, the Dutch governor, surrender the colony. On September 8, control over the colony shifted from the Dutch West India Company to James Stuart, the Duke of York, and brother of the English king. The Duke of York was a major shareholder in the Royal African Company, the corporation that held a monopoly over the British slave trade. Among the new regime's first actions was granting port privileges and the right to use warehouses to ships engaged in the slave trade. The transfer of the colony from the Dutch to British became official with the Treaty of Breda, signed in 1667 (Burrows & Wallace, 1999, pp. 70–74).

In Dutch New Netherland permanent, racially based, hereditary slavery was not a clearly established institution. However, this changed once the British took control. British authorities acknowledged the titles of Dutch settlers to the people they claimed to own and, in 1665, a law recognized the legal status of slavery in the colony. Twelve years later, in 1677, a court ruled that any person of African ancestry who was brought to trial was presumed to be a slave unless they could establish that they were free. The racial basis of enslavement was further reinforced through an edict issued by British Governor Edmund Andros in 1679. Andros forbade settlers from enslaving local Indians, but confirmed the legality of African enslavement (Lepore, 2005b, pp. 60–61).

This was followed by a series of measures designed to formalize the slave system. In 1682, local officials recognized the right of slaveholders to use physical violence, short of lethal force, to punish people they claimed as slaves. In 1684, a city ordinance prohibited more than four Africans and Native Americans from meeting together and Africans and Native Americans from possessing guns. In 1702, a curfew was imposed on enslaved men and women over the age of fourteen, and New York's first comprehensive slave code was adopted which equated slave status with being African. The 1702 act approved by the governor and council forbade "Trade with any slave either in buying or selling, without leave and Consent of the Master or Mistress"; reiterated the restrictions on assembly except "when it shall happen they meet in some servile employment for their Master's or Mistress's profit"; and confirmed the right of "any Master or Mistress of slaves to punish their slaves for their Crimes and offences." In 1706, a New York court ruled that conversion to Christianity did not change the legal status of enslaved Africans, and in 1711 the city's Common Council established the Wall Street waterfront "Meal Market" as the official location for the hiring of all slave labor (Katz, 1997, pp. 16–23; Hodges, 1999, pp. 36–38; O'Callaghan, 1851, v. 1, pp. 519–521 and v. 2, p. 458).

These legal actions reflected the growing size and economic importance of the African population in the New York colony. By 1712, 1,775 enslaved Africans made up roughly 15 percent of the population of the ten counties (New York, Kings, Richmond, Orange, Westchester, Queens, Suffolk, Albany, Ulster, and Duchess) that constituted the New York colony (O'Callaghan, 1851, v. IV, p. 469). They also reflected the difficulty colonial officials and settlers had in maintaining control over an enslaved population in an urban environment such as the port of New York that required worker mobility, and in scattered rural settlements on the periphery of the colony. Another concern was a potential "fifth column" rebellion by enslaved Africans in an area of the world where the British were vulnerable to attack by hostile natives and European competitors (Burrows & Wallace, 1999, pp. 146–148).

Resistance to Enslavement

Resistance to enslavement in the New York colony in the eighteenth century could be subtle or overt, passive or violent, and either individual or collective. Historians and students can discover it in legal documents such as the 1720 Will of Richard Smith of Smithtown, who requested that if his "mullato Dick continues villainous and stubborn then my overseers shall dispose of him and ye effects to be employed for the use of my wife and children" (Marcus, 1988/1995, p. 115), and the 1754 Will of Thomas Moore of Suffolk County, who left to his "Beloved wife Hannah . . . my Negro man called Pompie if he behaveth well, but if otherwise then my Executors to sell him & the money to be Disposed of by my Executors for the Good of my Estate at their Discretion" (Marcus, 1988/1995, p. 116).

Individual resistance to slavery often meant escaping to freedom. Graham Russell Hodges and Alan Brown (1994) have collected over six hundred runaway slave advertisements that appeared in New York and New Jersey newspapers during the colonial and revolutionary eras. Their book, *"Pretends to Be Free" Runaway Slave Advertisements from Colonial and Revolutionary New York and New Jersey,* takes its title from a line in a number of advertisements where a slaveholder complains about the dishonesty of an escapee who audaciously "Pretends to Be Free." The advertisements give insight into the lives of enslaved Africans, conditions in the colony, and the complicity of some of New York's leading citizens with the slave system.

An advertisement from the October 2, 1738 *New York Weekly Journal* demands the return of a "Runaway from Frederick Zepperly of Rhinebeck in Dutchess County, a copper colored Negro fellow named Jack, aged about 30 years, speaks nothing but English and reads English. Whoever takes up said run away and secures him so his master may have him again or gives notice of him to Harry Beekman or to John Peter Zenger shall have forty shillings and all reasonable charges" (Hodges & Brown, 1994, pp. 14–15). The John Peter Zenger mentioned in the advertisement is the publisher of the newspaper and also an iconic figure in American history for his defense of the right of the press to tell the truth about corrupt government officials. Other prominent names from New York history that appear in the advertisements include Philip Livingston, Jacobus Van Cortlandt, and Cornelius Van Wyke.

Many of the advertisements have detailed descriptions of the clothing worn by escaped Africans. According to *The New York Gazette* of July 24, 1758, "Runaway from Ide Meyer on the 20th of June last, a Mulatto wench named Ohnech, but goes by the name Hannah and pretends to be free: She is about 4 feet 4 inches high and 28 years of age; is well set and speaks both English and Dutch very well, had on when she went away a homespun stole, a petticoat, blue short cloak and white cap; whoever takes up and secures the said wench so that her Master may have her again shall have TWENTY SHILLINGS reward and all reasonable charges paid" (Hodges & Brown, 1994, p. 74). A number of things stand out in this advertisement. The enslaved woman is a "Mulatto," or person of mixed race. One of her parents or grandparents, probably her father or paternal grandfather, was White. Although she is twenty-eight years old and full grown, she is inordinately short at a little more than four feet tall, which suggests either a genetic disorder or a severe dietary deficiency. She is also fluent in both English, the language of the marketplace, and Dutch, the language of the household.

Students usually ask why runaways didn't change their clothes since they knew a description of what they were wearing was being circulated. The fact that they did not readily change clothing suggests at least two things. First, that unlike today, this was a time when a new set of clothes was not so easy to acquire and a Black attempting to purchase clothing would draw undesired attention. Also, because of the value of clothing, extra clothing could be exchanged for food or used to purchase help in escaping.

Reliable Witnesses

A problem for historians and teachers trying to piece together the past from primary sources is deciding which documents are reliable and which ones are tainted by faulty memory or intentional obfuscation. Sometimes we get lucky and find the same story told in different sources from radically different perspectives. When that happens, similarities in the accounts support the reliability of not just the overlapping stories, but of the rest of the narratives as well. This narrative confluence occurred in the case of Venture Smith of Long Island, where the historical record includes both his autobiographical history of his life and a runaway slave advertisement distributed by George Mumford, the man who claimed to own him (Singer, 2007a, pp. 2–6).

Smith published "A Narrative of the Life and Adventure of Venture" in 1798. The entire manuscript is available on line from the University of North Carolina at Chapel Hill at http://docsouth.unc.edu. The book recounts Smith's capture in Africa as a young boy, the trip across the Atlantic Ocean to Barbados, and his eventual arrival on Fisher's Island on the Long Island Sound between New York and Rhode Island. Smith goes on to discuss being mistreated by his master's son, a foiled escape attempt, and eventually being able to purchase his freedom and the freedom of his wife and children. It is the foiled escape attempt that interests me here.

According to Venture Smith, "My master owned a certain Irishman, named Heddy, who about that time formed a plan of secretly leaving his master. After he had long had this plan in meditation, he suggested it to me. At first I cast a deaf ear to it, and rebuked Heddy for harboring in his mind such a rash undertaking. But after he had persuaded and much enchanted me with the prospect of gaining my freedom by such a method, I at length agreed to accompany him. Heddy next inveigled two of his fellow-servants to accompany us. The place to which we designed to go was the Mississippi. We stole our master's boat, embarked, and then directed our course for the Mississippi River. We mutually confederated not to betray or desert one another on pain of death" (Smith, 1798, pp. 16–17).

The runaway slave advertisement published by his "owner" in *The New-York Gazette or, The Weekly Post-Boy* on April 1, 1754 verifies much of Venture Smith's story. According to the advertisement, "Run away from George Mumford of Fisher's-Island, the 27th Instant, four Men Servants, a white Man and Three Negroes, who hath taken a large two-mast Boat, with a square Stern, and a large white Pine Canoe; the Boat's Timbers are chiefly red Cedar. The White Man named Joseph Heday, says he is a Native of Newark, in the Jerseys, a short well set fellow of a rudy complection. . . . Venture had a Kersey dark colour'd Great Coat, three Kersey jackets, two pair of Breeches of the same, a new cloth colour'd Fly-Coat, with red shaloon lining, a green ratteen Jacket, almost new, a crimson birded stuff ditto, a pair of large Ozenbrigs Trowsers, a new felt hat, two pairs of shoes, one pair new, several pair of Stockings; he is a very tall fellow, 6 feet 2 inches high, thick, square shoulders, large bon'd, mark'd in the face, or scar'd with a knife in his own country" (Hodges & Brown, 1994, pp. 49–50). The location, the number of escapees, the name of the leader of the group, the boat, and Venture's African origins are all confirmed in the advertisement.

Trans-Atlantic Slave Trade

A major reason for the prosperity of the British colony, the growth of its enslaved population, and the social upheaval described above, was the increasing involvement of New York merchants in the trans-Atlantic slave trade. Some were established Dutch families like the Philipses, who sought workers for their Hudson River plantation, Philipsburgh Manor. Others had commercial ties to British Caribbean colonies, such as Nathaniel Sylvester, a Barbados sugar planter, who held twenty-four enslaved people on his Shelter Island estate (Philipsburg Manor, nd).

By 1720, half of the ships leaving the port of New York were engaged in the Caribbean trade. Most of the ships arriving in the port of New York that transported enslaved Africans had small human cargoes and were more involved in the trade of slave-produced commodities. One of the larger shipments of human beings included sixty-six Africans imported directly from Africa by Peter Livingston in May 1751 (Wilder, 2000, p. 34).

Slave auctions were held weekly, and sometimes daily, at the Wall Street Slave market established by the City Common Council and on the wharves where ships were unloaded. Advertisements for the sale of human beings regularly appeared in colonial newspapers. A typical notice in the *New York Weekly Post Boy* on June 10, 1754, announced: "Just arrived from Africa, a parcel of negroes, consisting of men, women, boys and girls, to be sold on board brig *York*, William Merciers, commander. Most of them have had the smallpox" (Wakeman, 1914).

Slaving voyages were especially profitable during this period. In 1725, the average price of an African loaded on a slave ship in West Africa was £11.87 (or $283.77 in modern United States money) and £23.92 when resold in British North America, a mark up of over 100 percent. On the eve of the American Revolution, a captive could be purchased for £17.04 ($398.51) in West Africa and resold in North America for £44.08 ($1030.88), a profit of 150% (U.S. Department of Commerce Bureau of the Census, 1975, Series Z, 165–168, p. 1174).

The two leading slave-trading families in eighteenth-century New York were the Philipses and the Livingstons. In 1685, a ship owned by Frederick Philipse brought enslaved Africans from Angola to Barbados. Eight captives, who were deemed too ill to be profitably sold, were brought to work at Philipsburg Manor in Rye, New York. By the mid-eighteenth century, the Philipse family held over 52,000 acres of land in Westchester County and had one of the largest slave-holdings in the colonial North. This included a community of twenty-three enslaved men, women, and children who lived and worked at Philipsburg Manor, where they helped operate a milling complex, bake house, farm, and dairy. Philip Livingston, second lord of the Livingston manor in Dutchess County, conducted extensive trade with the West Indies, including importing enslaved Africans, and was probably the New

York merchant most involved in the trans-Atlantic slave trade (Higgins, Dickstein, & Vetare, nd).

Besides being a landed aristocrat and a slave trader, Livingston was also a benefactor of Yale University, a New York City alderman, a representative at the 1754 Colonial Convention at Albany, and a delegate to the Continental Congress. Numerous places in the Hudson Valley still bear his family name, and former family homes and estates are state and national historic sites. In addition to these, Livingston owned a large mansion in Brooklyn Heights. It was located near where Livingston Street ends at Clinton Street today, about two blocks from the former New York City Board of Education headquarters at 110 Livingston Street (Singer, 2003e, 13).

Philip Livingston was one of four delegates from New York to sign the *Declaration of Independence*. The others, Francis Lewis, for whom a high school is named in Queens, William Floyd, and Lewis Morris, also claimed to "own" enslaved African Americans.

Because of mercantile taxation policies, many enslaved Africans were smuggled into the colony illegally by otherwise reputable merchants. One of the strangest business relationships in the colonial period was between members of the local elite, including Governor Bellomont, and Captain William Kidd, who they initially hired to attack Spanish shipping and import Africans from Madagascar. Kidd settled in New York City, married a wealthy local widow, and contributed to the construction of Trinity Church. He was later abandoned by his partners, arrested, and sent to London where he was executed as a pirate (Burrows & Wallace, 1999, pp. 112–114).

Rebellion and Repression

Resistance to enslavement and retribution by local authorities could be horrific. Questions that both students and teachers have to consider when they study slavery in the Americas include: Were attacks on slaveholders justified by the inherent cruelty of enslavement? Could authorities legitimately punish enslaved Africans for what were considered to be violent crimes?

In 1706, the governor of the colony expressed alarm at the "great insolency" of the city's African population. In response, he ordered justices of the peace in Kings County on Long Island to "kill or destroy" African escapees who were striking fear among the local colonists "if they cannot otherwise be taken" (Wilder, 2000, p. 16). In 1708, the English governor reported to the Board of Trade in London on the "most barbarous murder" with an ax of a White landowner in Queens County, his pregnant wife, and their five children by an enslaved Native male and his African wife. For their crimes, the woman was burned to death and the man was suspended in chains beside a blade that cut his flesh as he swayed in the breeze. According to reports, two other enslaved Africans were also executed (Hodges, 1999, p. 64).

The tension between increasingly restrictive regulations and the desire of enslaved Africans to be free came to a head in New York in 1712 and 1741. In the first case, there was a small, but well-documented, collective rebellion against slavery. In the second case, rumors about another "slave plot" were fueled by reports of violent upheavals in Guiana (1731), Jamaica (1733 and 1734), Antigua (1736), and Stono, South Carolina (1739). Coupled with the fear of an attack on the colony by Spain, these rumors led to mass public executions and exile to the Caribbean of over 100 enslaved Africans (Genovese, 1979, pp. 33–35; Lepore, 2005a, pp. xvi–xx, 11).

The 1712 uprising involved about two-dozen African men and women. They are believed to have set fire to a building in the middle of town. When White colonists tried to extinguish the blaze, the Africans killed at least nine of them and wounded six others. Militia units joined regular soldiers to defeat and capture the rebels. Twenty-one of them were executed and others are believed to have chosen suicide rather than allow their captors to torture them to death.

Governor Robert Hunter described the rebellion, the execution of the prisoners, and the aftermath in letters to the Board of Trade in London (O'Callaghan, 1856, V, pp. 341–342). According to one letter, one of the rebels was a pregnant woman whose execution was suspended. For the others, "Some were burnt, others hanged, one broke on the wheel, and one hung alive in chains in the town, so that there has been the most exemplary punishment inflicted that could be possibly thought of" (O'Callaghan, 1856, V, pp. 356–357).

The following year, new laws approved by the Common Council of the City of New York showed that tension in the city caused by the rebellion had not abated. These laws "prohibited Negro and Indian slaves above the age of fourteen years from going in the streets of this city after night without a lantern and a lighted candle" and established a curfew "an hour after sunset." The Common Council also allocated "the sum of thirty Six pounds & ten pence" to pay for the cost of the previous year's executions (O'Callaghan, 1856, III, pp. 27–31).

In 1715, Governor Hunter wrote to the Board of Trade in London complaining that some of the new legislation passed in response to the rebellion was having an unanticipated, deleterious impact. He specifically questioned a law that blocked the manumission of loyal slaves who were supposed to be freed upon the deaths of their masters. He feared that the restrictions would "make 'em not only careless servants, but excite 'em to insurrections more bloody than any they have yet attempted" (O'Callaghan, 1856, V, pp. 460–461).

Historian William L. Katz has described colonial New York at the beginning of the eighteenth century as a "turbulent urban world with four hundred taverns, one for every twelve adult males, and no police force. At night its streets were noisy, dangerous, and unhealthy. Disease and death lived in every block, and occasional epidemics tore through neighborhoods." Forty percent of New York City's White households owned enslaved Africans, though most families owned only one or two people (Katz, 1997, pp. 20–21).

By 1720, 5,740 enslaved Africans lived in New York; they made up over 15 percent of the total population of the colony. Their importance to the local economy continued to grow during the next three decades and, by 1750, their numbers had nearly doubled. The need for freedom of movement by enslaved Africans as they worked on the docks and in shops, and visited the markets, allowed them to mingle with each other, with poorer and indentured Whites, and with free Blacks. This put increasing pressure on colonial officials to maintain the mechanisms for control, and it increased fears that discontented enslaved Africans were plotting rebellion.

In 1730, New York attempted a general revision of its slave codes, increasing the restrictions on its Black community. It made it illegal for a free person, either Black or White, to trade with a slave without the knowledge and permission of their "master," or to "employ, harbour, conceal or entertain" another man's slave. To prevent conspiracies, it was unlawful for more than three enslaved Africans to meet together at any time. The penalty for violating this ordinance was up to forty strokes of the whip "upon the naked back." The carrying of any kind of weapon was strictly forbidden. To combat disobedience, thievery, or restive behavior in public, slaveowners could be fined if they failed to adequately punish and control their bondsmen. If an enslaved African committed a crime so serious that the penalty was execution, a master would be recompensed by the colony, but only up to £25. Enslaved Africans were to be punished by special tribunals and had no recourse to appeal. A master, however, anxious to protect his investment, could request a jury trial before twelve of the master's peers (Hartell, 1943, p. 62).

Despite these measures, or perhaps because of them, New York in 1741 was rife with talk of a slave conspiracy—a conspiracy the existence of which historians still debate. The hysteria was fed by appeals to racism and anti-Catholic prejudices. In his closing arguments at the trial, one of the prosecuting attorneys charged that the plan by the Africans was to kill all of the White men and have "the Women become a Prey to the rapacious Lust of these Villains!" (Lepore, 2005a, p. 10). Later, in a report to the Lords of Trade in London in August 1741, the Lieutenant-Governor of the New York colony charged they had discovered the "hand of Popery" and a "Romish Priest" behind the plot (O'Callaghan, 1856, v. 6, pp. 201–202).

The fear of an uprising by enslaved Africans in the city led to the arrest of 152 Blacks and twenty White coconspirators. Eighty-one of the Blacks confessed to participation in the conspiracy in order to save their own lives or the lives of loved ones. Thirty-four Blacks and four Whites were executed. Thirteen of the Blacks were burned alive. Seventy accused rebels had their lives spared and were transported to the sugar islands of the Caribbean (Lepore, 2005b, p. 85).

Even at the time, the existence of a slave conspiracy was challenged. A letter sent to Cadwaller Colden, a noted local scientist and historian, from an unknown correspondent, is very telling (Lepore, 2005a, p. xvi). The writer was from New England but had heard of "the bloody Tradegy" and stated that the wave of accusations, arrests, trials, and executions "puts me in mind of our New England Witchcraft in the year 1692." The star witness at the trial was a sixteen-year-old indentured Irish servant girl from Hughson's Tavern who was promised freedom and £100 for her cooperation. Criticism of colonial "justice" finally compelled Chief Justice Daniel Horsmanden (1744) to publish a comprehensive review of the case, presenting all of the evidence and testimony.

Crises expose the inner workings of a society, but what exactly was the crisis of 1741? The judge's report, instead of exposing the dangerous behavior of Africans in New York, actually documents the repression of enslaved Africans, the failure of the legal system, social conditions in the city, and the ways these factors contributed to what was in fact a deadly official conspiracy against the city's Black population. An excellent book on the topic was written by Jill Lepore (2005a), *New York Burning: Liberty, Slavery, and Conspiracy in Eighteenth-Century Manhattan*. After years of research, she remains uncertain about the reality of a slave conspiracy. For Lepore, what was historically most significant were the events leading up to the crisis, the "specter" of a slave conspiracy that made it so believable to White New Yorkers, and, of course, their brutal response.

Lepore argues that in the decade preceding the conspiracy trial, the New York colony was undergoing a crisis of the political order because of the authoritarian rule of British governor William Cosby. She finds it suspicious that most of the government officials who prosecuted the conspiracy case were from the faction that supported Cosby, while most of the enslaved Africans who were punished belonged to the group that opposed him. Later in the process, when enslaved Africans belonging to prominent Cosby supporters were accused of participating in the conspiracy, calls for ending the investigation increased and the trials and punishment stopped.

I have a slightly different take on the events than Lepore, based on the "revolutionary" idea that enslaved Africans should be perceived of as human beings. The winter of 1740–1741 was particularly harsh, the worst in the memory of anyone in the colony. The harbor and the Hudson River froze. Food and firewood were scarce. Everyone suffered, but the poor, the enslaved, and Blacks in general would have suffered the most. As winter turned into spring, a series of fires, including one that damaged the main fort, broke out in the city. Justice Horsmanden believed disgruntled slaves started the fires, and rumors quickly spread among White inhabitants of the colony that "The Negroes are rising!" (Lepore, 2005a: xvi).

If I were alive at the time, and were an enslaved African, I suspect I would have been especially bitter that winter. It was cold, my people were ill-fed and ill-clothed, and we were subject to increasing restriction and public humiliation under the slave codes. Normal human resentment would have led to individual acts of defiance, maybe the starting of fires, certainly increasing theft, and probably drunken boasting at taverns, like Hughson's, that were willing to serve us and provided a modicum of warmth and community.

Individual defiance is not collective rebellion, but it does explain what happened at the trial. One of the reasons that the charges seemed plausible and the "conspiracy" seemed so widespread is that people had been violating the slave codes and were involved in illegal activity just to stay alive. This would also explain, at least in part, why the accused confessed to crimes, especially when confession might save their lives or the lives of their loved ones. The joint "confessions" of two of the accused conspirators, Cuffee and Quaco, was made while they waited to be burned to death by an angry mob. Quaco, who hoped to save his wife and young son, said that his wife "was no ways concerned, for he never would trust her with it" and that the boy "knew nothing of the Matter" (Lepore, 2005a, pp. 105–106).

April Francis is one of the teachers who worked on the *New York and Slavery: Complicity and Resistance* curriculum. Students in her seventh-grade social studies class used documents from the curriculum guide to write and perform a "hip-hop rap opera" about the New York City Slave conspiracy trial. One of the students wrote the following, an analysis that I strongly support.

> It was the judge's report
> That we were the dangerous sort,
> In the slavery days of New York.
> There were many desires,
> And boasting by the liars,
> But no proof we started fires.
> "Negro rising" they screamed,
> They said that we had schemed,
> Of freedom we only dreamed.
> Conditions in the city,
> Fed fear of conspiracy,
> And proved to be deadly.
> Whites held the knife,
> So Quaco sacrificed his life,
> Hoping to save his wife.
> Yes we were defiant,
> Hoping to be self-reliant,
> The Whites were the tyrant.
> The legal system failed,
> When we were all jailed,
> Liberty was derailed.
> The documents proved repression,
> When Whites enslaved the African,
> They forgot that we were men.

The slave conspiracy trial led to another round of repressive laws. In 1742, the Minutes of the Common Council of the City of New York list a "Law to Restrain Negros from Going to Fetch Water on a Sunday" (Minutes, 1930, V, p. 59) and another "for Appointing: Establishing and Regulating a Good and Sufficient Night Watch" (Minutes, 1930, V, p. 77).

American Revolution

One of the ironies contained in most historical treatment of this period is that there actually was a major slave rebellion in the New York metropolitan area a few decades later during the American Revolution, but it rarely is presented that way. In 1775, the British colonial governor of Virginia, Earl of Dunmore, issued a proclamation promising enslaved Africans freedom if they joined the British forces trying to suppress the colonial independence movement (Hodges, 1999, pp. 139–153). One of the people who opted to fight for freedom, his own freedom, was Titus, an escaped slave formerly owned by John Corlies of Monmouth County, New Jersey. Eventually Titus, or Colonel Tye as he came to be known, led a band of as many as eight hundred Black and White guerrilla fighters in a series of campaigns on the Jersey shore and Staten Island. Other Black soldiers fighting for the British were stationed at Fort Negro in the Van Cortlandt Park section of the Bronx. While Titus did not survive the war, thousands of formerly enslaved Africans, who fought for freedom by fighting for the British, were later transported to Canada where they could live as free men and free women.

At least one New Yorker, Colonel Alexander Hamilton, aide-de-camp to George Washington, recognized the potential of African American troops fighting under the revolutionary banner. In 1779, he proposed recruiting four battalions of Negroes, whom he believed would be "very excellent soldiers." Hamilton was concerned that "if we do not make use of them in this way, the enemy probably will; and that the best way to counteract the temptations they will hold out will be to offer them ourselves. An essential part of the plan is to give them their freedom with their muskets. This will secure their fidelity, animate their courage, and I believe will have a good influence upon those who remain, by opening a door to their emancipation." Unfortunately for the future of the United States, Hamilton's proposal was never implemented (Kurland & Lerner, 1987, v. 1, p. 527).

White Opposition to Slavery

For our purposes as teachers, it is important to note that at the same time that some White New Yorkers were promoting slavery and the slave trade for financial purposes, others seriously questioned its legitimacy. As in England, many of the original proponents of abolition took a stand against slavery because of their religious beliefs. John Woolman, a Quaker and itinerant minister born in southern New Jersey, mobilized his coreligionists across the northern colonies as well as in England, to petition to end slavery and to emancipate their own slaves (Hochschild, 2005; Howlett, 2001, 30).

One of the more active antislavery Quaker meeting houses was in the town of Flushing, in Queens County. Its members would "have no unity" with slaveholders and refused their contributions. In 1765, it "dealt with" Samuel

Underhill, a member of the family that founded Oyster Bay on Long Island, for violating Quaker principles by "importing negroes from Africa." In 1775, a committee visited "such Friends as hold negro slaves, to inquire into the circumstances and manner of education of the slaves, and give such advice as the nature of the case requires." Another committee was appointed "to labor with Friends who keep these poor people in bondage, in the ability that truth may afford, for their release" (Hartell, 1943, p. 69).

A prominent secular opponent of slavery was Gouverneur Morris from what was then Westchester County but is today the Bronx. He represented Westchester County in New York's Revolutionary era Congress from 1775 to 1777. Although his family owned Morrisana, one of the largest slave-holding plantations in the north, Morris championed a motion at the state's constitutional convention to abolish slavery in New York. In 1779, Morris relocated to Philadelphia where he continued to fight against human bondage and represented Pennsylvania at the Federal Constitutional Convention. During debate at the convention, Morris described slavery as a "nefarious institution. . . . The curse of heaven on states where it prevailed" (Madison, 1840/1984, p. 411).

An important question for students to examine is why some people took a stand against injustice while other people, under similar circumstances, tolerated it or were actively complicit.

Chapter 6

Making Choices in a New Nation

> The rights of human nature and the principles of our holy religion call upon us to dispense the blessings of freedom to all mankind. . . . It is therefore recommended to the Legislatures of the State of New York to take measures consistent with the public safety for abolishing domestic slavery.
>
> —Gouverneur Morris (1777)

In "The Eighteen Brumaire of Louis Bonaparte," Karl Marx argued that "Men make their own history, but they do not make it just as they please; they do not make it under circumstances chosen by themselves, but under circumstances directly encountered, given and transmitted from the past" (Feuer, 1959, p. 320). Students should understand that we are all historical actors and have choices to make. While the past is a powerful influence on the present, and our individual and collective choices are circumscribed by our experience, the future is not preordained.

During the spring 2005 semester, I did a presentation on New York and slavery for about sixty eleventh-grade students at Francis Lewis High School in the New York City borough of Queens. The majority of the students in the group were ethnically South or East Asian, and either they or their parents were immigrants to the United States. Only three of the students were Black, and at least one of the three identified herself during the course of discussion as an immigrant born in the Caribbean.

A number of social studies educators discuss using a student's personal identification with the past to promote interest in historical analysis and empathy with the people whose lives are being examined (Barton & Levstik, 2004). When I do workshops like these, I like to begin with something from the local history of the area. It establishes that "history happened here," which leads into the idea that history happens everywhere and connects with the lives of all people. But this was a particularly difficult audience. I was not sure how much they identified with the community or connected their lives with the history of the United States. But I did not have to worry. What they identified with more than anything else was their high school.

Not that much is known about the life of Francis Lewis, for whom the high school was named. Much of what we do know comes from a combined biography of Lewis and his son Morgan. It was written by Morgan's granddaughter, Julia Delafield (1877).

In general, the students were aware that the Lewis estate was located not far from the school and that Francis Lewis was a signer of the *Declaration of Independence*, which established the timeframe for his life and the reason for his celebrity. When I asked whether it was legitimate to name a school after someone like Francis Lewis, I got some relatively low-key "yeses" and some polite nods. My opening question clearly had not generated either controversy or excitement.

I offered to read passages from the Delafield biography to help them learn a bit more about Lewis before continuing our discussion. Before I began, I explained that as they listened, they needed to "read between the lines." Delafield wrote the book because she was proud of her family's accomplishments. In some sense she was bragging. What they needed to discover were the broader historical events behind the story, events that she might lightly touch on or even gloss over because they are not the focus of her narrative.

The book is mainly anecdotal. In the first chapter, Delafield explained that her great-grandfather was born in Wales, orphaned, came into some money, and then migrated to the British American colonies while in his twenties. In New York City, he formed a partnership with a merchant named Edward Anglesey and married Anglesey's sister Elizabeth.

Delafield described a few of Francis Lewis' commercial enterprises in some detail. "In one of the ventures of Lewis to the coast of Africa, the captain ascended a river that empties into the Atlantic. What appeared to be signals of distress from an island in the stream, attracted his attention. He sent a boat to the spot, which returned, bringing with it two negro lads and a young girl. The story they told was that they were the children of an inland chief—that they had been kidnapped and afterwards abandoned by their captors upon the island from which they had been rescued. The Captain treated them kindly and brought them back with him to New York, where Lewis received them into his house" (17).

Delafield, who had heard the story from her father Morgan, claimed that the "princes" convinced Francis Lewis to return them to Africa with the promise of a large reward. The ship that he sent them on returned from Africa "laden with gold-dust, ivory, and other products of the tropics. Of the many ventures of Lewis, this was one of the most lucrative" (18). The trip was so profitable that Lewis attempted to establish a regular trade with this area of the African coast, but lost out to competition from the Dutch.

Why was Lewis's ship in Africa? What trade was going on between the American colonies and the African coast in the eighteenth century?

Students knew about the triangular trade and that the "commodity" loaded on boats bound for the New World was usually enslaved Africans. Was Francis Lewis a slave trader?

The text is suggestive, but not definitive. Lewis was a businessman, so what else could he be doing there? Why did he "rescue" the three young Africans and bring them back to New York rather than returning them to their family or just releasing them on the mainland? Why did he later decide to send them back to Africa? Was it out of a desire for philanthropy or profit? What, or who, was on the boat that returned from Africa with the exchange for the "princes"? Was it a human cargo? Delafield never says. Perhaps she did not know herself. Maybe she did not consider it important enough to report or assumed her readers would know the answers.

Students wanted to know whether I was certain that Lewis was a slave trader. I said I wasn't (although I later found evidence, see Donnan, 1932/1969, p. 507). Sometimes historians do not know the answer with certainty because the historical record is too incomplete or is disputed. We draw the best conclusions we can by using the information we have available, and then we look for additional documentation. Based on historical evidence such as port entry records about the slave trade between Africa, the Caribbean, and colonial New York, I suspected that Anglesey and Lewis were involved in slave trading.

From other passages in the book, we know that Francis Lewis definitely did own enslaved Africans. Julia Delafield described a dinner party given by Lewis's wife Elizabeth at the family house in Whitestone, Queens, where one of the servants was a "little colored girl." According to Delafield's grandfather Morgan Lewis, she was well treated and "(w)ith such a mistress [as Elizabeth Lewis] slavery, at least in childhood was no hardship."

I read the last line of the quotation a second time as students sat in total silence. "With such a mistress slavery, at least in childhood was no hardship." "Do you think it was true," I asked, "that being a slave in the Lewis household was not a hardship?" This they could not accept and many began to shout out. "She was just a girl." "Where did she come from?" "Where were her parents?" "They probably were working in his fields." "No type of slavery is okay." "Slavery is slavery."

I asked if they had any further questions, but no one did. So I asked a question. "Given what we now know, do you think the name of the school should be changed?"

Hands swept up and students began to argue with each other. Some students compared Francis Lewis to Thomas Jefferson and said they were both "damaged goods." Others responded that owning slaves did not negate the good things that they had done for the country and that all heroes had some flaws. "We celebrate Lewis and Jefferson because of the *Declaration of Independence* and their contributions to the birth of the new nation," a student said in summary of that position, "not because they owned slaves."

Finally one student said that I was not being fair because I was "judging Francis Lewis by today's standards, not what was acceptable in his time." I stopped everyone and conceded that the student had raised an important historical point. "But," I added," "I still have a problem."

I asked if anyone had heard of John Bowne High School and if they knew who John Bowne was. A significant number of students knew about the high school (it was less than a mile away) and a few even knew that John Bowne was "famous" because he permitted Quakers, in violation of local ordinances, to hold meetings at his house during the colonial era. Browne's wife was a Quaker and he was harassed by colonial authorities, fined, imprisoned, and once even banished from the colony for his support of their right to practice their religion. Because of Bowne's steadfastness under adversity the area, which is still known as Flushing, became a major Quaker center (Hartell, 1943, p. 69; Burrows & Wallace, 1999, p. 61).

It was at a 1716 meeting in Flushing that local Quakers first took up the antislavery crusade. The Flushing Meeting, as the Quaker congregation was called, formally condemned slavery as incompatible with the principles of Christianity in 1767, and in 1773 it urged its members not to purchase slaves. By the time of the American Revolution, most New York Quakers who had previously owned enslaved Africans had set them free. Those who refused faced expulsion from the religious community.

So my question was, "If other people in this very neighborhood were saying slavery was wrong and were freeing enslaved people, how can we excuse Francis Lewis for continuing to own slaves?"

The class erupted again and the arguments resumed. Finally, I had to wave my arms until they quieted. As there was very little time left, I said the issue would clearly not be resolved that day. I asked them to continue the discussion with their teachers and told them that my goal was not to convince them to change the name of the school, although I thought they should. I wanted them to recognize the complexity of historical issues, to question what they had previously learned about the past, and to use what they learned to become active in contemporary political debates.

What Kind of Country?

As teachers and students look at the Revolutionary era in American history and the creation of the new nation, we have to ask what kind of country this was? We also need to consider whether it had to follow the path that it took, a path that included human enslavement, Civil War, Jim Crow segregation, and racism.

The two quotes that open this chapter, the first by Gouverneur Morris and the second by Karl Marx, support the idea that historical developments are contingent, the result of specific factors interacting at any given time, and not predetermined. There are crucial turning points when individuals and societies have alternatives.

Four of the country's first five presidents owned enslaved Africans, as did the four New Yorkers who signed the *Declaration of Independence*. They made conscious choices to support slavery at a time when the path of history might have been changed. Slavery in the United States was being challenged on many fronts during the Revolutionary era. Pennsylvania, Connecticut, and Rhode Island approved gradual manumission proposals. Massachusetts's courts ruled that the state's constitution had, in effect, ended slavery. The Methodist Church declared slavery was "contrary to the golden laws of God" and other mainstream religious groups supported it. New Yorkers organized the Society for Promoting the Manumission of Slaves in 1785 and started a free school to educate African American students. The Northwest Ordinance, approved by the Articles of Confederation Congress, barred slavery in the Ohio territories.

In the South, cotton had not yet emerged as a major cash crop. Tobacco farmers, deeply in debt, with heavy investments in enslaved labor and resource-depleted lands, were facing bankruptcy. In response to economic pressure and political idealism, Virginia and North Carolina passed laws making it easier for plantation owners to manumit enslaved Africans. If men of goodwill had held out during the Revolutionary era and at the Constitutional Convention in 1787, slavery might have ended there and then (Franklin, 1974, pp. 96–98, 116). It was a crucial historical moment. The future, our past, could have been different.

In the movie *Analyze This* there is a great scene where a mob boss, played by Robert De Niro, explains that while he was trying to kill his psychologist, played by Billy Crystal, he was "conflicted." I think too much fuss is made about the fact that some founders of the new nation were personally "conflicted" about the institution of slavery. They had other options.

In New York, Lewis Morris's family owned one of the largest slave holding estates in the north, Morrisana, in what was then Westchester County but is today the Bronx, one of the five boroughs of New York City. While he remained committed to the institution of slavery, his half-brother, Gouverneur Morris, broke with the family and became an abolitionist. At the New York State Constitutional Convention in 1777, Gouverneur Morris proposed a motion, which was defeated, declaring that "The rights of human nature and the principles of our holy religion call upon us to dispense the blessings of freedom to all mankind . . . It is therefore recommended to the Legislatures of the State of New York to take measures consistent with the public safety for abolishing domestic slavery" (McManus, 1966, p. 161; Journals, 1842, vd. I, pp. 887–889). He later relocated to Philadelphia where he unsuccessfully fought to end slavery at the Federal Constitutional Convention.

John Jay was born in New York City in 1745 and raised on the family farm in Rye, New York. His father was one of the largest slave-owners in New York and although Jay personally owned slaves, he became a leading advocate of manumission. John Jay led an unsuccessful effort to include the abolition of slavery in New York State's first constitution. In 1785, he was a cofounder of the Society for Promoting the Manumission of Slaves and served as its president. In 1799, as governor of New York, he signed into law a gradual manumission act that would end slavery in the state by 1827 (Brady, 2001, p. 23).

Other New Yorkers made similar choices, and one pair of them is particularly ironic. Alexander Hamilton and Aaron Burr, who later became bitter political and personal enemies, were both involved in the establishment of the Manumission Society, and Burr helped John Jay shepherd the gradual manumission law through the New York state legislature.

Given the later hostility between Irish immigrants and New York City's African American population, it is important to note that many of the earliest arrivals in the United States compared the Irish under British rule, particularly the lives of landless laborers, with slavery. When Thomas Addis Emmet, who had been arrested and imprisoned for his part in the 1798 Irish Uprising, emigrated to New York in 1804, he established a legal practice and was hired by the Society of Friends (the Quakers) to defend runaway slaves (Emmet, 1915, pp. 8–9).

Recognizing Complexity

The possibility of historical "turning points," and of individual and collective choice, underscores the importance of teacher knowledge and research. They also support the focus on complexity and on the use of probing questions when teaching about slavery. Otherwise, it is too easy to fall into a pedagogy based on packaged lessons and simple answers.

In Fall 2005, my colleague Mary Carter and I gave a series of workshops for secondary school students in a suburban Long Island school district. The audience was nearly 100 percent White, although in the colonial era over 20 percent of the population in that area consisted of enslaved Africans. Our goal was to challenge students and teachers into rethinking their image of their community. "What happened to its Black people?"

We began by examining two primary source documents with the group. According to the will of a member of the town's founding family, they owned a number of enslaved Africans. Upon his death, his sons, daughter, and wife inherited the enslaved Africans. In addition, one of the schools was located on a street named after a local farmer who, according to a 1773 inventory, owned twenty-six enslaved Africans valued at £853 then, or over $128,000 today.

But we left something out which we did not learn about ourselves until later. The Reverend Henry Highland Garnet, a noted Black abolitionist, had escaped to freedom in the North with his parents and sister when he was eleven years old. When they were discovered in New York City by slave catchers, local

Quakers smuggled Henry out of the city and placed him in Suffolk County with a member of their fellowship named Epenetus Smith. A descendant of the same Long Island family that had owned enslaved Africans in the eighteenth century gave Garnet a job and a safe haven in the nineteenth century and nursed him when he suffered a severe injury. The lessons, of course, are that beliefs, families, and communities can change, and that family members are not automatically in agreement (Smith, 1865, pp. 25–26; Schor, 1977, pp. 3–24).

Yet the reality was that change in the condition of life for African Americans in New York, whether free or enslaved, was at best incremental and intermittent during the early years of the new nation. From 1790 to 1800, the number of enslaved Africans in the city actually increased by 22 percent and the number of slaveholders increased by one-third. According to the 1800 census, 43 percent of New York State's Black population remained enslaved. In Kings County (Brooklyn), 32 percent of the population was of African descent, and 82 percent of these people were still enslaved (Hodges, 1999, pp. 279–280; White, 1991, p. 17; Wilder, 2000, p. 37).

Part of the problem was the deep-seated racism that accompanied and justified enslavement. In both the North and the South, Whites debated what would become of the enslaved African population if it were to be freed.

In 1782, Thomas Jefferson (1787/1794, pp. 198–210) argued that the "real distinctions which nature has made" between the races would prevent Whites and Blacks from ever living together in a state of equality. Jefferson believed that the African's skin color, hair type, facial features, and "very strong and disagreeable odor" marked him as aesthetically inferior to Europeans. In addition, Jefferson believed their grief was "transient," their passions lustful, and their "reason much inferior." He concluded that "the blacks, whether originally a distinct race, or made distinct by time and circumstances, are inferior to the whites in the endowments both of body and mind" and recommended, "When freed, he is to be removed beyond the reach of mixture."

An anonymous article published in the *New-York Packet* on April 4, 1785, presented similar sentiments (Gellman and Quigley, 2003). The author argued that "It would be greatly injurious to this state if all the Negroes should be allowed the privileges of white men, unless there could be derived some possible means consistent with liberty, to separate them from white people, and prevent them from having any connection or intercourse with them." He concluded, "If they were free and on equal footing with us, God knows what use they would make of their power; a very bad one I fear" (pp. 34–35).

A major area of dispute in this debate was over the right to vote. At the 1821 New York State convention to revise the state constitution, Erastus Root of Delaware County argued that although Blacks were free, they should not be considered citizens, could be denied voting rights, and should be shut out of the political arena (Gellman & Quigley, 2003, pp. 114–117). Although debate ended without a formal decision, the issue of full citizenship rights continued to divide White New Yorkers and remained a threat to the rights of the state's

African American population after New York emancipation in 1827. Some New Yorkers ultimately supported the idea of resettling free Blacks in Africa. This included at least one prominent African American, John Russwurm, editor of *Freedom's Journal,* the first newspaper published by African Americans in the United States. Russwurm, who had been born enslaved in Jamaica, came to believe that African Americans should return to their African homeland and in 1829 he migrated to Liberia (Katz, 1997, pp. 58–60).

African Americans Demand Rights

An important theme in this historical period was the struggle of African Americans in New York for their rights, a struggle that intensified in the decades leading up to the American Civil War. Resistance to oppression took many forms. It included running away, fighting back, founding social and religious institutions, securing an education, and political organizing.

One of the most poignant personal stories of enslavement in New York and its impact on people's lives from this time period is the narrative of the life of Isabella Baumfree of Ulster County. Baumfree, who is better remembered by her chosen name, Sojourner Truth, dictated her memoirs in 1878 (Gilbert, 1884).

In the narrative, Truth described how she and "her youngest brother, remained, with their parents, the legal property of Charles Ardinburgh till his decease, which took place [in 1808] when Isabella was near nine years old" (17). According to Truth, she was sold at an auction "for the sum of one hundred dollars, to one John Nealy, of Ulster County," along with "a lot of sheep" (26). Sojourner Truth remembered that while the property of Nealy, she received "plenty to eat, and also plenty of whipping." On one occasion, "he gave her the most cruel whipping she was ever tortured with. He whipped her till the flesh was deeply lacerated, and the blood streamed from her wounds, and the scars remain to the present day to testify the fact" (27).

When she reached adulthood, Sojourner Truth had her own children illegally sold out of state and an owner deny her promised emancipation. Eventually she ran away and with the help of local Quakers was able to purchase her freedom and use the courts to secure the return of an infant son. She later went on to become an itinerant preacher and a champion of women's rights.

The struggle to end slavery in the new nation was assisted by the emergence of important African American institutions in the years after American independence. In 1796, Black congregants in New York City formed an independent Zion Church. The New York Manumission Society established African Free Schools that were later supported by the municipal government and the state legislature. Graduates of African Free Schools, including Henry Highland Garnet, Alexander Crummell, and James McCune Smith, became prominent community leaders, especially in the struggle for Black civil rights and for the abolition of slavery in the United States. Seneca Village, in an area that is now part of Central Park in New York City, emerged as a largely Black community (Katz, 1997, pp. 41–50).

One of the earliest leaders of the African American community in New York was Peter Williams, a founder of the New York Anti-Slavery Society. In 1808, Williams issued thanks to God on the occasion of the ban on the trans-Atlantic slave trade. What is most interesting in his prayer is the connection he drew between the American War for Independence and the campaign to end slavery. He argues that the revolution had made the new country a "temple sacred to liberty" (Aptheker, 1973, p. 51) and after quoting from the *Declaration of Independence*, calls for an extension of the "inherent rights of man" to the African race.

The struggle against slavery was also a struggle for racial equality. This was made very clear in William Hamilton's 1809 address to the New-York African Society. Hamilton directly challenged racism in American society and claims of African inferiority. To charges that Roman slaves had overcome their circumstances, Hamilton replied: "Among the Romans it was only necessary for the slave to be manumitted, in order to be eligible to all the offices of state . . . ; no sooner was he free than there was open before him a wide field of employment for his ambition, and learning and abilities with merit, were as sure to meet with their reward in him, as in any other citizen. But what station above the common employment of craftsmen and laborers would we fill did we possess both learning and abilities" (Aptheker, 1973, pp. 52–53).

One of the high points of the early struggle against slavery and a source of great racial pride was the Manumission Day Parade on July 4, 1827. Dr. James McCune Smith, an African American physician who studied medicine in Glasgow, described the New York procession he attended as a youth. It was led by a "splendid looking black man, mounted on a milk-white steed" with "colored bands of music and their banners appropriately lettered and painted." The sidewalks were crowded with "wives, daughters, sisters, and mothers of the celebrants, representing every state in the Union, and not a few with gay bandanna handkerchiefs, betraying their West Indian birth. Nor was Africa underrepresented. Hundreds who survived the middle passage and a youth in slavery joined in the joyful procession" (Hodges, 1999, pp. 223–224).

Chapter 7

Debate

In states where the slave system prevails, the masters directly or indirectly secure all political power and constitute a ruling aristocracy. In states where the free-labor system prevails, universal suffrage necessarily obtains and the state inevitably becomes sooner or later a republic or democracy. The two systems are at once perceived to be incongruous—they are incompatible. They never have permanently existed together in one country, and they never can . . . It is an irrepressible conflict between opposing and enduring forces, and it means that the United States must and will, sooner or later, become either entirely a slave-holding nation or entirely a free-labor nation.

—William Seward

With the formation of a national antislavery society in 1832, New York City emerged as the center of the American antislavery movement. Among the movement's White leaders were silk merchants Lewis and Arthur Tappan, who spearheaded a mailing campaign to flood the South with antislavery literature. Southern communities put a price on the Tappan brothers, including a $50,000 "wanted dead-or-alive" reward offered by East Feliciana, Louisiana (Richards, 1970, pp. 49–50; Burrows & Wallace, 1999, pp. 559–560).

Sections of this chapter were developed with the help of Kerri Creegan, a high school teacher from Massapequa, New York, and Stephanie Sienkiewicz, a teacher from James Fenimore Cooper Middle School in Virginia, who presented with me at the 2006 annual meeting of the Organization of American Historians. It was Kerri who insisted that New York be seen as a miscrosm of the national struggle over slavery. The material on the Draft Riots is the result of a long-term collaboration with Maureen Murphy.

The Tappans are best remembered for their financial support of Oberlin College in Ohio and for organizing a committee of New York City's leading abolitionists to aid in the defense of the kidnapped Africans on the Amistad. During the Amistad trial in Connecticut, Lewis Tappan wrote a series of reports for the *New York Journal of Commerce* defending their humanity and demanding protection for their legal rights. After the passage of the Fugitive Slave Law in 1850, Lewis Tappan declared it was now legitimate to disobey laws promoting the slave system, and he became an active supporter of the Underground Railroad.

The Tappans stand out because of the tacit or active complicity of most of New York City's business and political elite with slavery in the South and the Caribbean. At the annual meeting of the American Anti-Slavery Society in May, 1835, the Reverend Samuel J. May was confronted by a partner from one of New York City's prominent trading firms. In his memoir, May described their encounter. "(W)ith considerable emotion and emphasis," the unnamed businessman declared that "we are not such fools as not to know that slavery is a great evil, a great wrong. But it was consented to by the founders of our Republic. It was provided for in the Constitution of our Union. A great portion of the property of the Southerners is invested under its sanction; and the business of the North, as well as the South, has become adjusted to it. There are millions upon millions of dollars due from Southerners to the merchants and mechanics of this city alone, the payment of which would be jeopardized by any rupture between the North and the South. We cannot afford, sir, to let you and your associates succeed in your endeavor to overthrow slavery. It is not a matter of principle with us. It is a matter of business necessity. . . . We mean . . . to put you Abolitionists down—by fair means if we can, by foul means if we must" (Katz, 1995, p. 172).

Microcosm of Debate

From the American Revolution to the Civil War, but especially after local emancipation in 1827, New York was a microcosm of the national debate over human enslavement (Creegan, 2007). Black New Yorkers such as Henry Highland Garnet and Frederick Douglass saw the battle against slavery in the South as part of their continuing struggle for full human rights in the North. Local White abolitionists, many like the Tappans descended from Puritan and Congregationalist settlers or members of Quaker fellowships, viewed both slavery in the South and its toleration in the North as abominations that stained the moral character of the nation.

Prior to 1850, abolitionists in New York and the North, both Black and White, were demonized and marginalized. The rapid expansion of the anti-slavery crusade after the passage of the federal Fugitive Slave Act provides an arena for studying how a social movement moves from the margins of society to the mainstream and achieves at least some of its goals.

As with the prominent businessman quoted by May, prior to the Civil War most White Northerners and New Yorkers were comfortable compartmentalizing their values. If they commented on slavery at all, they claimed to recognize it was "evil" and approved its gradual abolition in the North. However, those with the power or influence to make a change either ignored its continued existence in the South or collaborated with the slave system by providing financial services to Southern and Caribbean planters and trading in commodities produced by enslaved labor.

There was a fine line between antipathy toward abolitionists and violent antagonism, and Northerners often stepped across the line. In 1835, a Boston mob dragged William Lloyd Garrison through the streets at the end of a rope (Richards, 1970, p. 64). In New York City, Lewis Tappan's house in lower Manhattan was attacked and destroyed in July 1834, and only armed resistance by his employees saved Arthur Tappan's shop. St. Philip's African Episcopal Church and the home of its minister, Peter Williams, were also destroyed during these anti-abolitionist riots (Burrows & Wallace, 1999, pp. 557–558).

At the highest levels of business and government, White Northerners made choices based on political and economic expediency. Leaders were willing to turn their backs on both the suffering of enslaved Africans and attacks against Blacks and abolitionists. During the 1863 Draft Riot in New York City, Governor Horatio Seymour and Tammany Hall leaders defended the rights of rioters and refused to call for martial law, even as the death count and property damage mounted (Bernstein, 1990, pp. 50–51).

Horatio Seymour, who was elected governor in 1862 as an antiwar and anti-emancipation candidate, was committed to restoring the union through concessions to the South. Along with financier August Belmont, corporate lawyer Samuel Tilden, and Samuel Morse, a leading nativist, he was a member of the Society for the Diffusion of Political Knowledge. The organization demanded the repeal of the Emancipation Proclamation because, they believed, an end to slavery undermined the economies of both the South and North. At a July 4th mass rally a little more than a week before the 1863 Draft Riots, Seymour declared that "the bloody and treasonable and revolutionary doctrine of public necessity can be proclaimed by a mob as well as by a government." The activities of New York's "Copperheads," minimized in most history texts and classrooms, expose as myth the story that a unified "free" North stood in opposition to slavery (Burrows & Wallace, 1999, pp. 886–888).

Even Abraham Lincoln, whom history recognizes as the Great Emancipator, equivocated. During the 1858 Illinois Senatorial race, Lincoln proclaimed that "this government cannot endure permanently half slave and half free" (Stern, 1940, p. 429). But four years later he wrote Horace Greeley, editor of the New York Tribune, "If I could save the Union without freeing any slave, I would do it" (Stern, 1940, p. 719).

Teachers often claim they present both sides of an argument. But in the case of Northern attitudes toward slavery, as in most cases, there are far more than just two sides, and disagreements can be quite nuanced. As students examine this debate, they learn about the dynamic of social movements, the importance of institutions such as colleges and churches for preparing leaders, the role religious beliefs have played in American history, and the operation of profit-driven capitalism, as well as about attitudes toward slavery.

Political Arena

In the political arena, there was a spectrum of views ranging from adamant challengers of the institution of slavery on the "left" to unabashed collaborators on the "right." The broad middle ground included those who, while unhappy with slavery in the South, were prepared to reach an accommodation to preserve the union and good business relationships.

Gerrit Smith (Singer, 2005a, pp. 189–190; *The Spartacus Internet Encyclopedia,* 2007) was probably the most radical White abolitionist engaged in electoral politics in the United States. In 1835, he joined the American Anti-Slavery Society after witnessing its speakers being attacked by a mob in Utica, New York. Five years later, Smith helped found the antislavery Liberty Party, which was based in New York State, and was its candidate for president of the United States in 1848 and 1852. Smith also served briefly as a congressman representing the upstate (Albany) Capital region in Washington DC.

Gerrit Smith used his family's fortune to finance the interracial Oneida Institute just outside of Utica and to establish communities for formerly enslaved Africans in the Adirondack region of the state. The Oneida Institute had a major role in training antislavery activists. Its president, Beriah Green, who was White, served as presiding officer of the 1833 founding convention of the American Anti-Slavery Society in Philadelphia. Former students who became prominent in the antislavery movement included Theodore Weld, a White man who became editor of the American Anti-Slavery Society newspaper; Alexander Crummel, a free Black from New York City who became a missionary in Liberia; Augustus Washington, one of the first Black photographers in the United States, who made portraits of leading abolitionists including John Brown and William Lloyd Garrison; Henry Highland Garnet, an escaped slave who was one of the most radical antislavery orators; and Jermain Loguen, an escaped slave who became a minister and the head station master for the Underground Railroad in Syracuse (Sernett, 1986).

Gerrit Smith was a supporter of John Brown's campaign against the extension of slavery into Kansas and was suspected of financing Brown's raid on a federal arsenal at Harpers Ferry, Virginia in 1859. When Brown's forces raided the federal arsenal at Harper's Ferry, Brown had in his possession a check for $100 from Gerrit Smith. Because of Smith's involvement at Harpers Ferry, students in Michael Pezone's law elective at Law, Government, and

Community Service Magnet High School have put him and Frederick Douglass on "trial" for violating the Patriot Act (2001) by materially supporting John Brown and others who were engaged in terrorist activities against the legitimate government of the United States. As one student noted during an evaluation of the project, "Terrorism is a subjective term. The thing that makes Douglass and Smith freedom fighters is that they were fighting for the inalienable rights of people. That is a fundamental premise of democracy. If you convict them of terrorism, then all of the people who participated in the Civil War should be declared terrorists also" (Singer et al, 2008, see Chapter 13, "Classroom Ideas").

William Seward (Singer, 2005a, p. 188; Foner, 1970, pp. 40–45; *The Spartacus Internet Encyclopedia*, 2007), a more prominent and successful politician, was an outspoken opponent of slavery during this period. He attended Union College in Schenectady, whose presidents included Jonathan Edwards, Jr. and Eliphalett Nott, both early abolitionists. Other Union alumni who became active in the antislavery cause were Chester Arthur (future President of the United States) and Preston King (U.S. congressman and senator).

William Seward witnessed the injustice of slavery firsthand as a young teacher in the state of Georgia. Later, as an opponent of the Fugitive Slave Act, he defended runaway slaves in court, and he and his wife Frances helped Harriet Tubman and the Underground Railroad by hiding fugitive slaves in their Auburn home.

In 1838 and 1840, Seward was elected governor of New York State, and in 1849 he was elected to the United States Senate, where he built a reputation as an antislavery senator. In one of his more powerful statements in opposition to slavery, Seward wrote that "The two systems [slavery and freed labor] are . . . incongruous—they are incompatible. They never have permanently existed together in one country, and they never can." He predicted "an irrepressible conflict between opposing and enduring forces" until the United States would "become either entirely a slave-holding nation or entirely a free-labor nation" (Baker, 1861/1972, IV, pp. 291–292). After Abraham Lincoln's election, Seward was appointed Secretary of State. He was a target in the Lincoln assassination plot but survived and continued to serve in office under Andrew Johnson. He died in Auburn, New York on October 10, 1872.

Principled opposition to slavery did not necessarily lead to militancy or a belief in human equality. Henry Ward Beecher (Singer, 2005a, p. 191; *The Spartacus Internet Encyclopedia*, 2007) was a minister at the Plymouth Congregationalist Church in Brooklyn, New York, and a leading opponent of slavery in the 1850s. In 1848, 1856, and 1859, to protest against the evil of slavery, Beecher raised money in his church to purchase the freedom of individual slaves. While Beecher believed it was a moral obligation to oppose the Fugitive Slave Law and the extension of slavery into the West, he thought it was a mistake to actively oppose slavery in the South or encourage slaves to run away.

William Cullen Bryant (Singer, 2005a, p. 187; Brown, 1971), editor of the *New York Evening Post* and a founder of the Republican Party, continually attacked the inhumanity of slavery and the slave trade. Bryant steadfastly opposed the expansion of slavery into the West and what he considered radical calls for the abolition of slavery; however, his primary concern as the nation approached civil war was preservation of the Union.

For many White New York politicians, political expediency may have been the primary factor in determining their position on slavery. Martin Van Buren, a founder of the modern Democratic Party and future President of the United States, grew up on a farm in Kinderhook, New York, where his father owned six enslaved African Americans. While Martin Van Buren opposed slavery for most of his adult life, he also owned an enslaved African man named "Tom." At one point, "Tom" escaped from Van Buren and remained free for ten years before he was recaptured. Van Buren sold him to his captor for fifty dollars (Singer, 2005a, p. 194; Shade, 1998, pp. 459–484; Cole, 1984, pp. 13 & 110).

While Van Buren voted against the Missouri Compromise because it admitted Missouri to the union as a slave state, he did not support citizenship rights for free Blacks. In 1821, he brokered a compromise at a convention rewriting the New York state constitution that extended the franchise to all adult White male citizens but maintained property restrictions for Black men (Quigley, 2005, p. 275).

As Van Buren became more prominent in the national Democratic Party, he tried to maintain a difficult balance on the slavery issue, just as many politicians today claim to personally oppose abortion while respecting a woman's freedom of choice. Van Buren argued that while slavery was morally wrong, attacking the slave system violated the constitutional principle of states' rights. As a candidate for President and in his inaugural address, Van Buren assured slave owners that he and the entire Northern White population had no desire to intervene in their local affairs and were prohibited from doing so by the *Constitution*. He promised that as President, he would protect their property rights as slave owners (Berlin & Harris, 2005, p. 5; Van Buren, 1837).

After his defeat for reelection in 1840 and an unsuccessful effort to secure the Democratic Party nomination in 1844, Van Buren blamed Southern intrigue for his defeats and changed his position on slavery (Foner, 1970, p. 151). He became a "Free Soiler" because he believed that free White labor could never compete economically with enslaved Africans, and he decided that Congress had the authority to prevent the extension of slavery into new territories and to abolish slavery in the District of Columbia.

Business connections inevitably led to political alliances between New York's merchants and Southern planters. During the summer of 1860, New York's leading merchants organized "The Volunteer Democratic Association of New York" to "save the federal Union from the calamities which would become inevitable consequences of the election of Lincoln and Hamlin" (Foner, 1941, p. 172). Members of the group included William Astor, merchant and heir to a real estate fortune, Moses Taylor, whose banking operations would eventually evolve into Citibank, sugar baron William Havemeyer, Erastus

Corning, President of the New York Central Railroad, and August Belmont, the American agent for the Rothchilds. After the election, they organized a Union Committee of Fifteen in an effort to ward off Southern secession. A meeting on December 15, 1860, on Pine Street in the Wall Street area was attended by over 2,000 people, including A. T. Stewart, a cotton merchant and founder of one of the country's first department stores, Abiel Low, whose import-export firm dominated the China trade, August Belmont, and Moses Taylor (Farrow et al, 2005, pp. 10–11). It was followed by an editorial in the *Journal of Commerce* pledging to defend the Constitutional rights of the slaveholders and the "fraternal relations established by it between you and us" (Foner, 1941, p. 228). Local merchants and politicians continued their effort to assuage the South and preserve slavery until the South finally fired on Fort Sumpter (Foner, 1941, p. 267).

The New York politician from this era most closely identified with support for slavery and the South was Fernando Wood (Singer, 2005a, p. 196; Mushkat, 1990), a wealthy merchant involved in the coastal trade with the South and a successful investor in local real estate, who served in Congress and as mayor of New York City. On January 8, 1861, the *New York Times* published the transcript of Mayor Wood's annual report to the city's Common Council. In this message, Wood spoke about the city's options as the United States federal union appeared to be dissolving and he called for the city to secede as well.

Woods told the Common Council, "It would seem that a dissolution of the Federal Union is inevitable." He reminded its members that with their "aggrieved brethren of the Slave States we have friendly relations and a common sympathy" because "[w]e have not participated in the warfare upon their constitutional rights or their domestic institutions." He proposed that "New York should endeavor to preserve a continuance of uninterrupted intercourse with every section," and to do this it should secede from the Union itself and become "a free City." He concluded, "When disunion has become a fixed and certain fact, why may not New York disrupt the bands which bind her to a corrupt and venal master. New York, as a *Free City,* may shed the only light and hope for a future reconstruction of our once blessed Confederacy" (p. 2).

Wood's sentiments were supported by the *New York Herald* and the *Journal of Commerce.* The *Herald* published a statement by department store magnet Alexander Stewart charging that "the refusal at Washington to concede costs us millions daily." The *Journal of Commerce* warned President-elect Lincoln that "[t]here are a million and a half mouths to be fed daily in this city and its dependencies; and they will not consent to be starved by any man's policies" (Ellis, 1966, p. 291).

While Wood backed away from this position once the actual fighting broke out, in 1864 he represented the city in Congress where he opposed the Thirteenth Amendment to the Constitution. In congressional debate he argued that an end to slavery would make it impossible for southern planters to repay their debts to New York City merchants. Once again, economic gain trumped ethnical considerations.

Politics, especially pro-slavery politics, makes very strange bedfellows. From as early as the 1830s, New York had a strong nativist contingent, usually anti-Irish and identified with the city's Protestant social elite. Samuel F. B. Morse, the inventor, was their candidate for mayor in 1836 and 1841. Morse disliked Roman Catholics, who he believed were part of a European conspiracy to destroy American liberty (Burrows & Wallace, 1999, p. 545), and supported the enslavement of Africans, which he thought was "divinely ordained" (Morse, 1863, p. 10). The nativists hated Wood because of his alliance with Irish and German immigrants and helped to oust him from office as mayor in 1857. However, during the Civil War, nativist opposition to emancipation and racial equality led to a marriage of convenience with pro-Southern politicians like Wood and Horatio Seymour who had support in the immigrant community.

Religion and Slavery

While many abolitionists, both White and Black, drew on religious principles to sustain them during a long, difficult and dangerous struggle, there were also prominent Northern religious leaders arrayed under the pro-slavery banner, including New York City's Roman Catholic Archbishop John Hughes (Singer, 2005a, pp. 195–196; Singer, 2003e, p. 13; Hassard, 1866; Andrews, 1934, pp. 60–78; Allen, 1994). Hughes, an immigrant from Ireland, became the acting head of the New York Roman Catholic diocese in 1838. He was appointed its bishop in 1842 and an archbishop of the church in 1850. Biographers speculate that Hughes's relationship with the Rodrigue family, refugees from the Haitian Revolution of 1793, and their accounts of massacres there contributed to an exaggerated fear of slave insurrection and a belief in the inferiority of Africans. His endorsement of the slave system also may have reflected the process of assimilation and Americanization by Irish immigrants who often competed with free and enslaved Black labor in the marketplace.

In 1853 and 1854, Archbishop Hughes traveled in Cuba and the American South where he was a guest on a number of plantations and witnessed the slave system firsthand. In May 1854, Hughes delivered a sermon at old St. Patrick's Cathedral, in what is now Soho, where he discussed his experiences during this trip and defended slavery.

In his sermon, Hughes cited passages from the *Gospel According to John* to justify slavery. He compared the slave master to the father of a family, and told his congregation, "Is not the father of the family invested with the power of God that he is sovereign, commanding and expecting to be obeyed as he should?" Hughes claimed to recognize that "slavery is an evil," but declared it was "not an absolute and unmitigated evil" because it brought Africans to Christianity. He believed that conditions for Africans were actually improved by enslavement. He claimed that during his trip he had "taken pains to inquire of some who had been brought to Cuba as slaves from the Coast of Africa, whether they wished to return, and they invariably stated they did not; and the reason is that their condition here, degraded as it is, is much better than it was at home, . . . it is really a mitigation of their lot to be sold into foreign bondage" (*New York Times*, 1854a, p. 4). In his column in the *Metropolitan Record,* he wrote: "We of course believe that no genuine Christian—no decent man— would be engaged in this kind of business: still, we cannot discover the crime, even of the slaver, in snatching them from the butcheries of their native land" (Andrews, 1934, p. 65).

Archbishop Hughes continued his public support for slavery during the Civil War. He warned Europeans who questioned his stance that the sudden emancipation of four million enslaved Africans would deprive them of the commodities on which their national economies depended. In May 1861, he declared that efforts to abolish slavery would violate the *United States Constitution* and demanded that Lincoln resign from the presidency if this was his goal (Allen, 1994, p. 190). Hughes wrote Secretary of War Cameron threatening that if "the purpose of the war is the abolition of slavery in the South," it would undermine efforts to recruit troops in New York City (Lee, 1943, p. 156; Allen, 1994, p. 182).

In an October 12, 1861 editorial in the *Metropolitan Record,* Hughes asserted that slavery exists by the "Divine permission of God's providence" and was desirable because it permitted "humane masters to . . . take care of unfortunate people" (Allen, 1994, 190). He dismissed the immorality of hereditary bondage by comparing it with the inheritance of original sin by each new generation.

Hughes wrote the Bishop of Charleston, South Carolina defending states' rights and denounced the Emancipation Proclamation as a violation of property rights (Allen, 1994, p. 190). In a letter to Secretary of State Seward, he blamed the 1863 New York City Draft Riots on an effort "to make black labor equal to white labor" (Allen, 1994, p. 192).

Fugitive Slave Law

In football, and in social struggles, the ball can take a funny and unanticipated bounce. In 1850, few commentators would have predicted a final victory for the abolitionists in the battle to end slavery. A legislative compromise allowing California to enter the Union as a free state included clauses in a new Fugitive Slave Law that allowed the seizure and transport back to enslavement of suspected runaways without due process. It also mandated that "all good citizens are hereby commanded to aid and assist in the prompt and efficient executive of this law" (Feder, 1967, p. 129).

Daniel Webster, Senator from Massachusetts and a leading Northern statesman, defended the compromise and the Fugitive Slave law as necessary for the "preservation of the Union" and to avoid a "convulsion" that would dismember the nation. In a speech delivered before the Senate, he charged abolitionists with "mischiefs" that tightened the "bonds of the slave . . . more firmly than before." He accused them of being impatient with the "slow progress of moral causes in the improvement of mankind" and charged, "They prefer the chance of running into utter darkness to living in heavenly light, if that heavenly light be not absolutely without any imperfection" (Webster, 1850; Shewmaker, 1990, pp. 121–130).

But Webster and the other proponents of the compromise with slavery had seriously miscalculated. The abandonment of due process was seen as a fundamental threat to constitutional liberty. The charge that all citizens were obligated by law to support slave catchers meant that every individual had to make a decision whether to be openly complicit with slavery or stand with those who resisted it. The plan, which was intended as a way of avoiding sectional conflict, ended up exacerbating it. Its failure was a major turning point in United States history and an underlying cause of the American Civil War.

In essence, the national compromise allowed no space for personal compromise. The law gave the forces of enslavement license to invade the North, and by organizing active resistance abolitionists now had a strategic weapon to mobilize opposition to slavery. In an 1851 speech in Concord, Massachusetts, Ralph Waldo Emerson declared "The act of Congress . . . is a law which every one of you will break on the earliest occasion—a law which no man can obey . . . without loss of self-respect" (Emerson, 1851).

Opposition to fugitive slave laws energized the antislavery movement in much the same way as the military draft and reproductive freedom energized the antiwar and woman's rights movements in recent decades. The success of these social movements offer historians, teachers, and students an important lesson on what happens when the "political becomes personal."

Defiance of the Compromise of 1850 began immediately and was covered in the first issues of the *New York Times*. On September 11, 1851, a posse of White men approached a two-story house near Christiana, Pennsylvania (Katz, 1974; Slaughter, 1991). The posse included a Maryland slave owner named Edward Gorsuch, members of his family, and U.S. Marshal Henry Kline. They had warrants for the arrest of several enslaved Africans who had escaped to the North and were being hidden by William Parker. Parker, a Black man, had been born into slavery in Maryland in 1822 and had escaped to Pennsylvania in 1839.

By 1851, William Parker was the head of a local Black self-defense organization. When he received word that slave catchers were in the area of Christiana, Parker, two other Black men, and two Black women decided to protect the escapees. They resisted the kidnappers, shots were fired, Edward Gorsuch was killed, and the rest of the posse retreated.

Following the battle at Christiana, thirty-six local Blacks and five local Whites, most of whom were bystanders during the battle, were charged with treason against the United States for resisting a U.S. marshal, violating the Fugitive Slave law, and rebelling against the government. William Parker avoided arrest by escaping to Canada with the help of Frederick Douglass and others. The Whites who were charged with treason were indicted because law enforcement officials did not believe that Parker and the other Blacks would have been able to resist the posse without the support and leadership of Whites.

The trial, which drew national attention, involved the largest group ever charged with treason at one time in United States history. Among the defense lawyers was a prominent abolitionist, Congressman Thaddeus Stevens.

Eventually, the people brought to trial were found not guilty of treason, and the other charges were dropped. The trial helped to convince Southerners that a Northern-dominated federal government would never respect their "property rights." It left Northerners increasingly angered by what they perceived as Southern attempts to force them to participate in maintaining and defending slavery. As a result of the antislavery resistance at Christiana, the country moved another step toward Civil War and the abolition of slavery.

Because of their proximity to Canada, their work opportunities, and their abolitionist traditions, cities located along the route of the Erie Canal in upstate New York were important sites on the Underground Railroad and in resistance to the Fugitive Slave Law (Sienkiewicz, 2007, pp. 67–68). In Syracuse, the Reverend Jermain Loguen (Loguen, 1859; Singer, 2005a, p. 202) led what has come to be called the "Jerry Rescue." In October 1851, federal marshals and local police arrested a man suspected of being an escaped slave. News of the arrest reached a political convention being held by the antislavery Liberty Party and an unsuccessful effort was made to free the prisoner. That evening a large crowd gathered in the street equipped for a more serious rescue attempt. When the door was broken in, authorities surrendered the prisoner. After several days in hiding, he was taken by wagon to Oswego where he crossed Lake Ontario into Canada.

Nineteen indictments were returned against the rescuers, including Loguen, who was a fugitive from slavery himself. The accused were bailed out by, among others, William Seward. Legal proceedings dragged on for two years and Loguen eventually escaped from the region.

Harriet Tubman (Singer, 2005a, p. 204; Bradford, 1886, pp. 124–127) led a similar resistance group in 1859 at Troy, New York. A fugitive named Charles Nalle was being held in the local office of the U.S. Commissioner. As police tried to lead him away, Tubman tore off her sunbonnet, tied herself to the fugitive, and dragged him to the Hudson River, where he was tumbled into a boat. Although Nalle was recaptured, he was able to escape again with the help of Tubman and local abolitionists.

Discussion of the abolitionist response to the Fugitive Slave Law introduces students to a number of essential questions. In its coverage of the "Christiana Incident," a *New York Times* editorial on September 19, 1851 declared, "Resistance to the law is always an offense against the peace of society. No government can exist without punishing breaches of the law, still less, without disaffecting opposition to it. And there is no country in the world, where obedience to law is more prompt and cheerful than in the United States" (*New York Times*, 1851, p. 2).

Did Northerners owe allegiance to the *Constitution* of the United States and the laws of the country, or to a set of "higher laws" that declared all human beings to be equal? Did free Blacks and formerly enslaved Africans have an obligation to obey the laws of the United States, or did they have the human right to resist the injustice of enslavement, even if it meant killing a slave owner? What happens when rights are in conflict—for example, the right to own property and the right to personal freedom? What happens to a country if resistance to its laws is recognized as a human right?

Draft Riot

One of the most disturbing events in the history of the United States was the Civil War Draft Riot in New York City in 1863. The Draft Riot was the country's largest urban upheaval of the nineteenth century. For four days, White mobs, primarily Irish, roamed Manhattan in defiance of the police and a small garrison of federal troops. More than 100 people, mostly African Americans, were killed during the riot and an estimated 12,000 people were injured (Bernstein, 1990; Bernstein, 2005; Singer, 2005a, pp. 259–263; Murphy, 2007, pp. 69–70).

The Draft Riot was a response to an unpopular military conscription law passed by Congress and signed by President Abraham Lincoln in May 1863. The new law allowed the affluent to avoid military service by providing substitutes or by paying $300. Many of the first draftees in New York were slated to be Irish immigrants who were too poor to pay this tax. While the Riots mark a low point in the history of Irish Americans, this story, as with most stories from the past, is more complicated than it appears on the surface.

For Irish Americans, the Civil War was the crucible in which they could demonstrate their loyalty to the United States and finally put a stop to nativist claims that Catholics were unfit for citizenship. The Irish volunteered for the Union Army in record numbers, including over 50,000 men in New York's Irish Brigade (consisting of the 63rd, the 69th, and the 88th regiments). These units suffered from high casualty rates during the early years of the war. The Fighting 69th lost 20 percent of its men at Bull Run. The Battle of Fredericksburg cost the Brigade nearly half of its soldiers. Following Chancellorsville, only five hundred men, enough for six companies were left to fight at Gettysburg. Heavy casualties added to the New York City Irish community's animosity toward the war, Republicans, Abraham Lincoln, and the Emancipation Proclamation.

New York City was ripe for an explosion when the draft lottery began on Saturday, July 11. Although they had lived side-by-side peacefully in some neighborhoods of the city, Blacks and White immigrant workers were often pitted against each other in competition for low paying jobs. In August 1862, two to three thousand Irish workers threatened to burn the Watson and Lorillard tobacco factories because they had hired Black women and children to replace White workers. In March 1863, one thousand strikers attacked Blacks hired by the Erie Railroad to move cotton bales housed at Pier 36 on Duane Street. After the outbreak of the Civil War, African Americans who had been freed were used to break strikes at the Staten Island ferry, the Customs House, and during dock strikes. "Copperhead," or pro-South, newspapers and politicians, including former Mayor Fernando Wood and Governor Horatio Seymour, contributed to the tension in the city by stirring up antiwar sentiment. The last straw was the release of the casualty lists from the Battle of Gettysburg that same weekend.

On Monday, July 13, a mass protest against the draft in New York City was transformed into a riot that attacked government buildings and the prowar press, and eventually turned on the city's African American population. From newspaper accounts, it appears that the rioters turned on the city's Black population after police had repeatedly opened fire on protesters, killing and wounding many people. They destroyed the city's orphanage for Black children, attacked and lynched African Americans caught on the streets, and threatened employers who hired Black workers. Hundreds of African American refugees from the rioting escaped to Weeksville and other largely Black settlements in Brooklyn. On the fourth day of the riot, federal troops from the Union army at Gettysburg arrived in the city and finally restored peace.

In his poem, "The House Top," Herman Melville (Singer 2005, p. 263) described the rioters as "tawny tigers . . . making apt for ravage," and as "ship-rats." However, according to *New York Times* coverage, most of the rioters were women and boys (*New York Times,* 1863, p. 1). Before the burning of the orphanage, which was perhaps the most horrendous of the events that took place, the rioters allowed the children to be evacuated and then looted the building looking for food and bedding. These were not the actions of "tigers" or "rats," but of desperately poor people.

In the last public appearance before his death, Archbishop John Hughes helped to calm the rioters and restore order to the city. My colleague Maureen Murphy (2007, p. 70) describes it as a "grace note" in what had otherwise been a poor record about slavery.

Commentators make a mistake when they talk about the Draft Riots as a single four-day action that was either directed from above or had a unified goal. At most, it represented a shifting coalition of different forces with different goals. Certainly there was an effort to provide direction from above by segments of the city's political and economic elite, but this was more an effort to manipulate popular unrest for political purposes than it was any actual control. An antidraft demonstration began at 6 a.m. on Monday, but the riot did not begin until 4 p.m. in the afternoon. A series of crucial turning points transformed a political protest that enlisted the city's organized workers and artisans into mob violence by unleashing the pent up anger and anguish of New York City's largely Irish preindustrial poor.

African American students with whom I discuss the Draft Riot usually find it a painful topic that, at least at first, supports anger and resentment toward American society. But many have also had experience with or witnessed some degree of urban unrest, official harassment of minority communities, and what they perceive of as biased media reports. As a concluding question, I ask them if they were sitting on a jury trying rioters for murder and other crimes, would they find them guilty based on the evidence? They cannot forgive them, but under the circumstances, they also cannot find them guilty of murder. However, they are much less sympathetic toward Seymour and the other public officials who stood by while Black people died.

Chapter 8

Profiting from Human Misery

New York is the chief port in the world for the Slave Trade. It is the greatest place in the universe for it. Neither in Cuba nor in the Brazils is it carried on so extensively. Ships that convey Slaves to the West Indies and South America are fitted out in New York.

—Captain James Smith (1854)

In 2000, the California Legislature passed a resolution that required insurance companies doing business in the state to file reports with the Department of Insurance about any involvement with slavery prior to the Civil War. In compliance with the law, New York Life disclosed that in the 1840s one of its predecessor companies, Nautilus Insurance Company, wrote over 300 life insurance policies on enslaved Africans in the American South. Aetna uncovered 7 life insurance policies taken out by plantation owners for enslaved Africans, some of which covered multiple lives. AIG admitted that one of its predecessors, United States Life Insurance Company in the City of New York (U.S. Life), also did business with plantation owners during the slavery era (Staples, 2003; California Department of Insurance, 2002).

A similar disclosure law in Chicago forced JP Morgan Chase to acknowledge that a corporate predecessor, Louisiana's Citizens Bank and Canal Bank, provided credit and mortgages to plantation owners with enslaved Africans as collateral. The bank, which eventually became Bank One and merged with JP Morgan Chase in 1994, took ownership of approximately 1,250 people when plantation owners defaulted (BBC, 2005).

Documents at the New York Historical Society and corporate records show that the founders of Brown Bros. Harriman, based in New York City, built the bank by lending millions of dollars to Southern planters and arranging for the shipment and sale of slave-grown cotton in New England and

Great Britain. At one point, the Brown family, which controlled a network of interlocking corporations with offices in New York, New Orleans, and Liverpool, took possession of three Louisiana plantations with 346 enslaved Africans (*USA Today*, 2002; Woodman, 1968, pp. 18, 124, 50n).

The push to expose corporate complicity with slavery in the United States has been spearheaded by Deadria Farmer-Paellman, a legal researcher based in Brooklyn, New York (Groanke, 2002; Farmer-Paellmann et al., 2006), and a team of reporters from the *Hartford* (Connecticut) *Courant* (Farrow et al., 2005). Their work shows the way the plantation system in the South and the Caribbean spawned a series of secondary industries in the North that fueled the region's commercial and industrial development. The trans-Atlantic slave trade and the shipping of commodities produced by slave labor supported the shipbuilding industry in Northern cities, which among other things meant work for sailors, carpenters, barrel, sail and rope makers, and longshoremen. They increased the demand for lumber and pine tar, required financing and insurance, and supported newspapers with their advertisements. Slave ships and plantations required foodstuffs and other supplies. Southern and Caribbean planters purchased luxury goods and services. Slave-produced products, initially sugar, but increasingly cotton, provided raw material for factories in European and Northern cities.

Economic historian Douglass North, in an analysis of the economic growth of the United States from independence through the Civil War, found that the North provided "not only the services to finance, transport, insure, and market the South's cotton, but also supplied the South with manufactured goods" (North, 1961, p. 68). Harold Woodman, another historian, argued that "[t]he financial center of the South was in the North" (Woodman, 1968, p. 169). The role played by Northern merchants and bankers was no secret at the time. In *The Impending Crisis* (1857), Hinton Rowan Helper, a Southern journalist, wrote that it is a "fact known to every intelligent Southerner that we are compelled to go to the North for almost every article of utility . . . that, owing to the absence of a proper system of business amongst us, the North becomes, in one way or another, the proprietor and dispenser of all our floating wealth" (Woodman, 1968, p. 145n).

A focus on the economic ties between the North and South and on individuals involved in cementing these connections, will help historians, teachers, and students explore a series of crucial historical questions. Did the economic relationship between the North and South parallel the earlier exploitative relationship between England and its American colonies? Could the South develop an effective modern economy while dependent on slave labor? How important were slavery-tainted profits in the growth of New York City, New York State, and the nation? Was the slave system in the South maintained in order to generate profits for the North? How aware were merchants, bankers, and other

Northern businessmen of their complicity with the slave system? It also raises an important question about the contemporary world. Can extractive (mineral-producing) or plantation (agricultural) economies such as the pre–Civil War American South, where production of commodities is based on the availability of natural resources and inexpensive (e.g., slave) labor, ever become advanced industrial or postindustrial (service-oriented) societies?

As we saw in the previous chapter, many Whites in the North, and in New York in particular, were involved in combating both slavery in the United States and the global slave trade. But despite the efforts of these individuals, the slave system supported the development of New York as a commercial and financial center. Prior to 1825, New York was a small town on the periphery of world development. By 1860, it was one of the world's major metropolises.

The standard historical narrative credits the Erie Canal with the rise of the port of New York. The canal, constructed between 1817 and 1825, created a waterway connecting the Hudson River and New York City with the Midwest (Ohio, Indiana, and Illinois) via the Great Lakes. Trade with newly settled western regions flowed East-West, rather than south along the Mississippi River system. But construction of the Erie Canal was only one of a series of factors that contributed to the rapid growth of New York City. The others were closely tied to the slave system, the shipment of cotton, and the production of sugar.

Cotton

At the time of the American Revolution, slavery looked like a dying institution. Tobacco had depleted the soil in Virginia and North Carolina, exports were down, and planters like Washington and Jefferson were in debt. What saved slavery in the American South was mechanization of the textile industry, development of the factory system, first in England and then in the American North, and the cotton gin, which made short-fibered American cotton easier to clean and profitable to produce. By 1850, two million enslaved Africans were involved in cotton production in the American South (Farrow, 2005, p. 10).

Cotton, tobacco, and Caribbean sugarcane were all marketed using a "factorage" or consignment system. Planters agreed in advance to provide the agriculture commodity to outside merchants. The merchant houses would loan them money to operate until the crop was picked, processed, shipped, and sold, provide them with necessities and luxury goods, arrange for shipping, and market the crop in different commercial centers at the best price (Woodman, 1968, pp. 8, 16, 18). Cotton factors charged for every service, and generally received a 2.5 percent commission on the gross price of the crop. Because of their need to purchase new land and labor in the form of enslaved Africans, the system often left the planters in debt to their factors (Woodman, 1968, p. 49).

Its role in the cotton trade as the homeport for a number of major cotton factors, and as a banking and shipping center, helped to transform New York City. Part of its success was due to a business innovation by a Manhattan-based merchant named Jerimiah Thompson, who first placed trans-Atlantic shipping between New York and Liverpool on a regular schedule. By 1822, cotton, shipped along coastal routes from the South to New York, where it was repackaged and loaded onto oceangoing vessels, made up 40 percent of the city's exports (Farrow, 2005, pp. 16–18). Three years later, as a result of the cotton trade, the port of New York exceeded the combined shipping of its two major American business rivals, Boston and Philadelphia, in both in volume and the value of goods being processed (Farrow, 2005, pp. 12).

If you have ever flown from the United States to Europe and tracked your progress on the flight map, you will understand why the port of New York was geographically, a logical starting point for trans-Atlantic vessels. On a two-dimensional map, the shortest route appears to be due east. But on a sphere such as the Earth, heading northeast toward Newfoundland, and then east toward London is the shortest arc, approximately 3,500 miles. Additionally, this route allows ships and planes to take advantage of prevailing winds that follow the Gulf Stream current across the Atlantic.

The financing and operation of the Southern cotton trade, and its ties with New York City merchants, was detailed in an 1852 report to Congress and in the first annual report of the Chamber of Commerce of the State of New York in 1859. According to the Chamber of Commerce, even when the Europe-bound cotton trade was not shipped through the port of New York, New York City merchants and bankers financed the exchange (Albion, 1961, p. 97). Commercial ties between the North and South also provided New York City merchants with other economic benefits. Southern merchants and their families made annual pilgrimages to the city, ordering imported and domestic luxury goods and patronizing hotels, restaurants and resorts (Albion, 1961, p. 120). Because of the cotton trade and all of its economic ramifications, Southern planters owed Northern merchants and bankers an estimated $200 million dollars at the outbreak of the Civil War (Ellis, 1966, p. 287).

Dependent on their economic ties with cotton planters, many New York merchants championed conciliation with the South and compromise with slavery even after the Southern states started to secede. William E. Dodge, one of the leading cotton factors based in New York City, generally identified himself as an abolitionist (Woodman, 1968, p. 158). However, in February 1861, Dodge issued an appeal to Abraham Lincoln calling on the President-elect to reach an accommodation with the South and slavery. Dodge declared, "I speak to you now as a business man, as a merchant of New York, the commercial metropolis of the nation. I am no politician . . . But let me assure you that even I can scarcely realize, much less describe the stagnation which has now settled upon the business and commerce of that great city, caused solely by the unsettled and uncertain conditions of the questions which we are endeavoring to arrange and settle here . . . Mr. President, . . . I have a deep and abiding interest in my country and sorrow as I witness the dangers by which it is surrounded. But I am here for peace" (Foner, 1941, p. 269). The economic ties between Southern planters and New York merchants were so strong that at the end of hostilities in 1865, prewar commercial arrangements were quickly reestablished (Woodman, 1968, pp. 246–247).

Sugar Cane

Between 1793 and 1802, Toussaint L'Ouverture led a revolutionary movement of enslaved Africans that liberated the French colony of St. Domingue in the Caribbean. St. Domingue, which was renamed Haiti, had been the world's largest and most profitable producer of sugar cane. The end of slavery there led to a shift in sugar production to other Caribbean Islands and South America. The problem for planters, shippers, and manufacturers was that the revolution in Haiti coincided with the abolition of the trans-Atlantic slave trade by Great Britain and the United States. At the same time that demand for slave labor was increasing, the supply was cut off. When Liverpool and Bristol in England were forced to pull out of the slave trade, it continued clandestinely, operating, according to the defendant in an 1854 slave-trading trial, primarily out of the port of New York (Singer, 2007b, 71–73).

Sugar cane was vital to the development of New York City and the prosperity of its merchant and political elite. William Havemeyer (Singer, 2005a, p. 251; New York Daily Tribune, 1874, p. 53), a prominent business leader elected mayor of New York City in 1845, 1848, and again in 1872, launched his successful political and business careers using wealth from his family's sugar refining business. First based in Manhattan and then in Williamsburg, Brooklyn (where a street still bears the Havemeyer name), this business later evolved into the American Sugar Company and Domino Sugar. In addition to being mayor, Havemeyer was a director of the Merchants' Exchange Bank, president of the Bank of North America, and a major investor in the Pennsylvania Coal Company, the Long Island Railroad, and numerous insurance companies. The raw material that provided the initial profit for all of these ventures, sugar, was imported from the deep South and the Caribbean, especially Cuba, which by 1860 produced over a quarter of the world's sugar supply. In all of these places, sugar was produced by slave labor.

What did Havemeyer's operation mean in human terms? In Cuba, African-born captives were known as bozales. After 1820, they were disproportionately men who did the most arduous work on the sugar plantations. Because of the difficulty and danger of the work, and because there were few women present, the population could not reproduce itself and more bozales continually had to be imported (Singer, 2005a, pp. 242–251; NYT, 1852, p. 1; Pérez, 1998, pp. X–XII).

According to records maintained by British Commissioners in Havana, the sale price for *bozales* in Cuba remained constant until 1846, which suggests that supply of captured Africans balanced the demand for new workers. From 1821 until 1827, an estimated four to five thousand newly enslaved Africans were brought to Cuba annually in violation of prohibitions on the trans-Atlantic slave trade. Between 1828 and 1841, about 125,000 *bozales* entered Cuba, approximately eight to ten thousand people per year. This boom in the slave trade reflected new lands being brought into production with the development of the railroad.

Congressional records show at least eight vessels intercepted while engaged in the trans-Atlantic slave trade between 1850 and 1858 were registered in New York City, and that a suspected twenty or more slavers sailed out of New York in 1857 alone. The last documented New York registered vessel to deliver enslaved Africans to Cuba was the Huntress in 1864 (DuBois, 1896/1965, pp. 296–297).

In 1852 and 1854, *The New York Times* explained in detail the workings of the illegal slave trade and the extent of involvement by the city's merchants and bankers (*New York Times*, 1852, p. 1; 1854b, p.4; 1854c, p. 4). The men who smuggled enslaved Africans referred to themselves as "blackbirders" and their illegal human cargo as "black ivory." Their favorite New York City meeting place was Sweet's Restaurant at the corner of Fulton and South streets. The men who profited by financing and participating in the illegal Atlantic Slave trade were generally able to avoid arrest and prosecution through a legal technicality that limited the jurisdiction of American courts to United States citizens (Singer, 2003c, pp. 17–30; Ellis, 1966, pp. 285–286).

Slave trading was a capital offense in the United States after 1820. Between 1837 and 1860, seventy-four cases were tried but there were few convictions and punishment tended to be minimal. In 1856, a New York City deputy marshal complained, "It is seldom that one or more vessels cannot be designated at the wharves, respecting which there is evidence that she is either in or has been concerned in the traffic [to Cuba]" (Thomas, 1997, p. 770).

The British counsel claimed that out of one hundred and seventy known slave trading expeditions for the Cuba slave market between 1859 and 1862, over one-third sailed from New York City. In the summer of 1859, the bark Emily set off from New York stocked as a slaver with a cargo of lumber, fresh water, barrels of rice, codfish, pork and bread, boxes of herring, dozens of pails, and two cases of medicines. It was returned to port under naval guard, but the case against its captain and owners was dismissed. Federal officials in New York were so ineffective in prosecuting slave trading cases that, in 1861, a *New York Times* editorial urged President Lincoln to replace the marshal and district attorney assigned to these cases (Thomas, 1997, pp. 771–772; DuBois, 1896/1965, pp. 178–182; NYT, 1861B; NYT, 1861c, p. 4).

In memoirs published in 1864 (Carleton, 1864/1968, pp. 408–411; Katz, 1995, pp. 30–31), Captain James Smith claimed that in 1859 eighty-five ships capable of carrying between thirty and sixty thousand enslaved Africans were outfitted in the port of New York to serve the slave markets of Cuba. Smith described New York as "the chief port in the world for the Slave Trade. It is the greatest place in the universe for it. Neither in Cuba, nor in the Brazils is it carried on so extensively. Ships that convey Slaves to the West Indies and South America are fitted out in New York. Now and then one sails from Boston and Philadelphia; but New York is our headquarters . . . I can go down to South Street, and go into a number of houses that help fit out ships for the business." The trade was so profitable that on one voyage in 1854, a ship that "cost $13,000 to fit her out completely," delivered a human cargo worth $220,000 to Cuba.

The *New York Times* regularly published updates on the Cuban sugar market for New York City merchants and bankers in reports issued by a special correspondent that were delivered by steam ship. A front page article in the *New York Times* on November 15, 1852 explained the workings of the Cuban sugar industry, which paid investors two and a half times the normal interest rate on loans, and which found it more profitable to smuggle in newly enslaved Africans than to allow for the internal reproduction of its work force. Another article (July 30, 1860) announced that "Business is quite active for this season of the year, and the sugar market firm. . . . Shipments of the week near 30,000 boxes. Sales large and some on speculation. Money somewhat easy to aid transactions. The stock of sugar is 270,000 boxes against 260,000 boxes last year at same date" (1).

Drawing the connection between New York City's history of complicity with slavery and particular individuals or businesses is difficult but not impossible. Because conviction as a slave trader carried a potential death sentence, prominent participants shielded themselves from prosecution by keeping their involvement as indirect as possible. The following case study illustrates just how deeply ran complicity with slavery, even in the most respected circles.

On May 24, 1882, the *New York Times* (p. 10) reported the death of Moses Taylor, "a well-known banker," at age 76. Taylor died of natural causes, leaving behind an estate valued at between forty and fifty million dollars, approximately forty-four billion in 2006 dollars (Uchitelle, 2007, pp. A1, A20–21).

Taylor (Burrows & Wallace, 1999, p. 657; Hodas, 1976; Singer, 2003d, p. 13; Albion, 1961, p. 182) had been born into a relatively prominent New York City family. His father, a cabinetmaker by trade, was also an alderman, state prison inspector, and real estate agent. Moses married as a young man, and he and his wife of fifty years had six children. Although raised as a Presbyterian, he later became a benefactor of St. George's Episcopal Church at East Sixteenth Street in Manhattan.

During his long career, Moses Taylor was a sugar merchant with offices on South Street at the East River seaport, finance capitalist, industrialist, and banker. He was a member of the New York City Chamber of Commerce and a major stockholder, board member, or officer in firms that later merged with or developed into Citibank, Con Edison, Bethlehem Steel, and ATT. During the Civil War, Taylor worked with Secretary of the Treasury Salmon Chase and New York City's leading bankers to finance the Northern war effort.

Clearly, Moses Taylor was much more than just "an old merchant." But what exactly was his role in New York City and United States history? The *New York Times* obituary gives us some other clues: "[I]t was the sugar trade with Cuba that first gave him his reputation as a merchant, and it was this trade that principally accumulated for him, his great fortune. . . . Upon this he concentrated his remarkable powers and to this he devoted his energies, until he became known throughout the world as one of the most prominent and successful of merchants."

As a result of his success in the sugar trade, Taylor became a member of the board of the City Bank in 1837 and served as its president from 1855 until his death. In the nineteenth century, City Bank, a predecessor of today's Citibank, primarily issued short-term credits to merchants to facilitate the import-export trade. Taylor's personal resources and role as business agent for the leading exporter of Cuban sugar to the United States proved invaluable to the bank, helping it survive financial panics in 1837 and 1857 that bankrupted many of its competitors.

Taylor generally earned a 5 percent commission for brokering the sale of Cuban sugar in the port of New York, as well as additional fees for exchanging currency and for facilitating as cargo was processed at the New York City Custom's House. He supervised the investment of profits by the sugar planters in United States banks, gas companies, railroads, and real estate, purchased and shipped supplies and machinery to Cuba, operated six of his own ships and numerous chartered vessels in the Cuban trade, repaired and equipped other ships with goods and provisions, provided sugar planters with financing to arrange for land purchases and the acquisition of a labor force, and even supervised the planters' children when they came to New York City as students or to serve as apprentices for mercantile firms.

On the face of it, these appear to be ordinary business ventures, except for one significant issue. The labor force that Taylor and City Bank were helping the Cuban planters acquire was slave labor, often smuggled illegally from Africa on ships outfitted in the port of New York, in violation of the international ban on the trans-Atlantic slave trade. Taylor and City Bank's financing of the Cuban sugar trade between 1830 and 1860 aided and abetted illegal slave trading.

Evidence shows that New York's merchants knew exactly what was happening. A *New York Times* editorial on December 7, 1860 bragged that the city's role in the cotton trade and its economic superiority were the result of its "position, skill, industry and wealth" (4).

Slave Trading

The city's involvement in the slave trade was also well known. In the 1850s, the amorphous "Portuguese Company," with connections to that country's consulate, operated out of offices on Pearl and Front streets in lower Manhattan.

Its legal representative was the firm of Beebe, Dean, & Donohue of 76 Wall Street (Howard, 1963, pp. 49–50). Between 1857 and 1860 alone, fifty-six ships were purchased in the port of New York for use in the illegal trans-Atlantic slave trade. (Howard, 1963, pp. 249–252).

Money flowed freely and public officials were easily corrupted. In May 1860, the *New York Leader* reported that "We have received information . . . to the effect that the price for the clearance of a slaver is as well-known to those in the trade as the price of a barrel of pork. It is said that a certain amount of gold is placed in the locker of the cabin . . . commonly ranging from $2,500 to $4,000, according to the size of the vessel" (Howard, 1963, p. 129).

The best-documented slave trading cases involving New York are the Julia Moulton, the Wanderer, and the Wildfire. In 1854 James Smith, the captain of the Julia Moulton, purchased the ship in Boston and sailed for New York where he hired a crew and loaded provisions, water, and lumber used to construct holding facilities for enslaved Africans. From New York, the ship sailed for Africa where six hundred and sixty-four captives were brought on board and stowed away as cargo in the hold of the brig. They were brought to Cuba where the Africans were sold and the ship destroyed. Smith was later arrested, tried, and convicted when a crewmember on the voyage, who claimed to have been underpaid, testified against him.

The *New York Times* (1854b) declared that this was "the *first* time in which a conviction of being engaged in the African Slave Trade has ever been had in this City," despite the fact that "scarcely a month passes in which there are not one or more vessels cleared at this port, which embark at once in the Slave-trade and land their cargoes on the coast of Cuba" (4). Smith was willing to testify at his trial because he was protected from the most severe penalties as an "unnaturalized German" in command of a ship whose registered owners were listed as Portuguese. He served two years in the King's County prison, but his $1,000 fine was remitted when President Buchanan pardoned Smith in 1857 (Howard, 1963, p. 195).

One of the successful slave ships that operated out of New York City was a ninety-five-foot long yacht known as the Wanderer, whose skipper and part-owner was a well-connected member of the New York Yacht Club (Calonius, 2006). The ship, which was built in 1857 in Setauket, New York, was refurbished for the slave trade at Port Jefferson, New York. In 1858, it was used to smuggle between four and six hundred kidnapped Africans from the Congo area into the Georgia South Sea Islands (Ellis, 1966, p. 286; Brown, 2002). Following the voyage, the ship and its captain were held temporarily at Port Jefferson and then released, with apologies from the authorities, for lack of evidence (*New York Times*, 1858a, p. 4; 1858b, p. 8).

As late as June 1860, *Harper's Weekly* reported the seizure off the coast of Cuba of the "bark Wildfire, lately owned in the city of New York" (pp. 344–346). The ship, which had left the Congo area thirty-six days before its capture, had on board a human cargo of "five hundred and ten native Africans."

According to the article, "About fifty of them were full-grown young men, and about four hundred were boys aged from ten to sixteen years . . . Ninety and upward had died on the voyage."

The companies founded by New York City merchants and bankers during this period, and the businesses they nurtured, all directly or indirectly benefited from slavery and the slave trade. As a *New York Times* editorial noted in 1852, "If the authorities plead that they cannot stop this, they simply confess their own imbecility. If they will not do it, the moral guilt they incur is scarcely less than that of the Slave-traders themselves" (*New York Times*, 1852b, p. 4).

Was slavery a tragic mistake? Or, was it central to the development of American capitalism and America democracy? In the song "Crossroads," Robert Johnson sings about a bluesman's pact with the devil made to achieve fame at the price of his soul. Was slavery America's and capitalism's pact with the devil?

Chapter 9

Resistance!

Let your motto be resistance! Resistance! Resistance! No oppressed people have ever secured their liberty without resistance.

—Henry Highland Garnet (1843)

There are names that need to be remembered. There are events that should be re-called. There are struggles that must be celebrated. These names, events, and struggles defined the nation. Knowledge of them helps historians, teachers, and students understand the past. Knowledge of them makes it possible to shape the future. Unfortunately, some have been erased from history. Others have been repackaged and transformed for political reasons into something entirely different.

The Civil Rights movement of the 1950s and 1960s is a good example of historical repackaging for political purposes. Now that Dr. Martin Luther King's birthday is a national holiday, every schoolchild can tell you the story of how Rosa Parks sat down, Martin Luther King stood up, and the world changed. But of course it did not happen quite this way. The magnitude of racial hatred and injustice in the United States, and the decades of organized opposition and mass struggle to overcome them, have been removed in this feel-good version of the past. It is a version of the past that makes it easier for those with power to deny racism and inequality in the present.

The history of slavery in the United States, especially the role of African Americans in the struggle to end slavery, has been erased and repackaged in a

---

Sections of this chapter were developed with the help of April Francis (2007, pp. 65–66), a middle school teacher from Uniondale, New York, and Stephanie Sienkiewicz (2007, pp. 67–68), a teacher from James Fenimore Cooper Middle School in Virginia, who presented with me at the 2006 annual meeting of the Organization of American Historians. April Francis piloted many of the lessons in the *New York and Slavery: Complicity and Resistance* curriculum with her students.

similar way. Today students learn that Harriet Beecher Stowe, a White woman, wrote a book explaining why slavery was wrong and then Abraham Lincoln, a White man, set it all right.

But how many people were actually freed when Abraham Lincoln issued the Emancipation Proclamation? All four million enslaved Africans? Four hundred thousand? Forty?

Although the United States honors Abraham Lincoln as the Great Emancipator, the answer is much closer to zero. The way the Emancipation Proclamation was written, it declared slavery over in the rebel states, areas where Lincoln had no authority to free anyone. However, other than small groups on offshore islands, it freed none of the people in territory under federal control.

Chapter 1 opened with a brief description of a walking tour of slavery sites in Lower Manhattan organized by a high school social studies class. As they walked from site to site, students chanted two slogans. "Time to tell the truth, our local history, New York was the land of slavery" and "Resist, Resist, Resist, Time to be free! Resist, Resist, Resist, No more slavery!" At each of eleven stops they hung up posters that detailed New York City's complicity with slavery and presented stories of heroic resistance. They also handed out hundreds of flyers to tourists, workers, and students on school trips.

The sites students visited included the former locations of an Abolitionist Meeting House, an African Free School, and the tavern where the 1741 "Slavery Conspiracy" was supposedly hatched. It also included the place where a group of approximately twenty enslaved Africans set fire to a building in 1712 and then ambushed Whites who tried to put out the blaze. For many of the students, the history of resistance was much more important than the history of oppression. They learned that freedom was not given to Black people. Freedom was something their ancestors fought for and seized (Pezone and Singer, 2006, pp. 32–35).

In essays written as a follow-up to the trip, students also commented on the importance of activism. According to Shiyanne Moore, a senior at Law, Government, and Community Service Magnet High School in Cambria Heights, Queens and a trip organizer, "I learned the truth about our city's past from this project. I also learned the more noise you make the more things can change. Permanent historical markers about slavery could inspire people to fight for change. I am proud that I was involved in helping to create the African American Slavery Trail" (32).

Students from Law, Government, and Community Service found their participation in social struggle, or what Henry Highland Garnet called "resistance," to be empowering. This chapter explores the struggle of Africa Americans to seize their freedom and hopefully will inspire future resistance. Once again, New York City and New York State were at the center of events, events that began even before enslaved Africans "got off the boat."

One of the best-known slave rebellions in United States history was on the slave ship Amistad. In July 1839, fifty-four enslaved Africans being transported from Havana to other ports in Cuba for resale took control of the vessel, killed most of the crew, and tried to force the survivors to return them to Africa. They were led by Sengbe Pieh (who is remembered as Cinqué), a member of the Mende tribe from the West African region near present day Sierra Leone (McMillan, 2002, pp. 104–105).

Eventually the Amistad arrived at Long Island, New York, off Montauk Point. The United States Navy captured the ship and the Africans were taken to New Haven, Connecticut, where federal courts had to decide their fate. Abolitionists, led by New York City silk merchant Lewis Tappan, and a legal team that included former President John Quincy Adams, finally secured a Supreme Court ruling allowing the Africans to be freed and to return home. While the case was ultimately decided on a technicality related to maritime law and established no legal precedents about slavery, it had symbolic importance at the time. Since then, journalistic, historical, fictional, and cinematic studies of the case have kept it alive as an emblem of resistance to oppression and the unquenchable human desire for freedom.

Many Forms of Resistance

Resistance to human bondage in New York, the North, and the nation took many forms. Records show that in New Amsterdam enslaved Africans collectively petitioned for wages as early as 1635, and used incessant colonial warfare and the Dutch need for soldiers as a wedge to negotiate for land and a measure of freedom in the 1640s. Resistance could simply mean insisting on your right to baptize a child, as Pieter and Susana San Tomé did in 1639, or to marry in church, as Lucie D'Angola and Anthony van Angola did in 1641 (Moore, 2005, pp. 38–45).

Resistance also meant running away, as hundreds of enslaved Africans did in eighteenth-century British New York, and refusing to abide by restrictive laws, stealing and bartering goods, illegally assembling at a local tavern such as Hughson's, murdering a particularly nasty owner, or plotting a collective rebellion. Resistance echoes through the voices of Caesar and Prince who proclaimed innocence during the 1741 slave conspiracy trials and refused to "name names," and of Quaco and Cuffee who "confessed" to participation in order to save their families from persecution. Resistance meant joining British forces during the Revolutionary War, as did Titus Corlis, Benjamin Whitecuff of Long Island, and Boston King (Lepore, 2005a; Hodges, 1999).

African American activists, ministers, and newspaper editors played a leading role in the campaign to abolish slavery in New York State, which finally ended on July 4, 1827. Their resistance to slavery and injustice in the new nation presaged many of the ideological positions and tactical strategies debated in the African American community throughout United States history. It included struggles for full citizenship rights and racial integration. Sometimes it took the form of calls for Black Nationalism and an acceptance of separatism, which included resettlement in Africa. African Americans networked, built communities and civic institutions, pursued their rights in the courts, participated in electoral politics, and engaged in civil disobedience and physical confrontations.

Community Building

The struggle for freedom and equality required the development of African American community institutions and indigenous leadership. While many of the institutions and leaders received support from White abolitionists, this was a long building process under what were largely hostile conditions. A key institution in the struggle to end slavery, as it was over 100 years later during the Civil Rights movement, was the Black church. Black churches nurtured internal community relationships, promoted numeracy, literacy, and oratory skills, offered financial support for ministers, and provided free space away from interference by both White allies and enemies (Rael, 2005).

By 1830, more than a dozen Black congregations rented or owned buildings in lower Manhattan alone. They included an African Methodist Episcopal Church founded by Peter Williams, the Demeter Presbyterian Church headed by Reverend Samuel Cornish, the First Colored Presbyterian Church under the leadership of Reverend Theodore Wright, who was the first Black graduate of Princeton's Theological Seminary, and Reverend William Hamilton's African Zion Church (Katz, 1997, p. 43, p. 57).

Many members of New York's growing African American professional and merchant class were parishioners and vestrymen at St. Philip's Episcopal Church. They were often graduates of the city's African Free Schools and founded voluntary associations that helped promote education and provided poor relief in the Black community (Rael, 2005, pp. 199–209).

One of the voluntary associations was the Phoenix Society, whose leaders included the Reverends Christopher Rush and Theodore Wright. It was founded in 1833 to elevate moral character and encourage both school and church attendance (Aptheker, 1973, pp. 140–141). The society later became involved in a petition drive aimed at the state legislature to secure the right to vote for all male citizens and protect the legal rights of people accused of being runaway slaves (Aptheker, 1973, pp. 164–165). Another voluntary association, the Garrison Literary and Benevolent Association of New York, was established by David Ruggles and Henry Highland Garnet to promote abolition and literacy (Aptheker, 1973, pp. 151–152). African American teachers also formed their own association committed to promoting education, temperance, and Black suffrage (Aptheker, 1973, pp. 211–212).

New York's African American community supported the first Black newspaper in the United States, *Freedom's Journal*. Its editors included Reverend Samuel Cornish and John Russwurm, a former slave and an immigrant to the city from Jamaica. In its first issue, the editors of *Freedom's Journal* argued for an end to slavery, demanded equal rights, and declared, "Too long have others spoken for us." Cornish, who was a founder of the New York Anti-Slavery Society, later edited the newspapers *The Rights of All, Weekly Advocate*, and *The Colored American*. As editor of *The Colored American*, he campaigned against White churches that would admit Black members but assign them to segregated pews (Katz, 1997, pp. 57–60, p. 72).

Debate over Colonization

In 1816, the American Colonization Society was founded by American Whites, including many abolitionists, to promote the repatriation of free Blacks in Africa. A national convention was held in New York City in 1823 and a local branch was started in 1831. Colonization was one of the most contentious issues facing New York's African American community. John Russwurm, one of the editors of *Freedom's Journal*, became a strong supporter of colonization efforts in Liberia. Samuel Cornish and Theodore Wright, however, were amongst its bitterest opponents.

During the Civil War, Abraham Lincoln endorsed a variety of colonization schemes, but by that time they received little support from the African American community. In 1862, a mass meeting held at Newtown in Queens County notified the President that "This is our native country; we have as strong attachment naturally to our native hills, valleys, plains, . . . and loft mountains, as any other people. . . . This is the country of our choice . . . we love this land and have contributed our share to its prosperity and wealth." They demanded that Lincoln abolish slavery and allow free Blacks to colonize the rebel states (Aptheker, 1973, pp. 471–473).

Social Equality

African Americans in New York and the North, even when free, were subject to countless indignities. In 1838, *The Liberator* published a letter from Thomas Van Renselaer of New York who complained that on a steamboat trip from Boston to Providence, Rhode Island, he was denied a cabin and forced to remain on deck because he was Black (Aptheker, 1973, p. 188). In 1848, an outraged Frederick Douglass protested when his nine-year-old daughter was assigned to a separate classroom in the Seward Seminary in Rochester because the parents and the headmistress would "not allow me to go into the room with the other scholars because I am colored" (Aptheker, 1973, pp. 274–275). Douglass finally had to transfer his daughter to another school.

Support for the abolition of slavery did not automatically mean support for legal and social equality. In 1837, at the annual convention of the New York State Anti-Slavery Society in Utica, the Reverend Theodore Wright denounced racism in the abolitionist movement. He protested that Black abolitionists could not get their statements published if they ran counter to the opinions of White opponents of slavery. He also excoriated a White abolitionist, a member of the

Society of Friends, who invited a Black minister to his house for dinner, but had him eat alone in the kitchen (Aptheker, 1973, pp. 169–173). White abolitionists could also be patronizing toward Black compatriots. In 1843, a leading Black abolitionist condemned *The Liberator* for publishing a statement that attacked his character and dismissed his views because "I have dared to think, and act, contrary to your opinion" (Aptheker, 1973, pp. 234–236).

New York's Rosa Parks

The battle for racial equality in New York led to civil disobedience in one of the first successful challenges to racial segregation laws (Singer, 2003b, pp. 77–79; *New York Tribune,* 1854, p. 7). On July 14, 1854, Elizabeth Jennings and her friend, Sarah Adams, walked to the corner of Pearl and Chatham streets in lower Manhattan. They planned to take a horse-drawn streetcar along Third Avenue to church. Instead, they entered into the pages of history when they were forcibly thrown-off a White-only streetcar.

Elizabeth was a young African American woman who taught Black children in New York City's racially segregated public schools. Her father, Thomas L. Jennings, was a leading local abolitionist. An account of what happened to Elizabeth was presented on July 17, at a protest meeting at the First Colored Congregational Church. The assembly passed resolutions protesting against her expulsion and segregated streetcars in general.

Jennings sued the streetcar company and was represented by a young White attorney named Chester A. Arthur, who later became a military officer during the Civil War and a politician. In 1880, Chester A. Arthur was elected vice president of the United States and he became President when James Garfield was murdered in 1881 (*New York Times,* 1880, p. 8).

Jennings's court case was successful. The judge instructed the jury that transit companies had to respect the rights of all respectable people, and the jury awarded Elizabeth Jennings money for damages and legal expenses. As a result of the protest by Elizabeth and Thomas Jennings, and their victory in court, the Third Avenue Railroad Company issued an order to permit African Americans to ride on their streetcars (*New York Tribune,* 1855, p. 7; Frederick Douglass's Paper, 1855, p. 2).

Battling Slave Catchers

African Americans, even when legally free, were continually at risk. In an 1836 letter to the *New York Sun,* David Ruggles described the kidnapping of a free Black on the streets of New York City. He was accused by police of "assault and battery" and brought to jail where slave catchers accused him of being a runaway. Unable to produce witnesses to counter their claims, "[I]n less than three hours after his arrest, he was bound in chains, dragged through the streets, like a beast to the shambles!" This kidnapping and others prompted African Americans in New York to form a vigilance committee that was headed by Ruggles as Secretary and the Reverend Theodore Wright as Chairman (Aptheker, 1973, pp. 159–161).

David Ruggles was a free Black, born in Connecticut, who became a major figure in the battle against slavery and for equal rights in the 1830s and 1840s. He operated a grocery and bookstore in Manhattan, founded a literary society that loaned books to African Americans denied access to the public library, published a newspaper, lectured, and wrote for the abolitionist press. He tirelessly worked for the right of accused runaways to jury trial and, until his vision failed, frequently put his body on the line to interfere with kidnappers. Ruggles is credited with helping over six hundred people escape from slave catchers, including Frederick Douglass (Katz, 1997, pp. 64–65).

Solomon Northup was a free Black man who lived in Saratoga Springs with his wife Anne and their three children. A skilled carpenter and violinist, he also worked on the Lake Champlain Canal and on construction of the Troy and Saratoga railroad. In 1841, while on a trip to Washington, DC, Northup was kidnapped by slave traders and his freedom papers were stolen. He was transported to Louisiana, sold as a slave, and worked on cotton plantations until he was able to smuggle a letter to his wife. Anne Northup petitioned the governor of New York to intercede and, using a New York State law designed to protect free Black citizens from being sold into slavery, secured her husband's freedom through the courts. Solomon Northup was finally released from bondage after twelve years as a slave (Eakin & Logsdon, 1967; Aptheker, 1973, pp. 334–335).

The Erie Canal, which runs east-to-west across New York State, was a major route on the Underground Railroad to Canada and freedom. The canal cities and towns were sites of numerous acts of physical resistance to slavery, particularly to efforts by slave catchers to trap free Blacks or return escapees to bondage in the South (Bordewich, 2005).

One of the most dramatic examples of resistance to slave catchers by African Americans was described by William Brown in his memoirs (Brown, 1849, pp. 109–124; Katz, 1995, pp. 154–155). Brown was born on a plantation near Lexington, Kentucky, in 1814 and escaped from slavery in 1834. He and his family moved to New York State where he began lecturing for the Western New York Anti-Slavery Society. Brown worked for nine years on a Lake Erie steamboat and as a conductor for the Underground Railroad in Buffalo, New York. He wrote about an 1836 battle between slave catchers supported by local police and Buffalo's Black community that had mobilized to prevent a kidnapping and reenslavement.

According to Brown's account, "The colored people of Buffalo are noted for their promptness in giving aid to the fugitive slave. The alarm was given just as the bells were ringing for church. I was in company with five or six others, when I heard that a brother slave with his family had been seized and dragged from his home during the night previous. We started on a run for the livery-stable, where we found as many more of our own color trying to hire horses to go in search of the fugitives."

The liberators cornered the kidnappers in a tavern, freed the captive and his family, and brought them to the Niagara River where there was a ferry to convey them to Canada. However, once there, "the sheriff and his men surrounded us. The sheriff came forward, and read something purporting to be a 'Riot Act,' and at the same time called upon all good citizens to aid him in keeping the 'peace.' This was a trick of his, to get possession of the slaves. His men rushed upon us with their clubs and stones and a general fight ensued. Our company had surrounded the slaves, and had succeeded in keeping the sheriff and his men off. We fought, and at the same time kept pushing on towards the ferry . . . After a hard-fought battle, of nearly two hours, we arrived at the ferry, the slaves still in our possession. Here another battle was to be fought, before the slaves could reach Canada. The boat was fastened at each end by a chain, and in the scuffle for the ascendancy, one party took charge of one end of the boat, while the other took the other end. The blacks were commanding the ferryman to carry them over, while the whites were commanding him not to. While each party was contending for power, the slaves were pushed on board, and the boat shoved from the wharf. Many of the blacks jumped on board of the boat, while the whites jumped on shore. And the swift current of the Niagara soon carried them off, amid the shouts of the blacks, and the oaths and imprecations of the whites. We on shore swung our hats and gave cheers, just as a reinforcement came to the whites. Seeing the odds entirely against us in numbers, and having gained the great victory, we gave up without resistance, and suffered ourselves to be arrested by the sheriff's posse . . . When the trials came on, we were fined more or less from five to fifty dollars each. Thus ended one of the most fearful fights for human freedom that I ever witnessed."

One of the most important conductors was the Reverend Jermain Loguen (Singer, 2005a, p. 201, 211; Loguen, 1859) of Syracuse who himself had been born into slavery. Jermain Loguen was trained as an abolitionist, teacher, and minister at the Oneida Institute in Whitesboro, New York (near Utica). In 1841, he moved to Syracuse, where as the "station master" of the local underground railroad "depot," he helped over one thousand "fugitives" escape to Canada.

Conventions and Ministries

National, state, and local conventions of Black activists became important weapons in the battle against slavery. The first annual "Negro Convention" was held in Philadelphia in 1831, with fifteen representatives from Pennsylvania, New York, Delaware, Maryland, and Virginia. In 1834, the venue shifted to New York City and the number of delegates reached fifty. The chair of the 1834 convention was William Hamilton (Aptheker, 1973, p. 154), an advocate for racial equality and a major opponent of colonization proposals.

Among the most prominent antislavery activist ministers in New York was the Reverend Henry Highland Garnet (Crummell, 1882; Ofari, 1972). Garnet escaped from enslavement when he was eleven and eventually settled in New York City where he attended the African Free School on Mott Street. His classmates included Alexander Crummell, Samuel Ringgold Ward, and James McCune Smith, the first African American to earn a medical degree.

Garnet was the target of racial violence on at least three separate occasions. In 1829, his family was forced to scatter after being besieged in their home by slave catchers, while sympathizers hid Garnet on a local farm. In 1835, he attended the interracial Noyes Academy in Canaan, New Hampshire. A mob destroyed the school and attacked the house where Garnet and the other Black students were living. They fought back but were eventually forced to flee the town. Garnet later graduated from the Oneida Institute and became pastor of a Presbyterian Church in Troy, New York. During the Civil War, he was a chaplain for Black troops stationed at Riker's Island. In July 1863, draft rioters stalked Garnet, forcing his family to hide with neighbors.

David Walker of Boston is usually considered the most militant African American opponent of slavery. In September 1829 (Aptheker, 1973, pp. 93–98), he published a widely circulated *Appeal to the Colored Citizens of the World,* which called for active rebellion. Unfortunately, Walker died less than a year later and was unable to organize resistance to slavery. This task fell to Garnet and others.

At a National Negro Convention held in Buffalo in 1843, Henry Highland Garnet issued a call for slaves to revolt against their masters. His ideas were considered dangerous by many abolitionists, including Frederick Douglass, who opposed violence and preferred using moral and economic arguments to challenge slavery. Garnet's words bear repeating (Aptheker, 1973, pp. 226–233).

Brethren, it is as wrong for your lordly oppressors to keep you in slavery, as it was for the man thief to steal our ancestors from the coast of Africa. You should therefore now use the same manner of resistance, as would have been just in our ancestors, when the bloody foot-prints of the first remorseless soul-thief was placed upon the shores of our fatherland. The humblest peasant is as free in the sight of God as the proudest monarch. Liberty is a spirit sent out from God and is no respecter of persons. Brethren, arise, arise! Strike for your lives and liberties. Now is the day and the hour. Let every slave throughout the land do this, and the days of slavery are numbered. You cannot be more oppressed than you have been, you cannot suffer greater cruelties than you have already. Rather die freemen than live to be slaves. Remember that you are four millions!

Garnet continued:

In the name of God, we ask, are you men? Where is the blood of your fathers? Has it all run out of your veins? Awake, awake; millions of voices are calling you! Your dead fathers speak to you from their graves. Heaven, as with a voice of thunder, calls on you to arise from the dust. Let your motto be resistance! resistance! resistance! No oppressed people have ever secured their liberty without resistance. Trust in the living God. Labor for the peace of the human race, and remember that you are four millions.

Garnet questioned whether Blacks, even after freedom, would ever be accepted in American society. In the 1850s he became a missionary in Jamaica and encouraged Blacks to move there. Later he founded the African Civilization Society to promote migration to Africa. In 1881, he was appointed a United States representative to Liberia, but he died shortly after his arrival (Ofari, 1972; Crummell, 1891).

Editor and Orator

Of all the Black activists engaged in the struggle to end slavery and secure equal rights for African Americans, the most prominent was Frederick Douglass of Rochester, New York (Douglass, 1892/1962). Frederick Washington Bailey was born in Maryland in 1817, the son of a White man and an enslaved African woman. As a boy he was taught to read in violation of state law. In 1838, he escaped to New York City where he married and changed his name to Frederick Douglass. William Lloyd Garrison arranged for Douglass to become an agent and lecturer for the American Anti-Slavery Society. In 1845, the society helped him publish his autobiography, *The Narrative of the Life of Frederick Douglass.* After the publication of his book, Douglass, afraid he might be recaptured by his former owner, traveled to Britain and Ireland where he lectured on slavery. He returned to New York after the purchase of his freedom and established an abolitionist newspaper, *The North Star,* in Rochester, New York. Frederick Douglass started out a strong ally of William Lloyd Garrison and his newspaper *The Liberator.* However, Douglass's views and those of Garrison eventually diverged. Garrison rejected the *United States Constitution* as a pro-slavery document. Douglass came to oppose the dissolution of the Union and believed that the *Constitution* in its "letter and spirit" was "an anti-slavery instrument" that could be used as a weapon in the fight to end slavery. Despite this position, Frederick Douglass delivered a Fourth of July speech in 1852 in Rochester, where he demanded to know, "What to the American slave is your Fourth of July?"

Few recall that Frederick Douglass was originally implicated in Brown's raid on Harpers Ferry and was forced to flee the country when a warrant for his arrest was issued in Virginia. He was also the subject of a congressional investigation into treasonous behavior just prior to the outbreak of the Civil War. In a later version of his memoirs, Douglass explained his decision not to join Brown on the raid and his final understanding of the historical importance of Brown's actions.

During the Civil War, Frederick Douglass, a Radical Republican, tried to persuade President Abraham Lincoln that formerly enslaved Africans should be allowed to join the Union Army. After the war, he campaigned for full civil rights for former slaves and was a strong supporter of women's suffrage. He also held several government positions including Marshall of the District of Columbia (1877–1881) and U.S. minister to Haiti (1889–1891). Frederick Douglass died in 1895 and was buried in Rochester, New York.

Douglass's "Fourth of July" speech in 1852 and his defense of John Brown and the 1859 raid on Harpers Ferry underscore the magnitude of the struggle Africans fought to end slavery in the United States and the magnitude of their success.

In his famous speech, Douglass demanded to know "What to the American slave is your Fourth of July? I answer, a day that reveals to him more than all other days of the year, the gross injustice and cruelty to which he is the constant victim. To him your celebration is a sham; your boasted liberty an unholy license; your national greatness, swelling vanity; your sounds of rejoicing are empty and heartless; your denunciation of tyrants, brass-fronted impudence; your shouts of liberty and equality . . . There is not a nation of the earth guilty of practices more shocking and bloody than are the people of these United States at this very hour" (Dunbar, 1914, pp. 42–47).

In his memoirs, Douglass wrote of the Harpers Ferry raid: "Did John Brown draw his sword against slavery and thereby lose his life in vain? . . . To this I answer ten thousand times, No! . . . John Brown began the war that ended American slavery and made this a free Republic. Until this blow was struck, the prospect for freedom was dim, shadowy and uncertain . . . When John Brown stretched forth his arm the sky was cleared. The time for compromises was gone . . . The South . . . drew the sword of rebellion and thus made her own, and not Brown's, the lost cause of the century" (Ruchames, 1969, pp. 278–299).

Civil War

After the Civil War broke out, Henry Highland Garnet, Frederick Douglass, and William Wells Brown campaigned to lift federal restrictions that prevented African Americans from enlisting in the Union Army and fighting to end slavery. In May, 1862, Brown told the annual meeting of the American Anti-Slavery Society in New York,

> All I demand for the black man is, that the white people shall take their heels off his neck, and let him have a chance to rise by his own efforts . . . I think that the present contest has shown clearly that the fidelity of the black people of this country to the cause of freedom is enough to put to shame every white man in the land who would think of driving us out of the country . . . I remember well, when Mr. Lincoln's proclamation went forth, calling for the first 75,000 men, that among the first to respond to that call were the colored men . . . Although the colored men in many of the free States were disfranchised, abused, taxed without representation,

their children turned out of the schools, nevertheless, they, went on, determined to try to discharge their duty to the country, and to save it from the tyrannical power of the slaveholders of the South. But the cry went forth—We won't have the Negroes; we won't have anything to do with them; we won't fight with them; we won't have them in the army, nor about us' . . . The black man welcomes your armies and your fleets, takes care of your sick, is ready to do anything, from cooking up to shouldering a musket; and yet these would-be patriots and professed lovers of the land talk about driving the Negro out! (Aptheker, 1973, pp. 470–471)

As war casualties mounted, the attitude of White politicians toward arming Black soldiers changed. In March 1863, Massachusetts started to recruit African Americans and, by December, New York had one thousand Black men enlisted in the Twentieth Regiment United States Colored Troops (Burrows & Wallace, 1999, p. 897). At the end of the Civil War, over 200,000 Black soldiers and sailors were engaged in the battle for freedom.

Chapter 10

What Students
Understand About Slavery

Our discussions evinced enormous disagreement regarding the issues of slavery and racism. What does disturb me is what I perceive as an underlying prejudice that many of my kids hold towards minorities. Unfortunately this clouds their thinking. We are the product of our upbringing I guess, although this does not excuse racist ideas.

—Jeffrey Cohen, high school social studies teacher

In 2000, a New York State Assistant Attorney General argued in court against a racial desegregation plan for Rochester, New York schools (Zehr, 2000, p. 5). "All children can learn," the lawyer contended, and "opportunities are not defined by who is sitting at the next desk." More recently, Chief Justice John Roberts argued in a controversial Supreme Court decision overturning school integration plans in Louisville and Seattle that remedies that assigned students to schools based on race were in effect continuing racial discrimination (Greenhouse, 2007, p. 1).

These claims may or may not be true. But while Black and White students who attend racially segregated schools in the United States may learn the same information, they often do not understand the same things about what they learn. Race, ethnic identification, and demographic isolation shape the way students navigate the secondary school curriculum, particularly when teachers introduce potentially difficult topics such as the history of slavery in the Americas.

This chapter was developed with the help of Ron McLean, Kean University, and Mary Carter, Hofstra University, with technical assistance from Jonathan Becker of Virginia Commonwealth University.

111

Divergent understanding about the past, and about conditions in the present is an especially serious phenomenon because United States schools are growing increasingly more segregated by race. More than 70 percent of Black (African American and Caribbean American) and Hispanic (as defined by the United States Census Bureau) students in the United States attended predominantly minority schools in 2000, a higher percentage than in 1970 (Orfield, 2001; Frankenberg, Lee & Orfield, 2003; Orfield & Lee, 2003; Orfield & Lee, 2004; Orfield & Lee, 2005). The impact of segregation on minority youth has been poignantly and angrily described by Jonathan Kozol (2005) as the creation of an apartheid society in the United States.

Educational research shows that student understanding is significantly shaped by racial and ethnic identity, and reflects a difference between academic and personal knowledge. Student understanding about slavery and race are definitely affected by "who is sitting at the next desk."

Terrie Epstein (1996; 1998; 2000) has explored the way racial identity shapes student understanding in social studies classes. In one study (2000), she analyzed the "historical narratives of 10 adolescents who completed the same 11th-grade history class. The analysis demonstrated that the adolescents' racialized identities significantly influenced their concepts of the historical experience of racial groups, the role of government in shaping these experiences, and the existence or lack of a common national history or identity" (185).

Catherine Cornbleth's research on high school student images of America (2002) found that "the major themes about which students agree play out differently for different individuals and groups, masking deep societal tensions and fissures" (519). She attributed this to the fact that they "simply have not experienced 'America' similarly . . . And, like other school messages, the images of America communicated by school curriculum and culture are not necessarily received by students or understood as intended" (544).

A study of Israeli high school students by Dan Porat (2004) suggests that "culturally comprehended" knowledge is so strongly rooted that students reformulate, or simply ignore, information that supports alternative explanations of historical events (963). Keith Barton reached similar conclusions in a study of how Roman Catholic and Protestant secondary school students understand the history of Northern Ireland (2005).

A number of researchers, including Patricia Espirutu Halagoa (2004), Keith Barton and Linda Levstik (1998), Terrie Epstein, and Peter Sexias (1993) have examined the impact on minority group students of finding themselves excluded from the standard curriculum. Halago found that "participants learned half-truths about themselves through the absence of their ethnic histories and cultures in the school curriculum and inherited colonized perspectives passed down from their parents" (476).

As part of the field test of the *New York: Complicity and Resistance* curriculum, approximately 450 students from seven racially segregated schools in the New York metropolitan area participated in a study about student understanding of what they had learned about slavery. Three of the schools, two high schools and a middle school, were from suburban communities with student populations that were overwhelmingly White. One suburban middle school had a student population that was entirely African American/Caribbean American, and Latino. Two high schools and one middle school were located in New York City. The student populations in the urban middle school and one of the high schools was largely Latino with an African American/Caribbean American minority. The other urban high school was overwhelmingly African American/Caribbean.

A questionnaire was designed to record student content knowledge and attitudes about slavery. Sixteen percent of the students in the study self-identified as Black or African American, 22 percent as Caribbean, 17 percent as Hispanic, 38 percent as White, and 7 percent as Asian, mixed, or other. Among these students, 68 percent reported their home language as English, 18 percent as Spanish, 7 percent as either Haitian Creole or Jamaica Patois, and 7 percent as other. Slightly more than half of the students reported that they and both of their parents were born in the United States. Twelve percent identified themselves as immigrants and 36 percent reported that one or both of their parents were immigrants.

On the "content knowledge" section of questionnaire, female students scored significantly better than male students, but there was no statistically significant difference between the scores of Black, Caribbean, and White students. Lower scores by Hispanic students appeared to result from language issues. However, there were major differences in student responses to the portion of the questionnaire designed to measure student understanding and attitudes. On the issue of whether slavery continues to impact on life in the United States, 84 percent of Black students said "yes," compared to a range of 67 to 75 percent for other student groups. On the issue of whether the United States has a responsibility to provide special help to the descendants of enslaved people, 69 percent of Black students and 71 percent of the Caribbean students said "yes," but only 42 percent of the White students and 49 percent of the Hispanic did. Eighty percent of the Black students described "Slavery and the Holocaust in Europe are equally horrible crimes against humanity," compared to 67 percent of the Caribbean and Hispanic students and only 62 percent of the White students. There was no statistically significant difference between students on the question of whether the motive for slavery was racism or profit.

Students were asked what they would emphasize if they were teaching younger children about slavery. There was a spectrum of opinion among the different groups of students who self-identified as members of distinct racial and ethnic communities. The greatest disparities were in the responses of Black, or African American, students and White, or European American, students. The responses of students who identified themselves as Caribbean tended to be closer on the spectrum to the responses of students who identified as African American. The responses of students who identified as Hispanic tended to be closer on the spectrum to the responses of students who identified as White. Not enough students identified as Asian, mixed, and other to make an examination of these categories meaningful.

Students from racially segregated schools who identified as Black or African American were twice as likely to say that the history of slavery in the United States is important to know than did students who identified themselves as Hispanic or White. However, what students considered "history" is also interesting. Black or African American students were significantly less likely than students from other groups to focus on "academic knowledge" and historical details, including conditions for enslaved Africans during the middle passage and on Southern plantations. They were also less concerned than students in other groups with the role of White abolitionists and the Civil War in bringing the era of slavery to a close.

Students from racially segregated schools who identified as Black or African American were much more concerned with "personal knowledge," the attitudes people have about the past, and the lessons people draw from the study of history. Much more than students from other groups, they believed that the social studies curriculum should focus on the following:

1. Resistance by people of African ancestry to slavery.
2. The continuation of racial oppression in the United States after the Civil War.
3. Racism in the United States in the present.
4. The continuing problem of slavery in the world today.

They were between three and four times more likely than students from any other group to press for the identification of slavery as a moral evil that violates fundamental human rights. They were significantly more likely than White students to argue that our society has a responsibility to rectify the injustices of the past.

Students from racially segregated schools who identified as White or European American agreed with African American, Caribbean, and Hispanic peers that White racism played a major role in the history of the United States. However, they were much more likely to argue that slavery is a thing of the past and that it is time to put it behind us. They were as knowledgeable about slavery as African American and Caribbean students, but their interest tended to be in "academic knowledge" or the details of history, rather than on the lessons that can be drawn from studying the past. They were also more likely than Black or African American students to believe that recent injustices, such as the

European Holocaust, outweigh past injustices, such as slavery and the trans-Atlantic slave trade, in the magnitude of horror and should be presented that way in the curriculum.

In 1903, W. E. B. DuBois (1961) wrote, "the problem of the Twentieth Century is the problem of the color line" (v). This study suggests that in social studies classrooms at the dawn of the twenty-first century, this division continues to shape the way secondary school students make meaning out of the past, has implications for they way they understand the present, and will influence their behavior in the future. The standards and testing movement in the United States rests on the assumption that education, like the mass production of factory goods, can be standardized. This in turn rests on the assumption that all students in a classroom are learning the same things regardless of culture and experience. This is an unwarranted assumption that ignores the diversity and positionality of student knowledge and human experience.

Chapter 11

Time to Teach the Truth

All people should know of and remember the human carnage and dehumanizing atrocities committed during the period of the African Slave Trade and slavery in America and of the vestiges of slavery in this Country.

—New York State Legislation establishing the Amistad Commission

In September 2005, the Associated Press reported that state legislatures were increasingly directing schools "to teach students more about the struggles and triumphs of different races and ethnic groups" in the United States. Among the initiatives was the establishment of a nineteen-member "Amistad" commission in New York, with members appointed by the governor and the legislature. The commission was charged with coordinating "educational and other programs on slavery and African-American history" and examining whether public schools were effectively teaching about the "physical and psychological terrorism" against Africans during the trans-Atlantic slave trade. States with similar curriculum initiatives included California, Illinois, Massachusetts, New Jersey, New Mexico, Rhode Island, Tennessee, and Virginia (New York State Assembly, 2005; Associated Press, 2005; Zehr, 2005).

For supporters of a more honest appraisal of the role of slavery in American history, and of an increased focus on the lives of ordinary people in general, these proposals seemed like significant victories. In reality, they tend to be little more than public relations pronouncements designed to pacify important voting blocks. A year after the New York State Amistad Commission was supposed to be created, only two members of the commission had been appointed.

In June 2007, the New York State Assembly approved a resolution that, if it is passed by the State Senate and signed by the governor, would amend Chapter 137 of the laws of 1817, one of a series of gradual emancipation laws that finally ended slavery in New York in 1827. The "apology" bill declared that the "government of the state of New York formally apologizes for its role in sanctioning and perpetuating slavery and its vestiges." It also acknowledged, "slavery, the transatlantic and the domestic slave trade were appalling tragedies in the history of New York state not only because of their abhorrent barbarism but also in terms of their magnitude, organized nature and especially their negation of the humanity of the enslaved person" (Gershman, 2007). Virginia, during the state's celebration of the 400th anniversary of the settlement of Jamestown, approved a similar resolution, as did lawmakers in Alabama, Arkansas, Maryland, New Jersey, and North Carolina. These resolutions, however, were largely symbolic and did not suggest methods for redressing what happened in the past or even how people would finally began to learn the truth about history. The New York State Senate's Majority Leader, while blocking the legislation, declared that "every one recognizes the sins," and that although he sympathized with the bill's intent, he had to protect the state against possible demands for reparations by descendants of the enslaved (Associated Press, 2007; Root 2007).

As the students from Law, Government, and Community Service Magnet High School in Cambria Heights, Queens learned when they planned a walking tour of slavery-related sites in lower Manhattan, decisions about what gets included in the social studies curriculum, and in official public history of the United States, are largely made for political reasons (English, 2006, A18; Pezone and Singer, 2006, pp. 32–35). If students are to learn the "truth" about slavery in New York, the North, and the United States, it will require committed activism. Illusions about the past and about American society today die hard, and as Frederick Douglass pointed out, "If there is no struggle, there is no progress" (Foner, 1950, p. 437).

There are powerful forces aligned against any genuine effort to rewrite the nation's past and to "teach the truth" about the history of slavery. They include conservative authors with close ties to Republican administrations, right-wing foundations, some traditional liberals such as the recently deceased Arthur Schlesinger, Jr., and even prominent historians who have sacrificed principle for position and privilege (Singer, 2005c, pp. 199–205; Brooks, 2006, p. A27).

For two decades, the right has vigorously attacked changes in the curriculum that promote a more "multicultural" framework as a "Trojan horse" designed to undermine American values. One of its leading spokespersons has been Diane Ravitch, a former undersecretary of education in the first Bush (1989–1993) administration, who is sponsored by the Educational Excellence Network, the Fordham Foundation, the John M. Olin Foundation, and the Manhattan Institute. Ravitch has dismissed multicultural education as a "pernicious" idea that promotes ethnocentrism (Ravitch, 1990b, p. 3). Following the attacks on the World Trade Center in New York and the Pentagon in

Washington DC on September 11, 2001, she virtually equated multicultural educators with the terrorists because, as advocates of diverse perspectives on world events, they were encouraging "cultural relativism" (Ravitch, 2001; Ravitch, 2002, pp. 6–9).

Major right-wing players in the war over what should be taught as history include Richard Gilder and Lewis E. Lehrman, cofounders of the Gilder Lehrman Institute of American History, who control the Board of Directors of the New York Historical Society. Richard Gilder is a founding member, and former chair, of the Board of Trustees of the Manhattan Institute. Lewis Lehrman is a trustee of the American Enterprise Institute, the Manhattan Institute, and the Heritage Foundation. In a *New York Times* interview (Pogrebin and Collins, 2004), Gilder acknowledged that their goal was to influence the national debate over history. Their view on slavery, as explained by Lehrman, is that it was "an institution supported throughout the world, but Americans took the initiative in destroying it." Lehrman deplored the belief that "American history consists of one failure after another to deal with the issue of slavery." However, he believes that "One of the triumphs of America was to have dealt directly with that issue in the agonies of a civil war, and to have passed the 13th, 14th and 15th Amendments" (p. E1).

The Gilder Lehrman Institute advisory board, which gives them an air of legitimacy, includes many prominent names from the history profession in the United States. As members of the advisory board, these historians are feted, paid consulting fees, and have their publications promoted. The historians on the Gilder Lehrman Institute advisory board tend to be from the liberal-left end of the political spectrum and not to see anything wrong with their involvement. As Upton Sinclair commented in a book about his unsuccessful campaign for governor of California during the Great Depression, "it is difficult to get a man to understand something when his salary depends on his not understanding it" (Sinclair, 1935/1994, p. 109).

Politics and privilege make very strange bedfellows. The advisory board also includes conservatives such as Roger Kimball, managing editor of the *New Criterion*, Richard Brookhiser, senior editor at *National Review*, Roger Hertog, former chairman of the Manhattan Institute, and Diane Ravitch.

This is not the only time in recent years that historians and their professional organizations have deluded themselves in a vain effort to influence public policy. In January 1995, the U.S. Senate voted 99 to 1 to reject National History Standards that were prepared by the National Center for History in the Schools with participation from the Organization of American Historians and the American Historical Association. The Senate charged that the standards, written under a grant from the federally funded National Endowment for the Humanities, failed to provide students with a decent respect for the contributions of Western civilization to the development of the United States. The sole dissenting vote was cast by a Democrat from Louisiana, who opposed the Senate's repudiation of the proposal as inadequate (Singer, 2005b, p. 8).

Following this debacle, the National Center for History in Schools issued revised national history standards that eliminated the classroom activities, which gave concrete form to what were otherwise broad blandishments (Thomas, 1996, p. 8). The new standards, minus the teaching suggestions, were almost as widely acclaimed as the original draft was condemned. Diane Ravitch and Arthur Schlesinger, Jr., praised them for acknowledging "our nation's troubled history of racial, ethnic and religious tension," while correctly focusing on "America's developing democratic tradition" and "continuing quest to make our practices conform to our ideals."

One of the sharpest and highest profile rightwing critics of multiculturalism and a revised history curriculum is Thomas Sowell (n.d.), the Rose and Milton Friedman Senior Fellow at the Hoover Institution at Stanford University. Part of the reason for Sowell's prominence is because he is African American.

In a speech available on his Web site, Sowell charged that advocates for multiculturalism are "quick to condemn the evils of 'our society'" even when the "sins" for which they condemn the West are "worse in many non-Western societies." He argued that the "classic case is slavery."

Sowell's position is very similar to that espoused by Lewis Lehrman. Lehrman argues that slavery, that "hideous institution," was defeated around the world by the West. He is upset because, instead of getting credit for this accomplishment, Western Civilization is condemned for its ties with slavery. Meanwhile, the non-Western world's "monumental" defense of slavery and the slave trade is ignored because "this is not the kind of story that appeals to the multiculturalists. If it had been the other way around—if Asian or African imperialists had stamped out slavery in Europe—it would still be celebrated, in story and song, on campuses across America" (Pogrebin & Collins, 2004, p. E1).

But as we saw when we looked at New York's long and torturous complicity with slavery and the trans-Atlantic slave trade, "Western Civilization" promoted this system for hundreds of years and deserves little credit for finally turning against its own creation. In the United States, the North did so haltingly and the South only because it lost the Civil War. It is ironic that the efforts of Toussaint L'Ouverture, Frederick Douglass, Henry Highland Garnet, Lewis Tappan, and John Brown, who fought so hard to destroy a slave system that was central to the development of both Western Civilization and capitalist industrialization, should be credited to the very system they fought to defeat.

We live in a difficult and dangerous world. Thomas Sowell, Lewis Lehrman, and his paid legions, the federal government, conservative propagandists, and even some traditional liberals, want schools to celebrate America, not encourage critical thinking about the past and its influence on the present. But it is precisely because the world is so difficult and dangerous that I join with the students of Law, Government, and Community Service Magnet High School and demand: "It is time to teach the truth."

Chapter 12

Books, Movies, and Web Sites

No book written today is produced without drawing on the work of others. The writing of history is a cumulative process as new historians add information and ideas to the intellectual pot and help build new understandings about the past. There are a number of books that are especially useful and are highly recommended.

John Hope Franklin's *From Slavery to Freedom* (NY: Knopf, 2000) is in its eighth edition. It remains the classic survey of African American life in the United States and is an important resource for every social studies teacher.

In *Slavery and the Making of America* (NY: Oxford University Press, 2005), James and Lois Horton have produced a highly readable textbook that is easily accessible to high school students. It is a companion to the PBS documentary series with the same name. The Hortons begin with a chapter on "The African Roots of Colonial America" and follow the story through the Reconstruction era after the Civil War. The four-part PBS documentary has two dramatic depictions of slavery in the New York area that are especially useful to teachers working on the *New York and Slavery* curriculum. The opening part focuses on the effort by enslaved Africans in the Dutch colony of New Amsterdam to secure their freedom. The second section looks at conditions in colonial New York City that contributed to the 1741 trial and execution of enslaved Africans who were accused of plotting a slave insurrection. The material on the American Revolution details the life and struggle of Colonel Tye, a runaway slave from New Jersey who fought for his freedom by fighting for the British.

Important books on slavery in the United States and the trans-Atlantic Slave Trade include the collected works of Eugene Genovese, especially *The Political Economy of Slavery: Studies in the Economy and Society of the Slave South* (NY: Vintage, 1967); *The World the Slaveholders Made: Two Essays in Interpretation* (1969); *Roll, Jordan, Roll, The World the Slaves Made* (NY: Pantheon, 1974); and *From Rebellion to Revolution, Afro-American Slave Revolts in the*

Making of the Modern World (Baton Rouge, LA: Louisiana State University Press, 1979). The notion of agency by the oppressed is at the center of the work of C. L. R. James (1938/1962) *The Black Jacobins, Toussaint L'Ouverture and the San Domingo Revolution* (NY: Vintage), which is a seminal work in the field.

Robin Blackburn, *The Making of New World Slavery* (NY: Verso, 1997) and *The Overthrow of Colonial Slavery 1776–1848* (NY: Verso, 1988), Eric Williams, *Capitalism & Slavery* (Chapel Hill, NC: UNC, 1944/1994), Marcus Rediker, *The Slave Ship, A Human History* (NY: Viking, 2007), and David Brion Davis, *Inhuman Bondage, The Rise and Fall of Slavery in the New World* (NY: Oxford, 2006) demonstrate the place of slavery within the evolving global capitalist system. Philip Foner, *Business and Slavery, The New York Merchants and the Irrepressible Conflict* (NY: Russell and Russell, 1941), documents the role of Northern and New York merchants in supporting Southern and Caribbean slavery by promoting the trade in slave-produced commodities. Foner's citations from local newspapers during the 1850s are often incomplete. The *New York Times,* however, now has a researchable database starting in 1851 that is available online.

Eric Foner and Joshua Brown collaborated on *Forever Free* (NY: Alfred Knopf, 2005), a book that examines the battles over emancipation and reconstruction. The opening chapter is a brief summary of the history of slavery in the United States that effectively introduces major themes and demonstrates its central role in the development of the nation.

Two books by William L. Katz are geared for use by secondary school students. In *Black Legacy, A History of New York's African Americans* (NY: Atheneum Books for Young Readers, 1997), Katz provides an overview of the African American experience in New York City from the time of the Dutch settlement through the end of the twentieth century. *Eyewitness: A Living Documentary of the African American Contribution to American History* (NY: Touchstone, 1995) has extensive narrative introductions that effectively place primary documents in their historical context. These documents have been edited with an eye toward classroom use. One of the documents cited by William Katz was of particular importance in shaping the curriculum guide. He has an excerpt from the memoir of a New York abolitionist named Reverend Samuel May (1997, p. 68). May describes an incident in 1835 with a New York City businessman who warns him that Northern merchants were committed to maintaining the slave system in the South in order to protect their investments.

In 2005, the New York Historical Society sponsored an exhibit on slavery in New York City. In conjunction with the exhibit, it helped publish a collection of essays edited by Ira Berlin and Leslie Harris (*Slavery in New York,* NY: The New Press, 2005). These essays and other works by the contributors provide a more in-depth look at the African American experience in New York and the North during "slavery days." The historians involved in the project included Jill Lepore, author of *New York Burning: Liberty, Slavery, and Conspiracy in Eighteenth-Century Manhattan* (NY: Knopf, 2005), who wrote about the evolution of the slave system in colonial New York. Graham Hodges, author of *Root and Branch, African Americans in New York and East Jersey 1613–1863* (Chapel Hill, NC: University of North Carolina, 1999), contributed a chapter on local Blacks during the American Revolution. David Quigley wrote a chapter on the economic relationship between New York merchants and bankers and Southern cotton planters. Iver Bernstein, author of *The New York Draft Riots: Their Significance for American Society and Politics in the Age of the Civil War* (NY: Oxford University Press, 1990), discussed efforts by New York's Black population to support the war against slavery and the impact of the anti-Black draft riots on life in the city.

Henry Louis Gates, Jr., described the African American "slave narrative" as a unique achievement in literature. As part of the campaign to abolish slavery, hundreds of ex-slaves and runaways told their personal accounts as lectures and in autobiographical narratives. Their stories provide eloquent testimony against their captors and the inhuman institution, and bear witness to the urge of formerly enslaved Africans to be both free and literate. Over 100 book length narratives were written before the end of the Civil War. By the 1940s, over six thousand former slaves had told their stories of human bond-age through interviews, essays, and books. Many of these stories are available on online at http://docsouth.unc.edu, http://newdeal.feri.org/asn and http://memory.loc.gov/ammem/snhtml/snhome.html. Especially useful for understanding African American lives in New York and the North are the narratives of Venture Smith, Solomon Northup, Sojourner Truth, William Brown, Thomas James, Samuel Ringgold Ward, Jermain Loguen, Harriet Jacobs, and of course, Frederick Douglass.

The most comprehensive annotated collection of documents on slavery in the United States is Herbert Aptheker's four-volume *A Documentary History of the Negro People in the United States* (NY: Citadel Press, 1974/1990). Primary source document collections that focus on New York history include Elizabeth Donnan, *Documents Illustrative of the History of the Slave Trade to America* (NY: Octagon Books, 1932/1969); E. B. O'Callaghan, *Documents Relative to the Colonial History of the State of New-York; Procured in Holland, England and France* (Albany, NY: Weeds, Parsons, 1856); and David Gellman and David Quigley, *Jim Crow New York, A Documentary History of Race and Citizenship 1777–1877* (NY: New York University, 2003).

Historical Fiction

Historical fiction and movies can help students and teachers imagine an elusive past. Frederick Douglass, *The Heroic Slave*, William Wells Brown, *Clotel*, and Harriet Wilson, *Our Nig*, are from the 1850s and are among the earliest published works by African American authors. They are collected in a single edition, *Three Classic African-American Novels* (edited by William Andrews, NY: Penguin, 1990). Recommended novels include *Uncle Tom's Cabin* by Harriet Beecher Stowe (NY: Penguin, 1852/1981), *The Adventures of Huckleberry Finn* by Mark Twain (NY: Oxford University Press, 1884/1996), *Sacred Hunger* by Barry Unsworth (NY: Norton, 1992), about the trans-Atlantic slave trade, Madison Smartt Bell's trilogy about Toussaint L'Overture and the Haitian Revolution (*All Soul's Rising*, NY: Knopf, 1995; *Master of the Crossroads*, NY: Knopf, 2000; and *The Stone the Builder Refused*, NY: Pantheon, 2004), Toni Morrison's *Beloved* (NY: Knopf, 1987), Russell Banks's novel *Cloudsplitter* about John Brown (NY: HarperCollins, 1998), and William Styron's *The Confessions of Nat Turner* (NY: Random House, 1967). Alex Haley's *Roots, The Saga of an American Family* (NY: Doubleday, 1976), whether viewed as a work of fact or of historical fiction, provides a powerful description of the slave system in the American South. Other useful works of fiction are Peter Hamill, *Forever* (Boston, MA: Little, Brown, 2003), which opens in colonial New York during the 1741 "Slave Conspiracy"; Walter Mosley's *47* (Boston, MA: Little, Brown, 2005), which blends history with science fiction; Virginia Hamilton's *The People Could Fly, American Black Folktales* (NY: Knopf, 1985) and *Anthony Burns* (NY: Knopf, 1988); and *Freedom's Crossing* by Margaret Goff Clark (NY: Scholastic, 1991), about the Underground Railroad in upstate New York. The books by Mosely, Hamilton, and Clark are written for young readers.

Movies

In *Slaves on Screen: Film and Historical Vision* (Davis: 2000), the historian Natalie Zemon Davis discusses (and recommends with reservations) four movies that portray slavery in the Americas. *Burn!* (1969) and *The Last Supper* (1976) are about slave revolts in the Caribbean. *Beloved* (1998) is about the psychological wounds of enslavement. *Amistad* (1997) is about the trans-Atlantic "middle passage" and attitudes toward the captives and slavery in the United States. *Middle Passage* (2000), which was not included in the Davis study, may actually be a better treatment of the trans-Atlantic slave trade than Amistad. There is no dialogue, however, the English version of its narrative, written by novelist Walter Mosely and delivered by the Academy Award nominated actor Djimon Hounsou, is very powerful.

Many movies that depict slavery are seriously flawed and should be used with care if at all. *Gone With the Wind* (1939) and *Songs of the South* (1946) essentially portray slavery as a benign institution, although Disney, which produced *Songs of the South,* and other supporters of the film claim that the scenes with happy, contented plantation workers actually represents the era after emancipation. *Roots* (1976) is a comprehensive chronicle of slavery in the South based on the book by Alex Haley. While it is supposed to be a true story of his family, much of it is conjecture. There is a "soap opera" quality to the movie, which was originally produced for television, and enslaved Africans are rarely shown working. *Solomon Northup's Odyssey* (1984), which was produced by PBS, is a much more accurate picture of plantation life and work. *Sankofa* (1993) is heavily spiritual, a woman visiting an Africa slave trading fort is possessed and plunged into the past, and can be difficult to follow.

Otherwise excellent movies are problematic because enslaved Africans appear peripheral to their own story. *Cold Mountain* (2003) is supposed to be about the Civil War, but enslaved Africans only appear in the background on a few occasions. *Glory* (1989), the story of the all-Black 54th Massachusetts Volunteer Regiment that fought during the Civil War, centers on the role of Colonel Robert Gould Shaw, the White abolitionist who commanded the forces. *Amazing Grace* (2007), which chronicles the antislavery campaign in Great Britain at the end of the eighteenth and beginning of the nineteenth centuries, credits its success to the work of White, religious, opponents of slavery, and neglects the crucial role played by the defeat of a British army invading Haiti by Toussaint L'Ouverture.

Web Sites

The Internet has been a great boon to research by historians, teachers, and students, although there are the continuing problems with search engines directing you to millions of sites (if you type in slavery, Google gives you almost twenty-five million hits), deciding which ones are reliable, and locating information once you arrive at a site that can be less than user friendly. This summary of Internet resources focuses on the sites that I found useful in editing the *New York and Slavery: Complicity and Resistance* curriculum guide and researching and writing this book.

The masthead of *The New York Times* (http://nytimes.com) proclaims that the newspaper covers "All the News That's Fit to Print." Whether you agree with that claim or not, its online historical archive, which covers 1851 to 1980, includes the complete text of every article ever published by the newspaper. The database can be searched by topic, headline, author, or date. While the *Times* charges for the service, it can also be accessed for free through some libraries using ProQuest.

The Library of Congress American Memory Web site has online resources on slavery and abolition in its "African-American Mosaic" (http://www.loc.gov/exhibits/african), "African-American Odyssey" (http://memory.loc.gov/ammem/aaohtml), and Federal Writer's Project (ttp://memory.loc.gov/ammem/snhtml/snhome.html) collections.

"Documenting the American South" (http://docsouth.unc.edu) is a project of he University of North Carolina at Chapel Hill. While it includes ten thematic collections of books, diaries, posters, artifacts, letters, oral history interviews, and songs, the collection I found most useful for my work is "North American Slave Narratives." It contains over three hundred narratives, although some of them are duplicate editions of the same account.

The Gilder Lehrman Institute of American History's Web site has a "module" on slavery (http://www.gilderlehrman.org/teachers/module7/

index.html) that includes primary source documents, teaching materials, and recommended Web links. Gilder Lehrman and the New York Historical Society maintain two additional Web sites that focus on material from exhibits "Slavery and the Making of New York" (http://www.slaveryinnewyork.org) and "New York Divided" (http://www.nydivided.org). Slavery in the New is also the focus of "Slavery in the North" (http://www.slavenorth.com), a Web site maintained by Douglas Harper, an independent historian.

PBS maintains Web sites paired with the documentaries "Africans in America" (http://www.pbs.org/wgbh/aia) and "Slavery and the Making of America" (http://www.pbs.org/wnet/slavery). "Africans in America" is organized chronologically and covers the years 1450–1865. "Slavery and the Making of America" can be viewed either chronologically or thematically. Both sites include documents, images, and lessons for teachers that are also useful for students. There is also an independent "Slavery and the Making of America" Web site (http://www.slaveryinamerica.org) that is supported by the New York Life corporation.

"Captive Passage," a Web site maintained by the Mariners' Museum in Liverpool, UK is an excellent resource on the Middle Passage (http://www.mariner. org/captivepassage). The site includes sections on Africa, the settlement of the Americas, and abolitionist campaigns.

I shy away from using online encyclopedias, however the *Spartacus Internet Encyclopedia*'s "Slavery in the United States" collection (http://www. spartacus.schoolnet.co.uk/USAslavery.htm) is truly invaluable. It includes thirty-two personal recollections of enslavement, and sections on the slave system, slave life, and abolitionist campaigns. Many entries contain excerpts from primary source documents.

A number of sites tell the story of the Underground Railroad. They include "Aboard the Underground Railroad," sponsored by the National Park Service (http://www.nps.gov/nr/travel/underground); the Cincinnati, Ohio based "National Underground Railroad Freedom Center" (http://www. freedomcenter.org); and National Geographic's "The Underground Railroad" (http://www.nationalgeographic.com/railroad).

Visual images are especially useful for classroom teachers. The Virginia Foundation for the Humanities and the University of Virginia maintain an incredible collection of drawings, maps, and photographs on their Web site "The Atlantic Slave Trade and Slave Life in the Americas" (http://hitchcock.itc. virginia.edu/Slavery/index.php). They are organized topically and include sections on African life, capture, the Middle Passage, slave life and work in the Americas, and the Civil War. The Slave Heritage Resource Center (http://www. sonofthesouth.net) Web site has photographs (although I am skeptical about the authenticity of some of them), and illustrations of slavery themes drawn by Thomas Nast. Articles and illustrations are also available at "Harpers' Weekly Reports on Black America 1857–1874" (http://blackhistory.harpweek.com).

Chapter 13

Classroom Ideas for Teaching About Slavery

Over eighty classroom teachers from the Hofstra University New Teachers Network and the "Gateway to the City" Teaching American History Grant were involved in developing and field-testing classroom ideas for the *New York and Slavery: Complicity and Resistance* curriculum guide. They are all available at the Web site of the New York State Council for the Social Studies (http://www.nyscss.org). Some of their classroom ideas were particularly effective.

Stephanie Hunte, Robert Kurtz, Adeola Tella, Randy Labella, April Francis, and Rachel Thompson where among teachers who worked on "Museum of Slavery" exhibits. For the museum project, middle school students select images from the history of slavery in the United States or the struggle by African Americans for freedom. They use them to create three-dimensional exhibits that are either dioramic representations or symbolic displays (exhibit A).

Andrea Libresco, a colleague from Hofstra University who has pioneered the use of "history-mysteries," suggested the idea for the history-mystery question in exhibit B. "History-mysteries" introduce students to primary source documents, some of which are edited. They require students to either use the documents to put together an historical narrative or to answer a specific question.

Kerri Creegan edited the trial transcript of the 1741 slave conspiracy trial for classroom use and organized a multiday lesson. Using Kerri's lesson, April Francis had students in her seventh-grade class translate the material into a "hip-hop rap opera." As students rewrote testimony in their own words, they figured out the meaning of what they read and drew conclusions about a disputed historical event (exhibit C).

Students in Michael Pezone's high school social studies class used the *New York and Slavery: Complicity and Resistance* curriculum guide to create and perform a play that put Frederick Douglass on trial as a "terrorist" for materially supporting John Brown. Students helped research the documents included in the play, edited the passages and organized the production. They insisted that Martin Luther King, Jr., be included as a defense witness because of his commitment to social struggle and parallels they saw between his career and the career of Frederick Douglass. The mock trial led to a serious discussion, quoted in the text, of slave uprisings and the African American struggle for freedom (exhibit D).

Exhibit A. Middle School Museum of Slavery

The centerpiece of the middle school "Museum of Slavery" we have created at the Hofstra University School of Education and Allied Human Services is a "Wall of Memory." It has consisted of over fifty white T-shirts, torn, stained, and dabbed with brown and red paint. The shirts represent both the pain of the slaver's lash and continuous resistance to bondage. Other exhibits have included dioramas of slave life and the slave trade, symbolic representations of the artifacts of slavery, and replicas of slavery-era documents. Images from the history of slavery can be found online at "The Atlantic Slave Trade and Slave Life in the Americas" (http://hitchcock.itc.virginia.edu/Slavery/index.php). Students have also presented African dances and plays, including ones based on short stories from Virginia Hamilton's *The People Could Fly, American Black Folktales* (NY: Alfred A. Knopf, 1985).

At the museum, exhibits are either hung or displayed on tables along with cards that explain what they depict. After visitors have a chance to browse, students present their exhibits to the entire group.

Teachers approach preparation for the Museum of Slavery differently. Students can work independently or in small groups either in or out of class. One teacher created a unit based on a "slavery document package" and used the museum exhibits as a final assessment of student learning. Another used the exhibits as "documents" for a document-based essay.

Possible themes for exhibits include:

1. Trans-Atlantic Slave Trade—By the 1700s a network to trade enslaved people between Africa and the Americas was well established. Re-create the conditions people endured on slave ships while in middle passage.
2. Horrors of Slavery—Many enslaved Africans who lived in servitude were subjected to harsh and unfair treatment. Create a replica of weapons or tools used to subjugate captives and control slaves.
3. Slave Resistance—Enslaved Africans fought against slavery in violent and nonviolent ways. Re-create a scene of resistance such as occurred at Harpers Ferry or an escape route taken to freedom on the Underground Railroad.

4. Contributions by African Americans—Many African Americans overcame injustices and went on to make important contributions to the world. Re-create a scene such as Sojourner Truth's "Ain't I a Woman" speech to a woman's rights convention.
5. Slavery in the World Today—Many people in the world are much less fortunate than we are and some still live under conditions of slavery. Create a scene representing slavery today.

Projects for the museum can also include:

1. Write a "slave song" in a modern style using information from slavery-era documents;
2. write a letter to an advocate of slavery challenging his or her views;
3. write a newspaper article about the discovery and impact of the cotton gin;
4. create a television broadcast on the issue of slavery;
5. design a giant poster illustrating an aspect of the slave trade or slavery; and
6. make reproductions of the artifacts of slavery including the tools and weapons of the slave trade.

Exhibit B. History-Mystery:
What was life like for enslaved
Africans in colonial New York?

Background information: During the colonial era and up until 1827, there was slavery in New York State. In Kings County, now called Brooklyn, there were many small farms with small groups of enslaved African workers. By 1664, the African population of the Dutch colony was about 800 people or 10 percent of the total population of the colony. In New Amsterdam, 375 Africans made up about a fourth of the settlement's total population. A 1664 tax list for New Amsterdam showed that approximately one out of eight citizens of the colony owned enslaved Africans. By 1750, more than eleven thousand people were enslaved in the colony of New York. At the time of the American Revolution, Kings County had a higher percentage of African Americans as part of its population than any other county in New York.

Task: A White male farm owner from Kings County (Brooklyn) in the eighteenth century could have made following statement. "The lives of slaves in the

New York colony are not so bad. It's not like in the South. And besides, we don't have that much slavery here anyway." Your task is to carefully read each of the documents and answer the document questions. After completing all of the documents and document questions, compare this statement against all of the evidence presented in your packets. Your goal is to decide how accurate his statement is.

Edited Documents:

1. Sale of Enslaved Africans

Source: E. Donnan (1932/1969). *Documents Illustrative of the History of the History of the Slave Trade to America* (NY: Octagon), p. 427.

> "Conditions and Terms on which the Director General and Council of New Netherland propose to sell to the highest bidder a lot of Negroes and Negresses May 29, 1664. The buyers shall immediately take possession of their purchased Negroes, and may use them as bond slaves, and also sell them to others."

Document Questions

- When are these events taking place?
- Who are the people being described in this passage?

2. An Act for Regulating Slaves (1702)

Source: The Colonial Laws of New York from the Year 1664 to the Revolution, vol. 1, pp. 519–521, in E. B. O'Callaghan, ed. (1851). *The Documentary History of the State of New-York.* Albany, NY: Charles Van Benthysen.

> "That no Person or Persons hereafter throughout this Province, do presume to Trade with any slave either in buying or selling, without leave and Consent of the Master or Mistress, on penalty of forfeiting Treble [three times] the value of the thing traded for, and for the sum of five pounds Current money of New-York, to the Master or Mistress of such slave . . . AND BE IT FURTHER ENACTED by the authority aforesaid, That hereafter it shall and may be lawful for any Master or Mistress of slaves to punish their slaves for their Crimes and offences at Discretion, not exceeding to life or Member."

Document Questions

- What does this law forbid?
- What does this law allow?

3. Death Penalty for Rebellious Slaves (1706)

Source: Wilder, C. (2000). *Race and Social Power in Brooklyn* (NY: Columbia University Press), p. 31.

> "Whereas, I am informed that several Negroes in Kings County have assembled themselves in a riotous manner, which, if not prevented, may prove of ill consequence; you and every one of you therefore hereby required and commanded to take all proper methods for seizing and apprehending all such Negroes in the said country . . . and to secure them in safe custody, that their crimes and actions may be inquired into; and if any of them refuse to submit themselves, then to fire on them, kill or destroy them. . . ."

Document Questions

- Why is the problem described in this statement?
- What solution is being proposed?

4. Law Appointing a Place for the More Convenient Hiring of Slaves (1711)

Source: Minutes of the Common Council of the City of New York, vol. II, p. 458, December 13, 1711 (New York Historical Society).

> "That all Negro and Indian slaves that are let out to hire within this City do take up their Standing in Order to be hired at the Market house at the Wall Street Slip until Such time as they are hired."

Document Questions

- What is the purpose of this law?
- In your view, why did the City Common Council decide to pass this ordinance?

5. Laws Restricting Enslaved Africans (1742)

Source: Minutes of the Common Council of the City of New York, vol. V, p. 59, 1742 (New York Historical Society).

> "That no Negro Mulatto or Indian Slave within this City after the Publication hereof Shall on any Lords Day or Sunday Presume to fetch any water other than from the Next well or pump the place of their Abode or Shall Presume to Ride any Horse through any of the Streets of this City or on the Common. Every

Slave So Offending Shall be Whipped at the Public Whipping Post at the Discretion of any one justice of the Peace Not Exceeding forty Lashes Unless the Master: Mistress or Owner of Such Slave So offending pay the sum of Three Shillings."

Document Questions

- What is the purpose of this law?
- What happened to enslaved Africans who disobeyed this law?

6. Runaway Slave Ad

Source: Wilder, C. (2000). *Race and Social Power in Brooklyn* (NY: Columbia University Press), p. 21.

"Run away from Barnet Van Deventer, of Flat-Bush, on Long-Island, in Kings County, a Negro man named Handrick, alias Hank, of middle stature, had on when he went away a linen striped shirt, a pair of homespun breeches, a bluish pair of stockings, and an old pair of shoes, a good felt hat. He speaks good English and Dutch, and tells people he is a free Negro. Whosoever takes up aid Negro and brings him to his said master, or secures him so that he may be had again, shall have 30 Shillings reward, and all reasonable charges paid by me, Barnet Van Deventer."—*The New York Evening Post,* September 29, 1746

Document Questions

- What do we learn about "Handrick" from this advertisement?
- What else do we learn about slavery in Kings County from this advertisement?

7. Characters from the Early History of Brooklyn

Source: Henry R. Stiles (1867–1870). *A History of the City of Brooklyn including the Old Town and Village of Brooklyn, the Town of Bushwick, and the Village and City of Williamsburgh, vol. II.* Brooklyn, NY: Pub. by subscription.

"Israel and Timothy Horsfield were men of mark [wealth] in their day. They were the sons of Timothy Horsfield, of Liverpool, England, where they were born. Israel came to this country in 1720, and became a freeman [citizen] of New York, on the 13th of December, of the same year. About three years after, his brother Timothy arrived and entered into business with him, as butchers. Long Island at that time furnished the New York market with most of its live stock. They built a wharf at the foot of the present Doughty Street, together with a slaughtering place and the necessary buildings for residence. The next year they leased the two best stands in the Old Slip Market in the city of New York; their dressed meats being brought over daily, in rowboats by their own slaves, to their stands in the market. Israel Horsfield, in 1738, had a family of ten persons, three of whom were colored men, and slaves. He and his brother afterwards had the misfortune to lose some of their 'chattels' [slaves] who were put to death for complicity in the 'Great Negro Plot' of 1741."

Document Questions

- Why were the Horsfields an important family in Brooklyn society?
- What happened to enslaved Africans accused of participating in the "Great Negro Plot" of 1741?

8. Farmers Who Owned the Most Enslaved Africans in Flatbush (1755)

Source: New York Slave Census for Kings County, Town of Flatbush (Brooklyn Collection, Brooklyn Public Library)

Owner' Name	Enslaved Africans (Male)	Enslaved Africans (Female)
Widow Clarkson	3	2
Henry Cruger	3	1
Engelbart Lott	2	2
Laurens Ditmars	1	3
Rem Martense	2	2
Antje Ver Kerck	3	4

Document Questions

- What is the average number of Africans held by the six largest slaveholders in the town of Flatbush in Kings County?
- Based on your knowledge of history, how does this compare with the number of people held as slaves on large plantations in the United States South and the Caribbean?

9.   Population of Kings County Towns (1791)

Sources: Wilder, Craig (2000). *A Covenant with Color: Race and Social Power in Brooklyn* (NY: Columbia University Press), p. 37.

Town	Enslaved Blacks	Free Black	White
Brooklyn	405	14	1,184
Flatbush	378	12	551
New Utrecht	206	10	346
Gravesend	135	5	286
Flatlands	137	0	286
Bushwick	171	5	364
Total	1,432	46	3,017

Document Questions

- Which town in Brooklyn had the largest number of enslaved Africans in 1791?
- What percentage of the Black population of Brooklyn was free in 1791?
- What percentage of the population of Brooklyn was enslaved in 1791?

10. An Old Farmer's Talk: Stephen L. Vanderveer's *New Lots* Recollections

Source: Brooklyn Eagle, September 19, 1886, p. 6.

"In those days there were as many Negroes as whites in this neighborhood. The latter were buried in front by the roadside and the former away back near the swamp . . . In 1824 our people thought it best to have a place of worship near the last resting place of our forefathers . . . In 1841 we saw the necessity of having a new burying ground, as the black people were overcrowding us in the old one. Therefore we purchased the ground alongside the church and removed a great many of the dead from across the road."

Document Questions

- Why was a new cemetery started?
- Who was buried in the new cemetery? Who was left behind?

Based on these documents, a student essay should include the following:

- Enslaved Africans played a major role in building the infra-structure (clearing the land, constructing housing and forti-fications, building roads) of the New York colony and did different kinds of work.
- Enslaved Africans were bought, sold, and rented in the colony.
- The New York colony had difficulty controlling its enslaved population and its relations with free Blacks and Whites and made laws to restrict their behavior and to punish them.
- Enslaved Africans were dissatisfied with conditions. They re-belled against enslavement, disobeyed laws, and ran away from bondage.
- Slave holdings, and probably the size of farms, in Kings County where much smaller than in the Southern and Carib-bean.
- In Kings County, enslaved Africans made up nearly have of the population of the colony.

Exhibit C. The New York City Slave Conspiracy Trial (1741): Who were the guilty parties?

Task: Write and perform a "hip-hop rap opera" about the New York City Slave conspiracy. Each part in the play will be a "rap," including the introductions and the testimony.

Background Information: Slavery in New York City in the first half of the eighteenth century created a potentially explosive situation. The city had a large population of enslaved Africans. In 1737, 16 percent of the 10,664 inhabitants of New York County (Manhattan Island) were of African ancestry. Conditions were very different from plantation life in the South and the Caribbean. Meet-ings between enslaved people were relatively easy and unsupervised and en-slaved Africans and free Blacks and White worked and lived in close proximity. The governors of the city lived in continuous fear of fire, attack by the enemies of England, a slave insurrection, or some combination of all three.

In 1712, Black rebels were accused of setting fire to a building in the mid-dle of the city and attacking White colonists who tried to extinguish the blaze. Nine Whites were shot, stabbed, or beaten to death and another six were wounded. Militia units from New York and Westchester and soldiers from a nearby fort captured twenty-seven rebels. Six captives took their own lives and the others were executed. The uprising led to a series of new legal restrictions on the rights of enslaved Africans. They included limits on their ability to meet, restrictions on manumission, bans on the use of firearms by slaves, the death penalty for involvement in a conspiracy to kill a White person, and greater threats of physical punishment.

In 1741, White New Yorkers, afraid of another slave revolt, responded to rumors and unexplained fires with the arrest of over one hundred and fifty enslaved Africans, the execution of thirty-four Blacks and four Whites, and the transport to other colonies of seventy enslaved people. Accusations were made by a young White female indentured servant, who received £100 and her freedom in exchange for her testimony. The joint "confessions" of two of the conspirators, Cuffee and Quaco, were made while they were waiting to be burned to death by an angry mob. Three years after the trials and executions, a record of the "New York Conspiracy" was published by one of the judges in the case. Historians continue to doubt whether a slave conspiracy ever existed. The convictions and executions are often compared with the hysteria surrounding the Salem Witch trials of 1692. The judges' report, instead of exposing the dangerous behavior of Africans in New York, actually documents the repression of enslaved Africans, the failure of the legal system, social conditions in the city, and the ways these factors contributed to a deadly official conspiracy against the city's Black population. The 1741 Slave Conspiracy lesson (http://www.nyscss.org) and the full text of the hip-hop rap opera are available on line (http://people.Hofstra.edu/faculty/alan_j_singer).

Prosecutor Frederick Philipse Addresses the Court

Source: Zabin, S., ed. (2004). *The New York Conspiracy Trials of 1741* (Boston, MA: Bedford/St. Martin's), pp. 64–65.

The many frights and terrors which the good people of this city have of late been put into, by repeated and unusual fires, and burning of houses, give us too much room to suspect, that some of them at least, did not proceed from mere chance, or common accidents; but on the contrary, from the premeditated malice and wicked pursuits of evil and designing persons; and therefore, it greatly behooves us to use our utmost diligence, by all lawful ways and means to discover the contrivers and perpetrators of such daring and flagitious undertakings: that, upon conviction, they may receive condign punishment . . .

I am told there are several prisoners now in jail, who have been committed by the city magistrates, upon suspicion of having been concerned in some of the late fire; and others, who under pretence of assisting the unhappy sufferers, by saving their goods from the flames, for stealing, or receiving them. This indeed, is adding affliction to the afflicted, and is a very great aggravation of such crime . . .

This crime is of so shocking a nature, that if we have any in this city, who, having been guilty thereof, should escape, who can say he is safe, or tell where will it end? . . . My charge, gentlemen, further is, to present all conspiracies, combinations, and other offenses, from treasons down to trespasses; and in your inquiries, the oath you, and each of you have just now taken will, I am persuaded, be your guide, and I pray God to direct and assist you in the discharge of your duty.

Prosecutor Frederick Philipse—
Student "Rap" Version

The good people of this city own slaves,
Who don't want to follow the ways,
Now the city we had just ain't the same
'Cause houses were burned down by flames.
Several prisoners who are now in jail
Want the chance to tell their tale,
Their crimes are shocking to nature you see,
The prisoners should all be found guilty.
My charge gentlemen is to prevent conspiracy,
By slaves and their friends in this city,
We must stop their crimes and stolen booty,
I pray that God directs you to your duty.

Exhibit D. United States v. Frederick Douglass
for Planning and Materially Supporting Terrorism

This "mock" trial uses primary source documents from the nineteenth century and some of the language may be difficult for students. While it is a trial of Frederick Douglass for planning and materially supporting terrorism against the United States, it also questions current definitions of terrorism and the Patriot Act. Rather than using the original material presented here, teachers may prefer to have students "translate" passages into contemporary language before acting out the play.

Discussion of the text and issues can take place between scenes or after the entire production is completed. The trial is divided into scenes so that more than one student can play a particular character.

The project is designed for three days although a more abbreviated version can be completed in one class period. On day 1, students discuss who Frederick Douglass and John Brown were, the attack on Harpers Ferry preceding the outbreak of the Civil War, the ideas of terrorism and conspiracy, and the Patriot Act. On day 2, students act out the play and discuss the issues highlighted in each of the scenes. We have included guiding questions that we found useful. For homework between days 2 and 3, students write their individual views on Douglass's guilt or innocence and whether they believe he was a freedom fighter or terrorist. They can use a standard essay format or present their views as a rap. On day 3, students deliberate in groups, present their views to the full class and debate their conclusions.

After acting out the mock trial, students in Michael Pezone's African American history class met as a "committee of the whole" to discuss whether Douglass was guilty as charged. Debate over the verdict was sharp.

Rhonda Daniel argued, "America was supposed to be founded on freedom, but for African Americans it meant enslavement. How can a country deny freedom and liberty to people because of the color of their skin? How can it be a crime to fight for your rights? Frederick Douglass was only defending the fundamental principles stated in the Declaration of Independence. The entire political system was corrupt and it was the government that was terrorist."

Clifford Pieroit replied to Rhonda arguing, "There is no denying that Frederick Douglass was a great man who accomplished many things as an abolitionist, author, political leader and spokesperson for human rights. Unfortunately, his achievements are tainted by his part in the conspiracy with John Brown. Even though slavery was wrong, it was the law in the South at that time. Terrorism means to act violently against people or property to influence public opinion and government policies. That is what John Brown did. Because Douglass helped him, he can justifiably be branded as a conspirator and even a terrorist."

"Terrorism is a subjective term," said Jamel Wells. "The thing that makes Douglass a freedom fighter and not a terrorist is that he was fighting for the inalienable rights of people that are part of democracy. Both the prosecution and the defense agreed that slavery was wrong and had to be abolished. If you convict Douglass of terrorism then all of the people who participated in the Civil War should be declared terrorists also."

Fiorella Leal was not so sure. "Frederick Douglass is guilty of the charges. He did help John Brown plan a rebellion against the government of the United States. It does not make him a bad guy. You can be guilty and be a good person. He should have been punished for breaking the law. He would have become a martyr like John Brown."

Ashley Willock countered, "There is nothing wrong with standing up for what you believe. Frederick Douglass was an antislavery activist who wanted to help his people. He did a wrong, but he did it to make a right. Douglass only agreed to use violence if they were provoked and had no choice. The courts accept that violence is legal in self-defense. When Douglass realized that the original plan had changed into something else that was too treacherous, he left the group. That is not the mind of a terrorist."

Diana Chavez suggested a compromise. "Douglass could be charged with conspiracy, but not with terrorism. Talking about something and doing something are not the same thing. Douglass thought terrorism was wrong. He went home. But either way, slavery ended with the Civil War. Douglass was fighting against slavery and should be found not guilty."

While it is written as a trial of Frederick Douglass, this activity is actually intended to stimulate discussion of current and past definitions of terrorism, conspiracy, and the Patriot Act (2001). The full text of the "mock" trial of Frederick Douglass was published in *Social Science Docket* (Winter-Spring 2008) and is available online at http://people.hofstra.edu/faculty/alan_j_singer.

United States v. Frederick Douglass

Background Information: Frederick Douglass (1817–1895) is probably the most noted African American figure from the nineteenth century. He was born in Maryland, the son of a White man and an enslaved African woman. As a boy, Douglass was taught to read in violation of state law. In 1838, he escaped to New York City. During the Civil War, Douglass tried to persuade President Abraham Lincoln that former slaves should be allowed to join the Union Army. After the war, he campaigned for full civil rights for former slaves and was a strong supporter of women's suffrage. He also held several government positions including Marshall of the District of Columbia (1877–1881) and U.S. minister to Haiti (1889–1891). Today, Douglass is honored as a former slave who escaped to freedom and became a noted abolitionist, public speaker, newspaper editor, author, international spokesperson for human rights, and political leader.

John Brown, on the other hand, remains one of the most controversial figures in United States history. On October 16, 1859, Brown and twenty-one other men, including five Blacks and sixteen Whites, attacked the federal arsenal at Harpers Ferry. Brown was wounded and captured. He was taken to Charlestown, Virginia, where he was put on trial and convicted of treason. John Brown was hanged on December 2, 1859. Although Northerners were initially shocked by Brown's actions, many prominent abolitionists soon began to speak favorably of his exploits.

Few recall that Douglass was originally implicated in Brown's raid on Harpers Ferry and was forced to flee the country when a warrant for his arrest was issued in Virginia. He was also the subject of a congressional investigation into treasonous behavior just prior to the outbreak of the Civil War.

The trial of Frederick Douglass for complicity in the "crimes" of John Brown never took place. In this mock trial, Douglass has an opportunity to defend himself against charges that he supported terrorism while his critics will finally have the opportunity to press their case.

The prosecutor is John Ashcroft, United States Attorney General from 2001 to 2005. Ashcroft was one of the architects of the Patriot Act after the attack on the United States on September 11, 2001. His questions directed at Douglass and other "witnesses" are fictional, however, their responses, the testimony, is from primary source documents. Anton Scalia, an Associate Justice of the United States Supreme Court serves as the judge in this case. Clarence Darrow, a noted defense attorney who frequently defended the civil liberties and legal rights of unpopular defendants, represents Douglass. Witnesses, in order of appearance, include John Brown, Henry Ward Beecher, Abraham Lincoln, Frederick Douglass, Patrick Henry, Thomas Jefferson, and Martin Luther King, Jr.

Since the failed attack on Harpers Ferry in 1859, political activists and historians have debated whether John Brown should be considered a freedom fighter or a traitor and terrorist? Do his ends or goals, the liberation of millions of enslaved Africans, justify his means, revolutionary violence against the government of the United States? Can violence by an enslaved human being or his or her supporters against an individual master or a system that denies their humanity be labeled as a form of terrorism or is the terrorist the person or oppressive system that denies liberty to others?

Frederick Douglass materially aided Brown and supported his goals, although he did not participate in the actual attack on Harpers Ferry. Should Douglass be remembered as a freedom fighter or a terrorist? Ladies and gentlemen, you are the jury in this trial. You must make the decision.

Scene from the United States v. Frederick Douglass

Ashcroft: I now call the defendant, Frederick Douglass, as a witness.

Scalia: Mr. Douglass, please take the stand.

Darrow: One minute, please, your honor. I wish to remind my client that he has the constitutional right not to testify against himself.

Douglass: I understand my rights. Your honor, I wish to testify.

Ashcroft: What exactly was your relationship with John Brown?

Douglass: From the time of my visit to him in Springfield, Massachusetts in 1847, our relations were friendly and confidential. I never passed through Springfield without calling on him, and he never came to Rochester without calling on me. He often stopped over night with me, when we talked over the feasibility of his plan for destroying the value of slave property.

Ashcroft: During these visits, did you plot with John Brown to use violence to overturn the laws of the United States?

Darrow: I object. Counsel is leading the witness.

Scalia: Mr. Douglass, are you pleading the Fifth Amendment right to remain silent?

Douglass: No. I am prepared to answer the question.

Scalia: Objection overruled. Please proceed Mr. Ashcroft.

Ashcroft: Let me repeat the question. Mr. Douglass, did you plot with John Brown to use violence to overturn the laws of the United States?

Douglass: "That plan . . . was to take twenty or twenty-five . . . trustworthy men into the mountains of Virginia and Maryland, and station them in squads of five, . . . They were to be well armed, but were to avoid battle or violence, unless compelled by pursuit or in self-defense. In that case, they were to make it as costly as possible to the assailing party, whether that party should be soldiers or citizens. . . . The work of going into the valley of Virginia and persuading the slaves to flee to the mountains, was to be committed to the most courageous and judicious man connected with each squad."

Ashcroft: What was your opinion of this plan?

Douglass: Hating slavery as I did, and making its abolition the object of my life, I was ready to welcome any new mode of attack upon the slave system which gave any promise of success. . . . In the worse case, too, if the plan should fail, and John Brown should be driven from the mountains, a new fact would be developed by which the nation would be kept awake to the existence of slavery. Hence, I assented [agreed] to this, John Brown's scheme or plan for running off slaves.

Darrow: I object. I object. I object. Your honor, what difference does it make what my client's opinions were. He is on trial because he is accused of terrorist actions against the United States government.

Ashcroft: We will get to the actions, your honor. We will get to them.

Scalia: By all means, continue Mr. Ashcroft. Objection overruled.

Source: Douglass, Frederick (1969). *Life and Times of Frederick Douglass*, 1892 edition (NY: Collier), 314–315.

References

Albion , R. (1961). *The Rise of New York Port [1815–1860]*. Hamden, Conn.: Archon Books.

Allen, T. (1994). *The Invention of the White Race, vol 1. Racial Oppression and Social Control*. N.Y.: Verso.

Andrews, R. (1934, March). "Slavery Views of a Northern Prelate," *Church History 3*(1), 60–78.

Annals of Congress (1820). 16 Congress, 1 session, vol. II, columns 1323–1328, in Bailey, T. & D. Kennedy (1984). *The American Spirit*, 5th ed., Lexington, Mass.: D. C. Heath, pp. 203–205.

Aptheker, H., ed. (1951/1973). *A Documentary History of the Negro People in the United States, vol. 1*. Secaucus, N.J.: The Citadel Press.

Associated Press (2005, September 28). "Schools Directed to Expand History Curriculums." Accessed on October 15, 2006 at http://www.cnn.com/2005/EDUCATION/09/28/ethnic. courses.ap.

Associated Press (2006, March 11). "Professors Seek to Shed Light on Legacy of Northern Slavery." Accessed June 8, 2007 at http://www.newsday.com/news/local/wire/ny-bc-ny—teachingslavery0311mar11,0,1452504.

Associated Press (2007, June 20). "Wednesday in Albany Includes Taxes, Slavery." Accessed June 24, 2007 at http://hosted.ap.org/dynamic/stories/N/NY_ALBANY_RDP_NYOL?SITE=NYITH&SECTION=HOME&TEMPLATE=DEFAULT.

Baker, G., ed. (1861/1972). *The Irrepressible Conflict. The Works of William H. Seward, vol. 4*. N.Y.: AMS Press.

Baldwin, J. (1998). *Collected Essays*. N.Y.: The Library of America.

Bailey, T., & D. Kennedy, eds. (1984). *The American Spirit, vol. 1*, 5th ed. Lexington, Mass.: D. C. Heath.

Barton, K., & L. Levstik (1998). "'It Wasn't a Good Part of History': National Identity and Students' Explanations of Historical Significance," *Teachers College Review, 99* (3), pp. 478–513.

Barton, K., & L. Levstik (2004). *Teaching History for the Common Good*. Mahwah, N.J.: Lawrence Erlbaum.

143

Barton, K. (2005). "Best Not to Forget Them": Secondary Students' Judgments of Historical Significance in Northern Ireland," *Theory and Research in Social Education, 33* (1), pp. 9–44.

BBC (2005, January 21). "JP Morgan Admits US Slavery Links." Accessed on October 12, 2006 at http://new.bbc.co.uk/2/hi/business/4193797.stm.

Berlin, I., & L. Harris, eds. (2005). *Slavery in New York.* N.Y.: The New Press.

Bernstein, I. (1990). *The New York City Draft Riots.* N.Y.: Oxford.

Bernstein, I. (2005). "Securing Freedom: The Challenges of Black Life in Civil War New York," in Berlin, I., & L. Harris, eds., *Slavery in New York.* N.Y.: The New Press.

Blackburn, R. (1997). *The Making of New World Slavery, From the Baroque to the Modern, 1492–1800.* N.Y.: Verso.

Bordewich, F. (2005). *Bound for Canaan, The Underground Railroad and the War for the Soul of America.* N.Y.: HarperCollins.

Bradford, S. (1886). *Harriet, The Moses of Her People.* N.Y.: G. R. Lockwood & Son.

Brady, Kevin (2001, Summer–Fall). "Abolitionists Among New York's 'Founding Fathers.'" *Social Science Docket, 1*(2).

Braudel, F. (1979) *The Perspective of the World, III: Civilization and Capitalism: 15th–18th Century.* N.Y.: Harper & Row.

Brooks, D. (2006, April 27). "The Death of Multiculturalism," *New York Times.*

Brown, C. (1971). *William Cullen Bryant.* N.Y.: Scribner.

Brown, J. (1997, November 17). "Slave Life at Lloyd Manor," *Newsday.* Accessed June 11, 2007 at http://www.newsday.com/community/guide/lihistory/ny-history-hs314a,0,6109118.story.

Brown, J. (2002). "The Wanderer Comes Home." *Newsday.* Accessed on October 12, 2006 at www.newsday.com/extras/lihistory/specfam/famwand.htm.

Brown, W. (1849). *Narrative of William W. Brown, an American Slave. Written by Himself.* London: C. Gilpin, 1849. Accessed at http://docsouth.unc.edu/fpn/brownw/menu.html on June 25, 2007.

Burrows, E., and M. Wallace (1999). *Gotham, A History of New York City to 1898.* N.Y.: Oxford University Press.

California Department of Insurance (2002, May). *Consumers: Slavery Era Insurance Registry Report.* Accessed June 28, 2007 at http://www.insurance.ca.gov/0100-consumers/0300-public-programs/0200-slavery-era-insur/slavery-era-report.cfm.

Calonius, E. (2006). *The Wanderer, The Last American Slave Ship and the Conspiracy That Set Its Sails.* N.Y.: St. Martin's Press.

Cardwell, D. (2000, August 12). "Seeking Out a Just Way to Make Amends for Slavery," *New York Times.*

Carleton, G. (1864/1968). *The Suppressed Book About Slavery,* N.Y.: Arno.

Cole, D. (1984). *Martin Van Buren and the American Political System.* Princeton, N.J.: Princeton University Press.

Collins, G. (2005, September 27). "A 'Main Event' in Old New York," *New York Times.*

Cornbeth, C., & D. Waugh (1995). *The Great Speckled Bird, Multicultural Politics and Education Policymaking*. N.Y.: St. Martin's Press.

Cornbleth, C. (2002). "Images of America: What Youth Do Know about the United States," *American Educational Research Journal, 39* (2), pp. 519–552.

Cotten, Stacey (2001, Summer–Fall). "Teachers Respond to Teaching About Slavery in the Americas," *Social Science Docket*.

Creegan, K. (2007, Summer–Fall). "New York State; A Microcosm of the Debate over Slavery," *Social Science Docket*.

Crummell, A. (1882). *The Eulogy on Henry Highland Garnet, D.D.* Washington, D.C.: Union Bethel Literary and Historical Association.

Davis, D. (2006). *Inhuman Bondage, The Rise and Fall of Slavery in the New World*. N.Y.: Oxford University.

Defoe, D. (1728). *A Plan of the English Commerce*. Cited in C. H. Wilson, "The Economic Decline of the Netherlands," *The Economic History Review, IX*(2), pp. 111–127.

Delafield, J. (1877). *Biographies of Francis Lewis and Morgan Lewis by Their Granddaughter*. N.Y.: Anson D. F. Randolph & Company.

Donnan, E. (1932/1969). *Documents Illustrative of the History of the Slave Trade to America, Vol. III. New England and the Middle Colonies*. N.Y.: Octagon.

Douglass, F. (1892/1962). *Life and Times of Frederick Douglass*. N.Y.: Collier.

DuBois, W. E. B. (1896/1965). *The Suppression of the African Slave Trade*. Baton Rouge, LA: Louisiana State University Press.

DuBois, W. E. B. (1961). *The Souls of Black Folk*. N.Y.: Fawcett, 1961.

Duberman, M. (1964). *In White America*. Boston, Mass.: Houghton Mifflin.

Dunbar, A. ed. (1914). *Masterpieces of Negro Eloquence*. N.Y.: The Bookery Pub. Co.

Eakin, S., & J. Logsdon, eds. (1967). *Twelve Years a Slave*. Baton Rouge, La.: Louisiana State University Press.

Eakin, S. (1990). *Solomon Northup's Twelve Years a Slave, 1841–1853*. Gretna, La.: Pelican Publishing.

Easton, K., & L. Guddat (1967). *Writings of the Young Marx on Philosophy and Society*. Garden City, N.Y.: Doubleday Anchor.

Ellis, E. (1966). *The Epic of New York City, A Narrative History*. N.Y.: Old Town Books.

Emerson, R. (1851). *The Fugitive Slave Law. The Complete Works of Ralph Waldo Emerson*. Accessed October 11, 2006 at http://www.rwe.org.

Emmet, T. (1915). *Memoirs of Thomas Addis and Robert Emmet*. N.Y.: Emmet Press.

English, M. (2006, June 2). "Signs of Slavery Taken Down," *New York Newsday*.

Epstein, T. (1996). "Historical Understanding Among Urban Adolescents: Differences in Black and White," *Theory and Research in Social Education, 26*, pp. 299–301.

Epstein, T. (1998). "Deconstructing differences in African-American and European-American adolescents' perspectives on U.S. history," *Curriculum Inquiry, 28*, pp. 397–423.

Epstein, T. (2000). "Adolescents' Perspectives on Racial Diversity in U.S. History: Case Studies from an Urban Classroom," *American Educational Research Journal, 37* (1), pp. 185–214.

Evans, M. (2005, September 13). "History of Slavery in NY 'Can't Be Ignored,'" *Newsday.*

Farmer-Paellmann, D., B. Afran, & C. Mayer (2006, September 22). *Corporate America's Uncashed Check: Disgorging the Ill-Gotten Gains of Slave Labor.* Accessed October 2, 2006 at http://CommonDreams.org.

Farrow, A., J. Lang, & J. Frank, (2005). *Complicity: How the North Promoted, Prolonged, and Profited from Slavery.* N.Y.: Ballantine Books.

Feder, B., ed. (1967). *Viewpoints: USA.* N.Y.: American Book Company.

Feuer, L., ed. (1959). *Marx & Engels, Basic Writings on Politics & Philosophy.* N.Y.: Anchor.

Finn, R. (2000, August 8). "Public Lives; Pressing the Cause of the Forgotten Slaves," *New York Times.*

Foner, E. (1970). *Free Soil, Free Labor, Free Men.* N.Y.: Oxford University Press.

Foner, E. (1991/1997). *Slavery, the Civil War and Reconstruction.* Washington, D.C.: AHA.

Foner, E. (2000, July 13). "Slavery's Fellow Travelers," *New York Times.*

Foner, P. (1941). *Business and Slavery, The New York Merchants and the Irrepressible Conflict.* Chapel Hill, N.C.: University of North Carolina Press.

Foner, P., ed. (1950). *The Life and Writings of Frederick Douglass, Vol. II, Pre-Civil War Decade 1850–1860.* N.Y.: International Publishers.

Francis, A. (2007, Summer–Fall). "African American New Yorkers and the Struggle to End Slavery," *Social Science Docket,* 7(2).

Frederick Douglass' Paper. "Legal Rights Vindicated," March 2, 1855.

Frankenberg, Orfield G., & C. Lee. (2003). *A Multiracial Society with Segregated Schools: Are We Losing the Dream?* Cambridge, Mass.: Civil Rights Project at Harvard University.

Franklin, J. (1974). *From Slavery to Freedom, A History of Negro Americans,* 4th ed. N.Y.: Knopf.

Gates, H., Jr. (2001, July 29). "The Future of Slavery's Past," *New York Times.*

Gellman, D., and D. Quigley, ed. (2003). *Jim Crow New York, A Documentary History of Race and Citizenship 1777–1877.* N.Y.: New York University Press.

Genovese, E. (1979). *From Rebellion to Revolution, Afro-American Slave Revolts in the Making of the Modern World.* Baton Rouge, La.: Louisiana State University.

Genovese, E., and E. Fox-Genovese (2005). *The Mind of the Master Class.* N.Y.: Cambridge University Press.

Gershman, J. (2007, June 13). "N.Y.'s Apology for Slavery Is Readied for 'Juneteenth'," *The Sun.* Accessed on June 24, 2007 at http://www.nysun.com/article/56415.

Gilbert, O. (1884). *Narrative of Sojourner Truth.* Battle Creek, Mich.: Review and Herald. Accessed on Oct. 9, 2006 at http://www.docsouth.unc.edu.

Greenhouse, L. (2007, June 29). "Justices, 5–4, Limit Use of Race for School Integration Plans," *New York Times*.

Groanke, Virginia (2002, May 5). "Slave Policies," *New York Times*.

Halagoa, P. (2004). "Holding Up in the Mirror: The Complexity of Seeing Your Ethnic Self in History," *Theory and Research in Social Education, 32* (4), pp. 459–483.

Hamilton, V. (1985). *The People Could Fly: American Black Folktales*. N.Y.: Knopf.

Hammon, J. (1787). *An address to the Negroes in the state of New-York, by Jupiter Hammon, servant of John Lloyd, Jun, Esq; of the manor of Queen's Village, Long-Island*. N.Y.: Carroll and Patterson. Accessed October 8, 2006 at http://etext.lib.virginia.edu/readex/20400.html.

Harper's Weekly (1860, June 2). The Africans of the Slave Bark Wildfire." Accessed on October 12, 2006 at http://blackhistory.harpweek.com/ SlaveryHome.htm.

Hartell, A. (1943, Fall). "Slavery on Long Island," *Nassau County Historical Journal, 6* (2).

Hassard, J. (1866). *Life of the Most Reverend John Hughes, DD, First Archbishop of New York, with Extracts from His Private Correspondence*. N.Y.: D. Appleton.

Higgins, R., L. Dickstein, & M. Vetare. *Establishing Slavery In Colonial New York*. Accessed October 8, 2006 at www.hudsonvalley.org/philipsburg/learn_ slavery_ny.htm.

Hochschild, A. (2005). *Bury the Chains, Prophets and Rebels in the Fight to Free an Empire's Slaves*. Boston, Mass.: Houghton Mifflin.

Hodas, D. (1976). *The Business Career of Moses Taylor, Merchant, Finance Capitalist, and Industrialist*. New York: New York University Press.

Hodges, G., & A. Brown, eds. (1994). *"Pretends to Be Free" Runaway Slave Advertisements from Colonial and Revolutionary New York and New Jersey*. N.Y.: Garland.

Hodges, G. (1996). *The Black Loyalist Directory: African Americans in Exile After the American Revolution*. New York: Garland Publishing.

Hodges, G. (1999). *Root & Branch: African Americans in New York & East Jersey, 1613–1863*, Chapel Hill, N.C.: University of North Carolina Press.

Horsmanden, D. (1744). *A Journal of the Proceedings in the Detection of the Conspiracy*, in Davis, T., ed. (1971). *The New York Conspiracy*. Boston, Mass.: Beacon.

Horton, J., & L. Horton (2005). *Slavery and the Making of America*. N.Y.: Oxford University Press.

Howard, Warren (1963). *American Slavers and the Federal Law, 1837–1862*. University of California, Berkeley.

Howlett, C. (2001, Summer–Fall). "John Woolman: New Jersey's Eighteen Century Quaker Abolitionist," *Social Science Docket, 1* (2).

Israel, J. (1995). *The Dutch Republic*. N.Y.: Oxford University Press.

Janofsky, M. (1994, October 8). "Mock Auction of Slaves: Education or Outrage?" *New York Times*.

Jefferson, T. (1787/1794). *Notes on the State of Virginia,* 2nd ed. Philadelphia, Pa.: Matthew Carey. Accessed October 9, 2006 at http://www.stolaf.edu/people/fitz/COURSES/Jefferson—Notes.htm.

Jensen, J. (2000, January 15). "Think Tank; Sermons on the Climb to the Mountaintop," *New York Times.*

Johnson, L. (1964, May 22). Remarks at the University of Michigan. Accessed June 8, 2007 at http://www.britannica.com/ebc/article-9116919.

Jordan, W. (1968). *White Over Black, American Attitudes Toward the Negro, 1550–1812.* Chapel Hill, N.C.: University of North Carolina.

Journals of the New York Provincial Congress (1842). Albany, N.Y.: Weed, Parsons.

Katz, J. (1974). *Resistance at Christiana.* N.Y.: Thomas Y. Crowell.

Katz, W. (1995). *Eyewitness, A Living Documentary of the African American Contribution to American History.* N.Y.: Simon & Schuster.

Katz, W. (1997). *Black Legacy: A History of New York's African Americans.* N.Y.: Atheneum Books for Young Readers.

King, B. (1798). "Memoirs of the Life of Boston King, A Black Preacher," *The Methodist Magazine,* May 1798, pp. 157–161. Accessed June 11, 2007 at http://antislavery.eserver.org/narratives/boston_king/.

Koch, A. (1966). *Notes of the Debates in the Federal Convention of 1787 Reported by James Madison.* Athens, Ohio: Ohio University Press.

Kozol, J. (2005, December). "Confections of Apartheid: A Stick-and-Carrot Pedagogy for the Children of Our Inner-City Poor," *Phi Delta Kappan, (87)* 4.

Kurland, P., and R. Lerner, eds. (1987) *The Founders' Constitution.* Chicago, Ill.: University of Chicago Press.

Lee, Brother B. (1943). *Discontent in New York City, 1861–1865.* Washington D.C.: Catholic University of America Press.

Lepore, J. (2005a). *New York Burning, Liberty, Slavery, and Conspiracy in Eighteenth-Century Manhattan.* N.Y.: Knopf.

Lepore, L. (2005b). "The Tightening Vise: Slavery and Freedom in British New York," in Berlin, I., & L. Harris, eds. *Slavery in New York.* N.Y.: The New Press.

Lerner, B. (2003, October 23). "Scholars Argue Over Legacy of Surgeon Who Was Lionized, Then Vilified," *New York Times.*

Loewen, J. (1995). *Lies My Teacher Told Me: Everything Your American History Textbook Got Wrong.* N.Y.: Simon and Schuster.

Loguen, J. (1859). *The Rev. J. W. Loguen, as a Slave and as a Freeman* (Syracuse, N.Y.: J. G. K. Truair). Accessed June 13, 2007 at http://docsouth.unc.edu/neh/loguen/loguen.html.

Madison, J. (1840/1984). *Notes of Debates in the Federal Convention of 1787.* Athens, Ohio: Ohio University Press.

Marcus, G. (1988/1995). *Discovering The African-American Experience in Suffolk County, 1620–1860.* Setauket, NY: Society for the Preservation of Long Island Antiquities.

McManus, E. (1966). *A History of Negro Slavery in New York*. Syracuse, N.Y.: Syracuse University Press.

McMillan, B., ed. (2002). *Captive Passage, The Transatlantic Slave Trade and the Making of the Americas*. Washington, D.C.: Smithsonian.

Meade, R. (1957). *Patrick Henry: Patriot in the Making*. Philadelphia, Pa.: Lippincott.

Minutes of the Common Council of the City of New York, 1675–1776 (1930). N.Y.: Dodd, Mead.

Moore, C. (2005). "A World of Possibilities: Slavery and Freedom in Dutch New Amsterdam," in Berlin, I. and L. Harris, eds., *Slavery in New York*. N.Y.: The New Press.

Morse, S. (1863). *An Argument on the Ethical Position of Slavery*. N.Y.: Society for the Diffusion of Political Knowledge, no. 12.

Murphy, M. (2007, Summer–Fall). "Reconsidering the Complex Relationship Between Blacks, the Irish, and Abolitionists," *Social Science Docket*, 7 (2).

Mushkat, J. (1990). *Fernando Wood, A Political Biography*. Kent, Ohio: Kent State Press.

Nanji, A. (2005, June 2). "Course Draws Debate," *Newsday*.

New York State Assembly (2005, March 10). *Regular Sessions 6362—B, 2005–2006*. Albany, N.Y.

New York State Assembly (2007). "An Act to Amend Chapter 137 of the Laws of 1817 Relating to Slaves and Servants, in Relation to Acknowledging the Tragedy of Slavery in New York State," *A00273B*. Accessed June 24, 2007 at http://assembly.state.ny.us/leg/?bn=A00273.

New York Daily Tribune (1874, December 1). "Obituary."

New York Times (1851, September 19). "Christiana Incident."

New York Times (1852, November 15). "Cuban Affairs."

New York Times (1854a, May 2). "The Slave Trade."

New York Times (1854b, November 10). "The Slave-Trade—An Important Trial."

New York Times (1854c, November 24). Editorial.

New York Times (1858a, June 11). "Mystery of the Yacht Wanderer."

New York Times (1858b, June 12). "The Yacht Wanderer's Mystery Explained."

New York Times (1860, July 30). "From Havana."

New York Times (1860, December 7). "The Commercial Relationship Between the North and South."

New York Times (1861a, January 8). "Message of the Mayor."

New York Times (1861b, March 18). "Editorial."

New York Times (1861c, March 19). "Escape of Capt. Latham."

New York Times (1863, July 14). "Burning of the Orphanage for Colored Children."

New York Times (1864, June 15). "The Anti-Slavery Constitutional Amendment."

New York Times (1882, May 24). "An Old Merchant's Death."

New York Times (1994, October 11). "Tears and Protest at Mock Slave Sale."

New York Times (2000, January 15). "Think Tank; Sermons on the Climb to the Mountaintop."

New York Tribune (1854, July 19). "Outrage Upon Colored Persons."

New York Tribune (1855, February 23). "A Wholesome Verdict."

Niebuhr, G. (1999, June 26). "Religion Journal; Church to Repent Its Ties to Slavery," *New York Times.*

North, D. (1961). *The Economic Growth of the United States 1790–1860.* New York: Prentice-Hall.

O'Callaghan, E. B. ed. (1851). *The Documentary History of the State of New-York.* Albany, N.Y.: Charles Van Benthysen.

O'Callaghan, E. B. ed. (1856). *Documents Relative to the Colonial History of the State of New-York; Procured in Holland, England and France.* Albany, N.Y.: Weeds, Parsons.

Ofari (Hutchinson), E. (1972). *"Let Resistance Be Your Motto": The Life and Thought of Henry Highland Garnet.* Boston, Mass.: Beacon.

Orfield, G. (2001). *Schools More Separate: Consequences of a Decade of Resegregation.* Cambridge, Mass.: Civil Rights Project at Harvard University.

Orfield, G., & Lee, C. (2004). *Brown at Fifty: King's Dream or Plessy's Nightmare?* Cambridge, Mass.: Civil Rights Project at Harvard University.

Orfield, G., & Lee, C. (2005). *Why Segregation Matters: Poverty and Educational Inequality.* Cambridge, Mass.: Civil Rights Project at Harvard University.

Pérez, L., ed. (1998). *Impressions of Cuba in the Nineteenth Century, The Travel Diary of Joseph J. Dimock.* Wilmington Del.: Scholarly Resources

Pezone, M. (2001, Summer-Fall). "Teachers Respond to Teaching About Slavery in the Americas," *Social Science Docket.*

Pezone, M. and A. Singer (2006, Winter). "Reclaiming Hidden History," *Rethinking Schools, 21*(2).

Philipsburg Manor (nd). *A Note on Large Slaveholdings in the North.* Accessed October 8, 2006 at http://www.hudsonvalley.org/philipsburg/learn_slaveholdings.htm.

Pogrebin, R., & and G. Collins (2004, July 19). "Shift at Historical Society Raises Concerns," *New York Times.*

Porat, D. (2004, Winter). "'It's Not Written Here, but This Is What Happened': Students' Cultural Comprehension of Textbook Narratives on the Israeli-Arab Conflict," *American Educational Research Journal, 41* (4), pp. 963–996.

Postma, J. (1990) *The Dutch in the Atlantic Slave Trade 1600–1815.* N.Y.: Cambridge University Press.

Quigley, D. (2005). "Southern Slavery in a Free City: Economy, Politics, and Culture," in Berlin, I., & L. Harris, eds. *Slavery in New York.* N.Y.: The New Press.

Rael, P. (2005). "The Long Death of Slavery," in Berlin, I., and L. Harris, eds., *Slavery in New York.* N.Y.: The New Press.

Ravitch, D. (1990a). *The American Reader.* N.Y.: HarperCollins.

Ravitch, D. (1990b, October, 24). "Multiculturalism Yes, Particularism No," *Chronicles of Higher Education, 34*(44).

Ravitch, D. (2001, October 17). "Now Is the Time to Teach Democracy," *Education Week, 21*(7).

Ravitch, D. (2002, October). "The World in the Classroom: September 11: Seven Lessons for the Schools," *Educational Leadership, 60* (2).

Rice, M. (1944). *American Catholic Opinion in the Slave Controversy.* N.Y.: Columbia University Press.

Richards, L. (1970). *Gentlemen of Property and Standing; Anti-Abolition Mobs in Jacksonian American.* N.Y.: Oxford University Press.

Rivera, R. (2007, May 31). "Council Rejects Street Name for Black Activist," *New York Times.*

Robinson, Randall (2001). *The Debt: What America Owes to Blacks,* New York: Plume.

Root, K. (2007, June 25). "Va. Leads in Regret for Slavery, but to Where?" Daily Press (Hampton Roads, Virginia). Accessed on June 28, 2007 at http://www. dailypress.com/news/local/dp-68103sy0jun25,0,395321.story?coll=dp-news-local-final.

Ruchames, L. (1969). *John Brown, The Making of a Revolutionary.* N.Y.: Grosset & Dunlap.

Schor, J. (1977). *Henry Highland Garnet, A Voice of Black Radicalism in the Nineteenth Century.* Westport, Conn.: Greenwood.

Seldes, G., ed. (1960). *The Great Quotations.* New York: Lyle Stuart.

Sernett, M. (1986). *Abolition's Axe.* N.Y.: Syracuse University Press.

Sexias, P. (1993). "Historical understanding among adolescents in a multicultural setting," *Curriculum Inquiry, 23,* pp. 301–373.

Shade, W. (1998, Autumn). "'The Most Delicate and Exciting Topics': Martin Van Buren, Slavery, and the Election of 1836," *Journal of the Early Republic, 18* (3).

Shewmaker, K., ed. (1990). *Daniel Webster, "The Completest Man": Documents from the Papers of Daniel Webster.* Hanover, N.H.: Dartmouth.

Sienkiewicz, S. (2007, Summer–Fall). "The Underground Railroad in New York State," *Social Science Docket, 7* (2).

Sinclair, Upton (1935/1994). *I, Candidate for Governor: And How I Got Licked.* Berkeley, CA: University of California. Accessed on June 13, 2007 at http:// www.gooznews.com/archives/000551.html.

Singer, A. (2001, Summer-Fall). "Teaching About Slavery in the Americas," *Social Science Docket.*

Singer, A. (2003a). *Social Studies for Secondary Schools, Teaching to learn, Learning to Teach,* 2nd ed. Mahwah, N.J.: LEA.

Singer, A. (2003b, Winter-Spring). "Elizabeth Jennings: New York City's Nineteenth Century Rosa Parks," *Social Science Docket, 3*(1).

Singer, A. (2003c, January–April). "19th Century New York City's Complicity with Slavery: The Case for Reparations," *The Negro Educational Review, 54*(1/2).

Singer, A. (2003d, February 6–February 12). "NYC's Complicity with Slavery Supports Call for Reparations," *Amsterdam News, 94*(6).

Singer, A. (2003e, July 31–August 6). "In United States and New York City History, It Is Hard to Tell the Good Guys from the Bad Guys," *Amsterdam News, 94* (31).

Singer, A. (2005a). *New York and Slavery: Complicity and Resistance.* New York State Council for the Social Studies. Accessed on October 10, 2006 at http://www.nyscss.org.

Singer, A (2005b, Winter–Spring). "Defending Social Studies," *Social Science Docket, 5*(1).

Singer, A. (2005c, September/October). "Strange Bedfellows: The Contradictory Goals of the Coalition Making War on Social Studies," *The Social Studies, 96* (5).

Singer, A. (2007a, January/February). "Venture Smith's Autobiography and Runaway Ad: Enslavement in Early New York," *MLL, Middle Level Learning Supplement to Social Education,* 28.

Singer, A. (2007b, Summer–Fall). "New York City's Role in the Illegal Trans-Atlantic Slave Trade," *Social Science Docket 7* (2).

Slaughter, T. (1991). *Bloody Dawn, The Christiana Riot and Racial Violence in the Antebellum North.* New York: Oxford.

Smith, J. M. (1865). *A Memorial Discourse by Henry Highland Garnet.* Philadelphia, Pa.: Wilson.

Smith, V. (1798). A Narrative of the Life and Adventures of Venture, a Native of Africa: But Resident Above Sixty Years in the United States of America. Related by Himself. New-London, Conn.: C. Holt. Accessed October 8, 2006 at http://docsouth.unc.edu/neh/venture/venture.html.

Sowell, T. (n.d.). "'Multicultural' Education." Accessed on October 15, 2006 at http://tsowell.com/spmultic.html.

The Spartacus Internet Encyclopedia (2007). "The Slave Trade." Accessed June 20, 2007 at http://www.spartacus.schoolnet.co.uk/slavery.htm.

Staples, B. (2000, January 9). "History Lessons from the Slaves of New York," *New York Times.*

Staples, B. (2003, June 15). "Slaves in the Family: One Generation's Shame Is Another's Revelation," *New York Times.*

Stern, P. (1940). *The Life and Writings of Abraham Lincoln.* N.Y.: Random House.

Stowe, C. (1911) *Harriet Beecher Stowe: The Story of Her Life.* 1911. Accessed June 8, 2007 at http://en.wikipedia.org/wiki/Harriet_Beecher_Stowe.

Stowe, H. (1852/1981). *Uncle Tom's Cabin.* N.Y.: Penguin.

Thomas, H. (1997). *The Slave Trade, 1440–1870.* N.Y.: Simon & Schuster.

Thomas, J. (1996, April 3). "Revised History Standards Defuse Explosive Issues," *New York Times.*

Thompson, E. (1963). *The Making of the English Working Class.* N.Y.: Vintage.

Thoreau, H. (1849). *Civil Disobedience.* Originally published as "Resistance to Civil Government," Elizabeth Peabody's *Aesthetic Papers,* in May 1849. Accessed June 8, 2007 at http://sunsite.berkeley.edu/Literature/Thoreau/Civil Disobedience.html.

U.S. Department of Commerce Bureau of the Census (1975). *Historical Statistics of the United States Colonial Times to 1970, part 2*. Washington, D.C.: United States Government Printing Office.

USA Today (February 21, 2002). "Brown Bros.: Loans gave planters cash to buy slaves." Accessed June 28, 2007 at http://www.usatoday.com/money/general/2002/02/21/slave-brown-bros.htm.

Uris, L. (1961). *Mila 18*. Garden City, N.Y.: Doubleday.

Van Buren, M. (1837). *Inaugural Address*. Accessed on June 24, 2007 at http://www.juntosociety.com/inaugural/vanburen.html.

Wakeman, A. (1914). *History and Reminiscences of Lower Wall Street and Vicinity*. N.Y.: Spice Mill.

Webster, D. (1850, March 7). *The Seventh of March Speech*. Accessed on October 11, 200oathttp://www.dartmouth.edu/~dwebster/speeches/seventh-march.html.

White, S. (1991). *Somewhat More Independent, The End of Slavery in New York City*. Athens, Ga.: University of Georgia Press.

Wilder, C. (2000). *A Covenant with Color: Race and Social Power in Brooklyn*. N.Y.: Columbia University Press.

Wilder, C. (2001). *In the Company of Black Men: The African Influence on African American Culture in New York City*. N.Y.: New York University Press.

Williams, E. (1944/1994) *Capitalism & Slavery*, Chapel Hill, N.C.: University of North Carolina.

Williams, J., & C. Harris (1970). *Amistad 1*. N.Y.: Vintage.

Williams, N. (2001, Summer-Fall). "Teachers Respond to Teaching About Slavery in the Americas," *Social Science Docket*.

Woodman, H. (1968). *King Cotton and his Retainers, Financing and Marketing the Cotton Crop of the South, 1800–1925*. Lexington, Ky.: University of Kentucky.

Zehr, M. (2000, November 29). "NY Judge Narrows Claims in Student Poverty Suit," *Education Week*.

Zehr, M. (2005, November 2). "States Still Grappling with Multicultural Curricula," *Education Week, 25* (10). Accessed on October 15, 2006 at http://www.edweek.org/ew/articles/ 2005/11/02/10ethnic.h25.html.

Zielbauer, P. (2000, July 6). "A Newspaper Apologizes for Slave-Era Ads," *New York Times*.

Biographical Note

Alan Singer is a historian and teacher educator at Hofstra University, former high school social studies teacher, and a political activist in the New York metropolitan area. He is editor of the award winning *New York and Slavery: Complicity and Resistance* curriculum guide and lead author of *Social Studies for Secondary Schools* (with members of the Hofstra New Teachers Network, 2nd edition, LEA, 2003) and *Teaching to Learn, Learning to Teach* (with Maureen Murphy, S. Maxwell Hines and the Hofstra New Teachers Network, LEA, 2003).

Index

Abdul-Jamal, Mumia, 22
abolition, 5, 77, 80, 83, 85, 103, 141;
    New York 7, 24, 32, 100
abolitionists, 11, 14, 17, 19, 21, 23, 25,
    27, 28, 63, 77, 83, 84, 85, 102, 103,
    104–107, 114, 125, 126, 138, 139;
    New York, 24, 25, 30, 31, 32, 69,
    70, 72, 76, 77, 78, 79, 85, 92, 100,
    101, 104–107, 122
Adams, John Quincy, 101
Adams, Sarah, 104
*Address to the Negroes in the State of New
    York, An* (Hammon), 52
Aetna Insurance Company, 34, 89
African (American) burial ground, 1, 28,
    32
African American community, 4, 30, 33,
    44, 57, 60, 72, 73, 101–103, 105
African free schools, 32, 72, 100, 102, 106
Alabama, 118
Alamo, 3
Algeria, 5
Algonquian tribe, 46
American Anti-Slavery Society, 31, 76,
    78, 108
American Colonization Society, 103
American Enterprise Institute, 119
American Historical Association, 119
American Revolution, 50, 52, 53, 57, 63,
    68, 76, 91, 123, 129; confiscated
    slave property, 50
American Sugar Company, 93
Amistad, 76, 100–101

Amistad (movie), 14, 136
Amistad Commission, 30, 117
Amistad Defense Committee and trial,
    31, 76
Amistad legislation, 33
Amsterdam (Netherlands), 37–39, 43, 55
Analyze This (movie), 69
Andros, Edmund, 53
Anglesey, Edward, 66–67
Anglo-Dutch wars, 47
Anthony, Susan B., 24
Appeal to the Colored Citizens of the World
    (Walker), 107
Aptheker, Herbert, 123
Ardinburgh, Charles, 72
Arkansas, 118
Arthur, Chester, 79, 104
Articles of Confederation, 69,
asiento, 38
Associated Press, 117
Astor, William, 80
Athena, 42
ATT, 95
Auburn, New York, 79

Baldwin, James, 22
Bank of North America, 93
Bank One, 89
Banks, Russell, 124
Barbados, 42, 56, 57
Barron, Charles, 35
Barton, Keith, 112
Baumfree, Isabella. *See* Truth, Sojourner

Becker, Jonathan, 111
Beebe, Dean, & Donohue, 97
Beecher, Henry Ward, 34, 79, 140
Beekman, Harry, 55
Bell, Madison Smartt, 124
Bellomont, Earl of, 58
Belmont, August, 77, 80
Berlin, Ira, 122
Bernstein, Iver, 123
Bethlehem Steel, 95
Black church, 102–103
black ivory, 30, 31, 94
Black newspapers, 72, 102–103, 107
Black Pioneers, 50
Black population: New Netherland
    colony, 9, 16; colonial New York,
    25, 54, 60, 70, 71, 129, 134, 135
blackbirders, 2, 40, 94
Blackburn, Robin, 39–40, 122.
Bonaparte, Napoleon, 3, 17
Book of Negroes, 50
Boston, Massachusetts, 10, 40, 77, 92,
    95, 97, 101, 113, 107, 92, 95
Bowne, John, 68
bozales, 93–94
Brazil, 16, 23, 37, 38, 39, 43, 45, 47, 89,
    95
Bristol, U.K., 7, 93
Bristol, R.I., 35
Bronx, New York, 63, 64, 69
Brookhiser, Richard 119
Brooklyn (Kings County), New York, 3,
    34, 44, 58, 71, 79, 87, 90, 129–135
Brooks, David, 2
Brown Bros. Harriman, 89–90
Brown, John, 9, 25, 49, 78, 79, 109, 120,
    124, 127, 137–141
Brown, Joshua, 122
Brown, William Wells, 9, 105, 109, 123
Brownsville (Kings County), 3
Bryant, William Cullen, 79–80
Buchanan, James, 97
Buffalo, New York, 10, 105, 107
Burr, Aaron, 70

Caesar, 102
California, 7, 83, 89, 117, 119
Callaghan, E.B., 123

Canada, 16, 25, 43, 50, 63, 84, 85, 105,
    106
Canaan, New Hampshire, 107
capitalism, 21, 40, ,41, 78, 98,
Capitalism & Slavery (Williams), 40, 122
Carleton, Guy, 50
Carter, Mary, 70, 111
Cartwright, Samuel, 18
Chase, Salmom, 96
Christiana, Pennsylvania, 84–85
churches: African Methodist Episcopal,
    102; African Zion, 102; Demeter
    Presbyterian, 102; Dutch Reformed,
    44, 46; First Colored Presbyterian,
    102; Methodist, 69; Plymouth Con-
    gregationalist, 34, 79; Presbyterian
    Church (Troy), 107; St. George's
    Episcopal, 95; St. Philip's African
    Episcopal, 77, 102; Theologicial
    Seminary (Princeton), 102; Trinity,
    28, 58; United Church of Christ, 35
Churchill, Winston, 3
Citibank. *See* City Bank
City Bank (Citibank), 31, 80, 95, 96
Civil Rights movement (1950–1960s),
    99, 102
Civil War, 1,4, 5, 6, 17, 22, 24, 28, 29,
    30, 31, 69, 72, 76, 80, 82, 83, 84,
    85, 86, 87, 89, 90, 91, 92, 96, 103,
    104, 107, 108, 109, 110, 114, 119,
    120, 121, 123, 125, 126, 137, 138,
    139; battles, 86–87
Clark, Margaret Goff, 124
classroom ideas, 18–22, 127–141
Cohen, Jeffrey, 111
Colden, Cadwaller, 60
Coleman, Christy, 13
Colonel Tye. *See* Titus
Colonial Williamsburg, 13,
colonization movement, 24, 103, 106
Compromise of 1850, 84
Con Edison, 95
Congo, Simon, 43, 47
Constitution (New York State), 70, 71,
    80
Constitution (United States), 23, 32, 40,
    53, 64, 76, 80, 81, 83, 84, 86, 108,
    140

constitutional amendments, 32, 81, 119, 140
constitutional conventions (New York State), 69, 71, 80
constitutional convention (United States), 69
Continental Congress, 58
Conyers, John, Jr,. 35
Copperhead, 77, 87
Corlies, John, 63
Cornbleth, Catherine, 112
Corning, Erastus, 80–81
Cornish, Samuel, 102, 103
Cosby, William, 61
Cotten, Stacey, 15
cotton, 6, 21, 34, 69, 90, 91–93, 105, 129; New York connection, 29, 81, 86, 89, 90, 91–93, 96, 123
Creegan, Kerri, 5, 75, 127
Crummell, Alexander, 72, 78, 106
Crystal, Billy, 69
Cuba, 31, 32, 82, 89, 93–97, 101
Cuffee, 62, 101, 136
Curaçao, 39
curriculum and pedagogy, 14–16, 26, 29–34, 41, 111–112, 114–115, 117–120
Curriculum of Inclusion, 29

d'Angola, Lucie, 46, 101
d'Angola, Paul, 43
da Costa, Matthieu, 43
da Verrazano, Giovanni, 42
Davis, Angela, 22
Davis, David Brion, 40, 122
Davis, Natalie Zemon, 124
De Bow's Review, 18
de Fries, Jan, 44
de Gerritt, Manuel, 46, 47
De Niro, Robert, 69
Declaration of Independence, 23, 24, 49, 50, 53, 58, 68, 69, 138
Defoe, Daniel, 38
Delafield, Julia, 66
Delaware, 106
Delaware County, New York, 71
Democratic Party, 2, 80
Dew, Thomas, 22

Die Presse, 6
Disney, 4, 124
Dodge, William, 92
Domino Sugar, 93
Donnan, Elizabeth, 123
Douglass, Frederick (Bailey, Frederick Washington), 1, 9–11, 24, 33, 76, 79, 84, 103, 105, 107, 108–109, 118, 120, 123; Fourth of July speech, 11, 108–109; Trial of Frederick Douglass, 127–128, 137–141
draft riot (1863), 77, 83, 86–88, 107
drapetomia, 18
Duberman, Martin, 19
DuBois, W.E.B., 2–3, 8, 22, 23, 115
Dunmore, Earl of, 63
Dutch colony. See New Netherland
Dutch East India Company (VOC), 38
Dutch West India Company (WIC), 16, 38, 43–47, 53
Dutchess County, New York, 55, 57
dysaethesia aethiopica, 18

education, slaves and freedmen, 64, 102
Educational Excellence Network, 118
Edwards, Jr., Jonathan, 79
The Eighteen Brumaire of Louis Bonaparte (Marx), 65
emancipation, 25, 34, 63, 72, 122, 124; gradual 4, 20, 42, 69, 70, 77, 117; New York State, 9, 30, 72, 76; West Indies, 10
Emancipation Proclamation, 77, 83, 86, 100
Emerson, Ralph Waldo, 84
Emmet, Thomas Addis, 70
Epsetin, Terrie, 112
Equiano, Olaudah, 18
Erie Canal, 5, 16, 25, 29, 85, 91, 105
Erie Railroad, 86
essential questions, 7–10, 28, 41–42, 85
Ethiopian Regiment, 50
Eyckenboon, 45

factorage, 91
Fanon, Franz, 5
Farmer-Paellmann, Deadria, 34, 90
Federalist Papers, 53

Fisher's Island, New York, 56
Flushing (Queens County), 63, 68
Floyd, William, 58
Foley Square executions, 31
folk songs, 21
Foner, Eric, 28–29, 34, 122
Foner, Philip, 122
Fordham Foundation, 118
Fort Orange, New York, 44
Fox-Genovese, Elizabeth, 40
France and French colonial settlements, 17, 38, 39, 42, 43, 93, 123
Francis, April, 20, 62, 99, 127
Francis Lewis High School (Queens County), 65
Francisco, John, 43
Franklin, John Hope, 121
Freeport, New York, 15
free press, 51
Free Soil Party, 80
Fugitive Slave Act (1850), 27, 76, 79, 83–86

Garfield, James, 104
Garnet, Henry Highland, 9, 10, 70–72, 76, 78, 99, 100, 102, 106–109, 120
Garrison, William Lloyd, 10, 11, 34, 77, 78, 108
Garrison Literary and Benevolent Association, 102
Gates, Henry Louis, Jr., 35, 123
Gateway to the City, 127
Gellman, David, 123
Genovese, Eugene, 40, 121
Georgia, 79, 97
Gilder, Richard, 119
Gilder Lehrman Institute of American History, 119, 125–126
Gold Coast (Africa), 38
Gómez, Estéban, 42
Gorsuch, Edward, 84
Gouda (Netherlands), 39
Great Britain (England) and English colonial settlements, 4, 7, 16, 17, 23, 24, 25, 38, 39, 41, 42, 43, 44, 47, 49–64, 66, 70, 90, 91, 93, 94, 101, 121, 125, 132, 135

Greeley, Horace, 77
Green, Beriah, 78

Haarlem (Netherlands), 39
Haiti. *See* Santo Domingue
Halagoa, Patricia, 112
Haley, Alex,124
half-freedom, 45
Half Moon, 43
Hamill, Peter, 124
Hamilton, Alexander, 53, 63, 70
Hamilton, Virginia, 19, 124, 128
Hamilton, William, 73, 102, 106
Hammon, Jupiter, 49–52
Harper, Douglas, 126
Harper's New Monthly Magazine, 2, 97, 126
Harpers Ferry, 10, 78, 108, 109, 128, 131, 137, 139, 140,
Harris, Leslie, 122
Hartford Courant, 34–35, 90
Havemeyer, William, 32, 80, 93
Heday, Joseph, 56
Helper, Hinton, 90
Henry, Patrick, 51, 140
Heritage Foundation, 119
Hertog, Roger, 119
hip-hop rap opera,19, 20, 62, 127, 135–136
historical fiction, 123–124
history: Black history as American history, 2–7, 117–118; complexity, 65, 68, 70–73; connections, 34–36, 41; contingent nature, 69; curriculum, 29–34, 117–120; explanation, 6–7; multiple versions, 4, 16–18; slavery erased, 1–11, 28–29, 99; texts, 77; themes, 52; turning points, 84
History Channel, 4
history-mysteries, 127, 129–135
Hodges, Graham, 54
Hofstra University: New Teachers Network, 127; School of Education and Allied Human Services, 33, 127, 128
Holocaust (European), 15, 20, 30, 113, 115
Hoover Institution, 120
Horsmanden, Daniel, 61

Horton, James, 121
Horton, Lois, 121
Howard University, 28
Hudson, Henry, 43
Hughes, John, 82–83, 87
Hughson's Tavern, 32, 61, 101
human rights, 6, 7, 20, 88, 114, 138, 139
Hunte, Stephanie, 127
Hunter, Robert,59

Illinois, 77, 91, 117
Impending Crisis, The (Helper), 90
In White America (Duberman), 19
Ireland, 82, 108
Irish and Irish Americans, 56, 61, 70, 82, 86–87
Irish Brigade, 86

Jacobs, Harriet, 9, 123
Jamaica, 16, 42, 59, 72, 102, 108, 113
James, C.L.R., 23, 122
James, Thomas, 123
Jamestown, Virginia, 16, 118
Janvier, Thomas, 2
Jay, John, 53, 70
Jefferson, Thomas, 40, 53, 68, 71, 91, 140
Jennings, Elizabeth, 104
Jennings, Thomas, 104
John Bowne High School (Queens County), 68
Johnson, Andrew, 79
Johnson, Lyndon, 35
Johnson, Robert, 98
Jordan, Winthrop, 40
JP Morgan Chase, 89
Julia Moulton, 97

Katz, William, 18, 59, 122
Kansas, 78
Kidd, William, 58
Kieft, Willem, 44, 46
Kimball, Roger, 119
Kinderhook, New York, 80
King, Boston, 50, 101
King, Martin Luther, Jr., 49, 99, 128, 140
King, Preston, 79
Kline, Henry, 84

Kozol, Jonathan, 112
Kurtz, Robert, 127

Labella, Randy, 127
Lake Champlain Canal, 105
Lake Ontario, 85
Law, Government, and Community Service Magnet High School, 31, 39–40, 78–79, 100, 118, 120
Lehrman, Lewis, 119–120
Leiden (Netherlands), 39
Lepore, Jill, 61, 122
Levstik, Linda, 112
Lewis, Francis, 58, 66–68
Lewis, Elizabeth, 66
Lewis, Morgan, 66
Liberator, 10, 34, 103, 108
Liberia, 72, 78, 103, 108
Liberty Party, 85
Libresco, Andrea, 127
Lies My Teacher Told Me (Loewen), 4
Lincoln, Abraham, 27, 36, 77, 79, 80, 83, 86, 92, 94, 100, 103, 108, 109, 139, 140
Liverpool, U.K., 7, 93
Livingston, Peter, 57
Livingston, Philip, 55, 57–58
Lloyd, James, 52
Lloyd, Henry, 52
Lloyd's Neck (Queens County), 52
Loewen, James, 3, 4
Loguen, Jermain, 9, 16, 78, 85, 106, 123
Long Island, New York, 14, 44, 52, 56, 58, 64, 70, 71, 93, 101, 133
Long Island Railroad, 93
Louisiana's Citizens Bank and Canal Bank, 89
L'Ouverture, Toussaint, 16, 93, 120, 122, 124, 125
Low, Abiel, 81
Lower Manhattan walking tour, 1–2, 31–33, 100, 118

Madison, James, 53
Malcolm X, 49
Manhattan Institute, 118, 119
Manumission Day Parade, 73

Marable, Manning, 22
March on Washington (1963), 49
Mariners' Museum, 126
Marx, Karl, 6, 65, 69,
Maryland, 10, 11, 84, 106, 108, 118,
    139, 141
Massachusetts, 83, 110, 117, 125
Mayflower Compact, 16
May, Samuel, 76, 122
McLean, Ron, 111
meal (grain) market, 31, 54
Melville, Herman, 87
Merchants' Exchange Bank, 93
Mila 18 (Uris), 15
Missouri Compromise, 40, 80
mock slave auction, 13–14
Monmouth County (New Jersey), 63
Moore, Queen Mother, 35
Moore, Shiyanne, 100
Moore, Thomas, 54
Morris, Gouverneur, 64, 65, 79
Morris, Lewis, 58
Morrisana, 64, 69
Morrison, Toni, 124
Morse, Samuel, 77, 82
Mosley, Walter, 124
Mossel, Thijs, 43
Mount Vernon, 3
movies, 124–125: *Amazing Grace, Amistad,
    Beloved, Burn!, Cold Mountain, Glory,
    Gone with the Wind, The Last Supper,
    Middle Passage Roots, Sankofa,
    Solomon Northup's Odyssey*
multicultural education, 2, 118–120
Mumford, George, 56
Murphy, Maureen, 75, 87
Museum of Slavery, 127–129
museums, 1, 20, 29, 30, 37, 126

Nalle, Charles, 85
*Narrative of the Life of Frederick Douglass,
    The* (Douglass), 108
Nast, Thomas, 126
National Association for the Advancement
    of Colored People, 13
National Center for History in the
    Schools, 119–120

National Council for the Social Studies,
    33
National Endowment for the Humanities,
    119
National History Standards, 119
National Negro Conventions, 10, 106, 107
National Review, 119
nationalism, 102–103
nativism, 77, 82, 86
Nealy, John, 72
Negro convention movement, 106–108
Nehru, Jawaharal, 3
Netherlands (Holland, United Provinces,
    Dutch Republic), 7, 37–46, 52, 67
New Amsterdam, 28, 42–47, 101, 129,
New Criterion, 119
New England, 5, 16, 60, 89
New Haven, Connecticut, 101
New Holland, 39
New Jersey, 5, 49, 50, 54, 63, 118, 121
New Jersey Council for the Social Studies,
    33
New Mexico, 117
New Netherland (Dutch colony), 2, 9, 24,
    28, 37– 47, 53, 101, 121, 122, 129
New York (city): Board of Education, 58;
    Chamber of Commerce, 95: City
    Hall, 32; City Council, 35; Common
    Council, 31, 54, 57, 59, 62, 81;
    merchants and bankers, 20, 24, 29,
    81, 86, 89–98, 123; secession crisis,
    81; segregation, 104; slave laws
    (ordinances), 46, 51–53, 59, 60, 72,
    131; statues and monuments, 51
New York (state): Assembly, 2, 117;
    Chamber of Commerce, 92; colonial
    convention (1754), 58; constitutional
    convention (1777), 69; Education
    Department, 29–30, 33; freedom
    trail, 30; gradual manumission, 70;
    Great Irish Famine curriculum, 30,
    33; human rights curriculum, 30;
    Senate, 2, 117–118
*New York and Slavery: Complicity and
    Resistance* curriculum guide, 1, 5, 16,
    19, 31, 62, 121, 122, 125, 127
New-York African Society, 73

New York Anti-Slavery Society, 73, 103, 105

New York Burning: Liberty, Slavery, and Conspiracy in Eighteenth-Century Manhattan (Lepore), 61, 122

New York Central Railroad, 81

New York Emancipation Day (1827), 102

New York Evening Post, 79

New-York Gazette or, The Weekly Post-Boy, 55, 56

New York Herald, 81

New York Historical Society, 14, 30, 89, 119, 122, 126

New York Journal of Commerce, 76, 81

New York Leader, 97

New York Manumission Society, 32, 70, 72

New-York Packet, 71

New York State Council for the Social Studies, 127

New York Sun, 104

New York Times, 2, 28, 81, 84, 85, 87, 94–98, 119, 122, 125,

New York Tribune, 6, 77, 93

New York Weekly Journal, 55

New York Yacht Club, 97

Newport, R.I., 35

Newtown (Queens County), 103

Niagara River, 105

Nicholson, Asenath, 32

Nieu Amsterdam woodcut, 44

North Carolina, 69, 91, 118, 123, 125

North, Douglass, 90

North Star, 108

Northern Ireland, 112

Northup, Solomon, 9, 10, 21, 105, 123, 125

Northwest Ordinance (1787), 5, 69

Notes on the State of Virginia (Jefferson), 40

Nott, Eliphalett, 79

Noyes Academy, 107

Oberlin College (Ohio), 76

Ogletree, Charles, 35

Olin Foundation, 118

Oneida Institute, 10, 78, 106, 107

Orange Town, New York, 50

Orange County, New York, 54

Organization of American Historians, 119

Oswego, New York, 85

Oyster Bay, New York, 64

Paine, Thomas, 53

Parenti, Michael, 22

Parker, William, 84

Parks, Rosa, 99, 104

Patriot Act, 79 139

PBS (Public Broadcasting System), 21, 121, 135, 136

pedagogy. *See* curriculum and pedagogy; teaching ideas; essential questions; student projects

Pennsylvania, 4, 64, 69, 84, 93, 106

Pennsylvania Coal Company, 93

Pentagon, 118

The People Could Fly (Hamilton), 19, 124, 128

Pezone, Michael, 1–2, 22, 78, 127, 138

Philadelphia, Pennsylvania, 4, 49, 64, 69, 78, 92, 95, 106

"Pretends to Be Free" Runaway Slave Advertisements from Colonial and Revolutionary New York and New Jersey (Hodges & Brown), 54

Philipsburgh Manor, 57

Philipse, Frederick, 136–137

Phoenix Society, 102

Pinckney, Charles, 22, 40

Porat, Dan, 112

Port Jefferson, New York 97

Portugal and Portuguese colonial settlements, 38, 39, 42, 47

Portugies, Anthony, 33, 43

Portuguese Company, 96–97

Prince, 102

Providence Bank of Rhode Island (FleetBoston Financial Corporation), 34

Quaco, 62, 101, 136

Quakers. *See* Society of Friends

Quigley, David, 123

Queens County, 31, 54, 58, 63, 75, 77, 100, 103, 118

racial and ethnic identity, 112
racial and social equality, 24, 45, 49, 71,
    73, 79, 82, 99, 102–104, 106, 109
racism, 3, 4, 5, 8, 9, 13–14, 18, 22, 25,
    40, 60, 69, 71, 73, 99, 103–104,
    111, 113–114
Ravitch, Diane, 16, 118–120
religion, 4, 6, 23, 46, 63, 65, 78, 79, 82–83
Republican Party, 2, 79, 86, 108, 118
Rhode Island, 34, 35, 56, 69, 103, 117
Riker's Island, 107
Roberts, John, 111
Robinson Crusoe (Defoe), 38
Robinson, Randall, 35
Rochester, New York, 10, 11, 103, 108,
    109, 111, 140
Rodriguez, Jan, 43
Roman Catholic Church, 38, 60, 82, 86,
    112
Root, Erastus, 71
Royal African Company, 53
Ruggles, David, 33, 102, 104, 105
runaway slave advertisements, 35, 49, 51,
    52, 54–56, 132
Rush, Christopher, 102
Russwurm, John, 72, 102
Rye, New York, 57, 70

St. Patrick's Cathedral, 82
San Tomé, Pieter, 102
San Tomé, Susana, 102
Santo Domingue (Haiti), 16, 23, 82, 93,
    109, 113, 124, 125, 139
Saratoga Springs, 9, 21, 105
Schlesinger, Arthur, Jr., 118, 120
Schomburg Center for Research in Black
    Culture, 17, 20
Seminole, 17
Seneca Village (Central Park), 33
Sengbe Pieh (Cinqué), 101
Setauket, New York, 97
Seward, Frances, 79
Seward Seminary (Rochester), 103
Seward, William, 75, 79, 83, 85
sex and sexuality: interracial relations, 44;
    sexual abuse, 27; sexuality, 44, 51
Sexias, Peter, 112

Seymour, Horatio, 77, 82, 87, 88
Shelter Island, 57
Shiva, 6
Sienkiewicz, Stephanie, 75, 99
Sierra Leone, 101
Sims, James Marion, 18
Sinclair, Upton, 119
skilled trades, 21, 45, 105
slave conspiracy trial (1741), 2, 19, 20,
    32–33, 59–61, 100–101, 121, 124,
    127, 133–136
slave narratives, 123
slave rebellion (1712), 2, 32, 59, 100, 135
slave trade, 1–9, 14, 15, 21, 22–25, 27,
    30, 31, 34–35, 38–41, 43, 47, 53,
    57–58, 63, 67, 73, 80, 89–91,
    93–98, 105, 115, 117, 118, 120,
    121, 123, 124, 126, 128, 129; prof-
    its, 5, 6, 7, 20, 22–23, 24, 34–35,
    38–39, 57, 67, 89–98, 125; trial
    (1854), 97
slavery: in Africa, 23; in ancient world,
    40, 73; apologists, 22, 34, 40, 41;
    apologies for, 117–118; banks in-
    volved, 31, 80, 89–90, 95, 96; Chris-
    tianity, 23, 27, 28, 46, 54, 68, 82, 83;
    corporations built on slave profits,
    93–95; development as an institu-
    tion, 53–54; insurance companies
    involved, 89; insurrections, 10, 82,
    121, 135; main ideas about, 22–26;
    profits, 4, 34; reparations, 2, 35–36,
    118; resistance, 23, 54–56, 58–62,
    99–110; student attitudes toward, 9,
    111–115; white opposition, 63–64
Smith, Epenentus, 71
Smith, Gerrit, 9, 78–79
Smith, James, 89, 94–97
Smith, James McCune, 72, 73, 106
Smith, Richard, 14, 54
Smith, Venture, 56, 123
Smithtown, New York, 14, 54
Social Darwinism, 23
Society for Promoting the Manumission
    of Slaves, 69–70
Society for the Diffusion of Political
    Knowledge, 77

Society of Friends (Quakers), 68, 70, 71, 72, 104
Songs of the South (movie), 4, 124
South Street Seaport, 1, 30, 31, 94–95
South Sea Islands, 97
Southern Christian Leadership Conference, 13
Sowell, Thomas, 120
Spain and Spanish colonial settlements, 16, 17, 38, 39, 42, 58, 59, 113
spice trade, 38–39
Squash, Deborah, 50
Squash, Harry, 50
Stalin, Joseph, 3
Staples, Brent, 28, 34,
Stevens, Thaddeus, 85
Stewart, Alexander, 81
Stowe, Harriet Beecher, 14, 27–28, 100, 124
Stuart, James, 53
student projects, 128–129
student understanding, 111–115
Stuyvesant, Peter, 45–46, 51, 53
Styron, William, 124
Sugar, 31, 38–40, 47, 90, 91, 93–96; merchants and refining, 31–32, 80, 93, 95–96; plantations 57, 60
Supreme Court, 101, 111, 139
Surinam, 42, 47
Sweet's Restaurant, 30, 31, 94
Sylvester, Nathaniel, 57

Tammany Hall, 77
Tappan, Arthur, 31, 75–77
Tappan, Lewis, 9, 31, 75–77, 101, 120
Taylor, Moses, 30, 31, 80, 95, 96
Teaching American History grant, 3, 33, 127
teaching ideas, 18–22, 127–141
Tennessee, 117
terrorism, 10, 30, 49, 50, 79, 117, 119, 127, 137–141
Testament (Bible), Old and New, 22, 40
Third Avenue Railroad Company, 104
Thoreau, Henry David, 13, 21–22, 26
The Souls of Black Folk (DuBois), 2, 8
Thompson, Jerimiah, 92

Thompson, Rachel, 127
Tilden, Samuel ,77, 82,
Titus (Colonel Tye), 16, 49, 63, 101, 121
tobacco, 39, 44, 45, 69, 91
TransAfrica, 35
Trans-Atlantic slave trade. *See* slave trade
Treaty of Breda (1667), 47, 53
Treaty of Westminster (1674), 47
Trinidad, 39
Troy, New York, 10, 85, 105
Truth, Sojourner, 72, 123, 129
Tubman, Harriet, 79, 85
Twain, Mark, 124
Twentieth Regiment United States Colored Troops, 110

Ulster County, New York, 54, 72
Uncle Tom's Cabin (Stowe), 14, 23, 27, 124
underground railroad, 16, 17, 30, 76, 78, 79, 85, 105–106, 124, 126, 128
Underhill, Samuel, 64
Union College, 79
Union Committee of Fifteen, 81
Union of Utrecht, 38
United States Holocaust Memorial, 20
United States Senate, 79, 83
Uris, Leon, 15

van Angola, Anthony, 46, 101
Van Buren, Martin, 80
Van Cortlandt, Jacobus, 55
Van Renselaer, Thomas, 103
van Vaes, Anthony Jansen, 44
Van Wyke, Cornelius, 55
Virginia, 4, 10, 13, 16, 19, 22, 40, 50, 51, 63, 69, 75, 78, 91, 99, 106, 108, 117, 118, 126, 139, 141
voluntary societies, 102
Volunteer Democratic Association of New York, 80

Walker, David, 107
Wall Street, 28, 51, 81, 119
Wall Street slave market, 2, 30–31, 54, 57, 131
Wanderer, 97

Ward, Samuel Ringgold, 106, 123
Warsaw Ghetto, 15
Washington, Augustus, 78
Washington, D.C., 20, 21, 27, 78, 81, 105, 119
Washington, George, 4, 50, 51, 63, 91
Washington Square Park, 33, 47
Watson and Lorillard, 86
websites (Africans in America, Atlantic Slave Trade and Slave Life in the Americas, Captive Passage, Documenting the American South, Library of Congress American Memory, National Geographic, National Park Service, National Underground Railroad Freedom Center, Slave Heritage Resource Center Slavery and the Making of America, Spartacus Internet Encyclopedia), 125–126
Webster, Daniel, 83–84
Weeksville (Kings County), 87
Weld, Theodore, 78

Westchester County, New York, 54, 57, 64, 69, 135
Whitecuff, Benjamin, 102
Whitesboro, New York, 106
Whitestone (Queens County), 67
Wildfire, 97–98
Williams, Eric, 40, 122
Williams, Nichole, 17
Williams, Peter, 73, 77, 102
Williamsburg (Kings County), 93
Wilson, Harriet, 123
Wood, Fernando, 29, 32, 81–82, 85
Woodman, Harold, 90
Woolman, John, 63
World Trade Center, 118
Wright, Theodore, 102, 103, 104

Yale University, 58

Zenger, John Peter, 55
Zepperly, Frederick, 55
Zeus, 42
Zinn, Howard, 22